L. P. ALFORD

AND

THE EVOLUTION OF MODERN
INDUSTRIAL MANAGEMENT

L. P. Alford

L. P. ALFORD

AND

THE EVOLUTION OF
MODERN INDUSTRIAL MANAGEMENT

BY

WILLIAM J. JAFFE

Professor in Management Engineering
Newark College of Engineering

WITH AN INTRODUCTION BY
DAVID B. PORTER

NEW YORK UNIVERSITY PRESS

New York · 1957

TO

RALPH I. ALFORD, M.D.

BUT FOR WHOSE FILIAL DEVOTION

THIS VOLUME WOULD NOT HAVE BEEN POSSIBLE

INTRODUCTION

Leon Pratt Alford, engineer, editor, author, and educator, occupies a unique and prominent place in the field of scientific management. Possessed of an analytical mind tempered with rare appreciation of human values, his counsel was eagerly sought by and unstintingly given to the many committees of professional societies and governmental bodies on which he served. He was a contemporary of and knew intimately the pioneers of scientific management. His interpretation and evaluation of their work, together with his own distillation of fundamental principles out of management practice from ancient to modern times and his creation of the "kilo-man-hour" unit of measurement, have been recognized as his outstanding contributions. These principles form a firm foundation on which any manager at any time, now or in the future, may build his own practice.

The writer of this book has had access to Alford's letters and unpublished manuscripts that were found in his files and library and that throw additional light on his work beyond his published material. He has capably synthesized all of Alford's writings so that the serious student will see in this volume the unfolding and development of scientific management, as seen through the eyes of one whose business it was, as an editor and author, to interpret the times, and whose qualifications for that mission were eminent.

Lastly (because it came at the end of his career) Alford as educator and professor will be revered by his students and those who served with him because of his vision, kindness, sincerity, and selfless dedication to the service of others.

DAVID B. PORTER

University Heights
New York University
October 22, 1956

PREFACE

According to the popular conception, a biography presents, in the main, the story of a man's life, with the greatest emphasis resting upon the day-to-day events of his life. These events may be "ordinary" or "extraordinary," depending on the subject, the author, and the audience.

Fortunately or unfortunately, as the case may be, the present study does not fit in this category. Nor does this presentation purport to be an attempt at a psychological analysis of a man's life with the intent of explaining the subject's character and personality.

However, if the study of a man's work is effectively presented, it should result in a clearer picture of his environment and a clarification of the present scene and its implications. This is especially true of a man who has spent his life in many different environments. It is even more important if he has succeeded in them all.

This is the case with L. P. Alford.

He was an electrical engineer, a mechanical engineer, an inventor, a shop foreman, a production superintendent, a writer on such subjects as drilling machines and bearings, management and ammunition manufacture, an engineering editor, an editor in chief of engineering and industrial publications, periodicals, and books, a commentator on shop procedures, a propounder of management laws and principles, a founder of a production control system that extended far beyond the production shop, one of the earliest of standardization advocates, an adherent of the examination and analysis of the costing aspects of industry, a student of industrial and human relations, a founder and furtherer of engineering and management organizations, an aide to governmental committees and commissions, a diagnostician and a prognostician of the economic ills of our times, an adviser on industrial problems involved in the nation's defense, a biographer of one of the great engineers of modern times, an engineering educator, a historian of engineering's past developments, a philosopher of its present, and a prophet of its future, and the recipient of some of the highest honors American engineering can offer.

Such were the man's professional accomplishments. In recounting and analyzing his work in these fields, this study presents the development of an important phase of engineering—call it *administrative, industrial, management,* or what you will—together with its present significance.

A study of the history of the sciences has had its advocates from Dampier through Cajori. Its value need not be stressed here other than to quote the following statement from the announcement of Ostwald's *Klassiker der exacten Wissenschaften,* which Cajori, writing in 1898, used in the preface to the first edition of his *A History of Physics:*

> While by the present methods of teaching, a knowledge of science in its present state of advancement is imparted very successfully, eminent and far-sighted men have repeatedly been obliged to point out a defect which too often attaches to the present scientific education . . . *it is the absence of the historical sense and the want of knowledge of the great researches upon which the edifice of science rests.*

If this has been a weak point of the *sciences,* it is no stronger as far as engineering is concerned. And this is particularly true of the more recent developments that have, as yet, not had time to be recorded to any great extent.

Furthermore, the history of science reveals that its early leaders had wide interests. One does not, for example, tie Archimedes down to such "limited" fields as hydrostatics or even mechanics: his work is well recognized in the more compre-

hensive fields of physics, mathematics, geography, and astronomy. Da Vinci's fame was as great in the arts as it was in the
sciences. However, as the sciences developed, the work of the
leaders became more detailed—but narrower. By the time Gauss
had finished his work, science had probably seen the last of the
all-encompassing genius. Today, for example, one is seldom considered an algebraist or a geometrician—much less a "mathematician"—but rather a student in, say, group theory or in
Peano spaces. The engineer is no different. Even today's *civil
engineer* is not always the same as his predecessor who practiced "nonmilitary" engineering. Whether this situation is good
or bad is another matter: however, these are the facts as they
exist.

The case of management—or industrial or administrative—
engineering is much the same. Today one considers oneself a
practitioner of production control or of quality control or of
some other phase. As a matter of fact, even some of the so-called
pioneers were limited in their interests. Taylor was basically interested in the production aspects of *scientific management* despite his later assertions of its wider applications: Kimball, for
example, pointed out that the important field of distribution
had been neglected. Cooke, too, was interested, to a great degree, in institutional and governmental applications. This does
not necessarily mean that the early leaders were restricted in
their efforts to a single phase: the Gilbreths' interests were beyond motion study, Church's beyond costs, Gantt's greater than
mere production. Even Emerson could be credited with work
in production and costing and organization. But none had the
wide interests of Alford! And probably no one, in the future,
will ever duplicate his wide scope!

Certainly biographical data are unavoidable in this study of
Alford's work. However, in it a serious attempt has been made
to use his work as a medium by which to examine the development of an important phase of engineering through the first
forty years of this century. It can hopefully engage on so ambitious an undertaking only because of the potency of Alford's
accomplishments—as well as the period in which he lived, the

environment in which he worked, and the skills which he possessed and utilized.

This study may be called *An Examination and Analysis of the Development of Management Engineering, Industrial Relations, Production Control, Costing, Standardization, Engineering Education,* etc., etc.

For the sake of brevity, it is simply titled: *L. P. Alford and the Evolution of Modern Industrial Management.*

In its original version, in 1953, this study bore the title, "Alfordian Analyses, Principles, and Laws," and was a doctoral dissertation at the Graduate College of Engineering, New York University, in whose library a copy is on file. In its present form, it must be noted, in addition to a title change and additional "personal" data, some of the more technical details have been eliminated, and the work has been so revised as to give to it a more general appeal. Nevertheless, it is hoped that it still remains a means of acquainting all who are interested in today's and tomorrow's management with the debt they—too often unknowingly—owe to Alford, who played so important but so little publicized a role in helping to bring "scientific management" from its early period of questionable popularity to its present state of distinction.

Unfortunately, too many present-day writers on management topics and practitioners of management techniques continue to use Alford's work without any due regard to the recognition of the man who was responsible for so much of today's management concepts.

This lack of recognition can be traced to several sources: the man himself, the manner in which this work was presented, and the consequent unfamiliarities of some of the newer writers and practitioners with the behind-the-scenes occurrences during the early days of industrial management here in the United States.

As for Alford himself, he lacked both the brash aggressiveness that Taylor used in setting forth his ideas, as well as the almost too smooth eloquence that Emerson employed in capturing, for the movement and for himself, the popular fancy.

He was rugged but sensitive, and always, to use Lillian Gilbreth's description, a "gentleman of the old school." Although
Alford had great faith in his beliefs, he was too engrossed in
his work to be really conscious of the fact that he should have
spent more time in "selling" his ideas.

Once his ideas were committed to paper or conveyed orally
to a group of engineers—"No engineering work is complete," he
wrote in his private papers, "until the doer has told his brother
engineers what he did and why he did it"—he felt that the
major work was done. As for furthering himself as the origi-
nator of the concepts he presented, nothing was more remote
from his mind.

Rooted in his heritage and nurtured by his devotion to Gantt,
Alford had a keen sense of duty both as an engineer and as a
member of society and, once the task was set before him, he
accomplished it. It was the task that interested him and not
the accompanying credit. (And when some little recognition was
afforded him, he accepted it with almost unbounded gratitude.)
Lillian Gilbreth clearly analyzed the matter: he was an engineer
keenly aware of his responsibilities to his profession, his community, and his country. Senator Ralph Flanders holds a similar opinion.

Although Gantt exerted great influence on his protégé's devotion to "service," only Alford himself can be held account-
able for the unflinching devotion with which he applied himself. His steadfastness might be called "slave-driving" were it
not that he drove himself even harder than he did his associates and subordinates.

Yet seldom did the question of credit come to his mind.
When, for example, Alford was asked to conduct the ASME's
study of the status of industrial management in 1912, he accepted the task with the same devotion that he performed his
daily work assignments. Only in his private papers—and then
in a spirit of a job well done—did he admit sole authorship of
the report that was presented as a joint venture. Many of his
articles and all his editorials in the *American Machinist, Industrial Management, Manufacturing Industries,* and other pe-

riodicals, as well as the writings in handbooks and committee reports bear no publicly apparent identification of his authorship. Yet all who were intimately connected with the work were indeed conscious of his influence. Thus, even though some of the American Engineering Council's reports—*Waste in Industry, Twelve Hour Shift,* etc.—bear the mark of committee authorship, L. W. Wallace attests to his significant contributions.

Although he was co-author with Church on *The Principles of Management,* few even now are aware of the major role he played. As Church's name had become familiar to readers, not many realized, as will be pointed out further on, that Church himself admitted to Alford's greater part in the collaboration.

Thus, Alford was always more interested in the *fait accompli* than in any glory connected with it. Only that too-fast-disappearing group of engineers who lived and worked on the scene with Alford is aware of the facts, while those writers whose familiarity with the scientific management movement is limited to an examination of published works are slow to realize the Alford contribution.

For example, Alford's work, except for his authorship of the Gantt biography, is almost entirely unrecognized by Filipetti's *Industrial Management in Transition,* which includes résumés of "people who have either made direct contributions to the managerial evolution or who have interpreted some phases of it or its impact." On the other hand, only too infrequently does there appear a report such as Lyndall Urwick's "Management's Debt to Engineers," [1] which was presented at the ASME Calvin W. Rice Lecture, on September 8, 1952, at the Centennial of Engineering in Chicago. In this, although reference is made to only three of Alford's accomplishments—his secretaryship of the ASME Committee that made the 1912 Report, his role as management's historian, and his work in connection with the handbooks—Urwick does pay public homage to him: "With Lillian Gilbreth he was a bridge between the early pioneering days and the stupendous development of the subject we see

[1] "Advanced Management," *SAM, 17,* No. 12, 5-12, December (1952).

around us today." Yet even Urwick's citations are but a small part of Alford's accomplishments.

One may wonder whether this lack of universal recognition is justified. But nothing can be further from the truth. Nor is an occasional medal—in commemoration of either Gantt or Melville—necessary as concrete evidence. The fact that so much of Alford's work appeared under the anonymity of committee reports or as unsigned articles belies the important force he was in every committee he served or in connection with any article he edited. The writing of so many of the reports fell to him because of the recognition of his writing ability coupled with his eagerness to serve. And the fact that he presented so many writings by others is no indication that he added nothing to these works: if anything, he not only published their views but, in his presentation, clarified their thinking and made it more readily acceptable to a wider audience. Thus, the tenyear report on the progress of management that appeared less than a year after his death needed the writing efforts of about a dozen people in order to attain the breadth of the standard set by Alford.

Even more important testimonials to Alford's work are those of the people who worked with him in the early development of engineering and who strongly encouraged this study. Every one of them agreed that the accomplishments and recognition of Alford had been left to word of mouth for too long a time. Although the statements of those persons whose names are listed below attest to Alford's importance, typical of all are the following excerpts from a letter received by the author from Dr. L. W. Wallace, whose name has become practically synonymous with that great and important body, the American Engineering Council:

I was gratified to learn that you have selected for the subject . . . the late L. P. Alford. Since you have read several things I have written about him, you know of my very high esteem for his ability, his character, and his contribution to American Life. No more able and true man ever labored among us than L. P.

It is my feeling you are quite right in believing that Henry L.

Gantt influenced Alford as much as or more than anyone else. Alford and I discussed Gantt many times; we were both admirers of the sound, fair, and human philosophies of Gantt. Gantt's philosophy appealed very much to Alford; moveover it was a philosophy closely akin to the spirit and character of Alford, himself.

Again I think that you are correct in maintaining that if there is any one trait by which Alford may be characterized it was his deep sense of duty and responsibility as an engineer to his profession and to Society. He had a very deep sense of responsibility and loyalty to his friends, his profession, and his country—even further, he was tenacious about it and had little patience for those who manifested a lack of such qualities. There was nothing false or facetious in his makeup, as manifested by his writing and speaking. He was one of those rugged, but sensitive, fine characters too little appreciated. We suffer for the lack of more like him.

I agree that his conception and pronouncement of management laws and principles was a very significant contribution. However he made other contributions as profound and far-reaching. A careful study of his writings will disclose this. Perhaps I have sensed this more than many others because of my intimate relationship with him through his membership on committees of, and with respect to the various studies made by, American Engineering Council. Among some which come to mind, where the unseen mind and heart of Alford contributed greatly, are these: The Constitution of the American Engineering Council; aspects of the report, *Waste in Industry;* the dynamic import of the report on *Twelve Hour Shift in Industry.* Into these and others went keen analysis, human interest, the philosophy and spirit of Alford.

May I say in closing, that for a long time before Alford passed on I had the deep conviction that he was one of those among us— including the ASME and the engineering profession—who had never been appreciated to the degree his character and contributions warranted.

Further comment may be unnecessary, but it would be pertinent to add that, although a man's work is his own monument, it was the Rev. George Crabbe who, more than a century ago, in *The Borough,* pointed out that "Monuments themselves memorials need."

Among the many who willingly and anxiously gave of their time and efforts so that Alford's true worth be recognized, I should like to give particular thanks to the following people, whose help has been invaluable to me in the preparation of this study.

First and foremost, I would like to thank Dr. Ralph I. Alford, without whose aid and co-operation this volume would not have been possible. Dr. Alford made accessible his father's private files and papers, many of which had never been published. Continuing his role of university benefactor, he has since presented many of the original papers of his father to the Department of Industrial and Management Engineering of New York University's College of Engineering. Moreover, it is only by virtue of his generosity that this book is being published.

On the staff of New York University, Professor Alex W. Rathe, under whose advisement the original dissertation was written, suggested the topic, and his personal guidance and encouragement were ever present during the writing of the original version of this work. He chaired the original Advisement Committee on which Professor David B. Porter, Professor Emeritus Charles W. Lytle, and Dr. John W. Enell were members. Professor Norman N. Barish, Chairman of the Department of Industrial and Management Engineering, played an important part in recommending the publication of the present version of this work and offered valuable suggestions in its preparation as well. The author also gratefully acknowledges the courtesies extended to him by the American Society of Mechanical Engineers in making available the Alford File at the Society together with the letters accumulated by Professor Emeritus Joseph W. Roe in the writing of the Alford Obituary for ASME when Alford's death seemed still a shocking unreality.

Although it is impossible to mention and evaluate separately all of those to whom I am deeply indebted, I should like specifically to thank the following people, all of whom have written or personally spoken to me about Alford or have allowed examination of magazines, letters, or files in their charge:

Miss Dora Albert, L. P. Alford's secretary at NYU.

The late Mrs. L. P. Alford (nee Grace Agnes Hutchins), L. P. Alford's widow.

Mrs. Ralph I. Alford, L. P. Alford's daughter-in-law.

Miss Mabel Allen, daughter of Mrs. L. P. Alford's sister.

Professor William Stewart Ayars, engineer, educator, a member of Diemer's Industrial Engineering Department at Pennsylvania State College.

Dean William R. Bryans, engineer, educator, and compiler of a history of NYU's College of Engineering.

Mrs. Pearl Franklin Clark, widow and partner of Wallace Clark.

Mr. Harold V. Coes, engineer, past President of ASME, and friend of L. P. Alford.

Mr. Fred H. Colvin, engineer, editor, and L. P. Alford's associate on the *American Machinist*.

Professor Henry A. Cozzens, Jr., engineer, educator, and friend of L. P. Alford.

Col. Clarence E. Davies, Secretary of ASME and friend of L. P. Alford.

Miss Francis I. Duck, Librarian at Stevens Institute of Technology and in charge of the Taylor Collection.

Dr. John W. Enell, engineer, educator, and management adviser.

Senator Ralph E. Flanders, engineer, past President of ASME, U.S. Senator from Vermont, and associate and friend of L. P. Alford.

Dr. Lillian M. Gilbreth, engineer, scientific management pioneer, widow and associate of Frank B. Gilbreth, and friend and neighbor of L. P. Alford.

Mr. George E. Hagemann, engineer, editor, friend, and associate of L. P. Alford.

Mr. Ernest Hartford, Executive Assistant Secretary of ASME.

Miss Elizabeth Hayward, compiler of the Taylor Collection.

Dr. Joseph M. Juran, engineer, educator, and management consultant.

Professor Emeritus Charles W. Lytle, engineer, educator, and associate of L. P. Alford.

Dean Henry J. Masson, engineer and educator.

Mr. Joseph A. Piacitelli, engineer and L. P. Alford's associate on the Textile Work Assignment and the Telephone Projects.

Professor David B. Porter, engineer, educator, and associate of L. P. Alford.

Dean Thorndike Saville, engineer, educator, and past President of ASEE.

Miss Frances Selig, secretary to Col. Davies.

Mr. Erik G. Sellman, editor, associate of L. P. Alford, and friend of the Alford family.

Dr. C. A. Slocum, formerly SAM Executive Director, who was in charge of SAM's collection of Taylor Society Bulletins.

Mr. George A. Stetson, Editor Emeritus, ASME publications.

Mrs. Thomas T. Taber (nee "Peggy" Gantt), daughter of H. L. Gantt.

Dr. L. W. Wallace, engineer and L. P. Alford's associate on the American Engineering Council.

The author owes an additional debt of gratitude to Professor Porter, who distinguishes this book by his Introduction.

Finally, grateful acknowledgment is extended to all authors and publishers—particularly The Ronald Press Company and the McGraw-Hill Company and its *American Machinist,* pioneers in scientific management publications—to whom detailed credit is given throughout the book.

WILLIAM J. JAFFE

Newark, New Jersey
October 31, 1956

CONTENTS

". . . One of these days a new generation of engineers will revive this vision and at that time what we did and what we failed to do may be of assistance to the leaders."

L. P. ALFORD TO C. E. DAVIES

July 14, 1941

Chapter I

BEFORE 1912

ALFORD—BEFORE 1910

Leon Pratt Alford was born on January 3, 1877, at Simsbury, Connecticut, and it would be most fitting to relate this date to matters and persons of great concern to him throughout his life. Because of his great devotion to his country and to his profession, to management and to the great humanist of the management movement, it can appropriately be added that his year of birth was one in which the United States was beginning to recover from the Panic of 1873; the ASME was still three years away from its founding at the offices of the *American Machinist;* Towne would not, until nine more years had passed, be ready to discuss *The Engineer as an Economist;* and Gantt, at the age of sixteen, was still at McDonogh School.

Alford's lineage can be easily traced. Interested in genealogy, his private files contain many references to his heritage, and his walls were hung with framed pictures of his family coat of arms. Among his papers a note from his friend and neighbor, Arthur H. Churchill, refers to a London publication in 1908, compiled by John G. Alford and edited by W. P. W. Phillimore, called *Alford Family Notes, Ancient and Modern,* which deals with his family both here and abroad.

According to the Coronation Edition (London, 1937) of Burke's *Landed Gentry,* the family, on his father's side, came from Whitestaunton, near Chard, Somerset, England, and was probably a branch of the family from Alford ("Old Ford") in the same county. The family, at least the English branch, "pro-

3

duced an extraordinary number of Clergymen ranging from Curates to Bishop." Most famous of these was Henry Alford, D.D., Dean of Canterbury, who was also known as a poet, Greek scholar, and Biblical commentator.

As for the American branch, Benedict Alford was the first to arrive in the United States. It is definitely known that he came to Windsor Colony in 1634. He may have come here directly from England, but Alford, in one of his notes, claimed that his ancestor was a member of the Hooker party—which refers to the followers of the Rev. Thomas Hooker [1] who, displeased with the oligarchic order that prevailed in the Massachusetts Bay Colony, gathered his congregation from Newton and other environs of what is now Boston and voluntarily left that colony for the fertile valley of the Connecticut River. In any event, it is definitely known that Benedict Alford is credited with having commanded the Colony of Connecticut in the Pequot Indian War.

Although the Alford family was well established in Connecticut for many years, it does not necessarily mean that all the descendants remained here, for his father, Emerson Alford (1825-1899), was born in Frederick County, Virginia.

Emerson Alford left the South for New England, where he lived, in turn, at North Canton, Connecticut, Worcester, Massachusetts, New Britain, and Plainville, both in Connecticut. Although he spent his childhood in a Baptist environment, he became a Congregationalist and, later, in North Canton, he associated himself with the Methodist Episcopal Church. In New Britain, he paid the first subscription toward the new Trinity Church. Finally, when he came to Plainville in 1894, he continued his church interests and served as Steward and President of the Board of Trustees. An old newspaper clipping describes him:

He was gentle in his disposition, strong in his self control, liberal in his gifts, regular in his church attendance, active in all movements for the welfare of the community. His judgment arising from

[1] Wish, *Society and Thought in Early America*, pp. 35-36.

a liberal education and observations in extensive travels was excellent, his counsel clear, unselfish and just. He constantly grew in favor of God and man.

He planned for his death and funeral services as one would do for a day's outing, with composure and anticipated joy. Never robust, he battled successively against disease. The duration of his last sickness was about a week, during which he suffered intensely, but exhibited an excellent spirit of submission and patience.

On the distaff side, Leon Alford was descended from the Pratt family. The first American ancestor of his mother, Sarah Merriam Pratt (1829-1887), was Thomas Pratt, who came to this country about 1647, settling in Watertown, Massachusetts. On both her mother's and father's side, Alford's mother was related to the Merriam family—another one of New England's early settlers.

L. P. Alford's parents were married on April 23, 1851, and had five children: Clara J. (1852-1923), Ephraim B. (1854-1856), Ralph E. (1857-1926), Frank I. (1864-1923), and lastly, Leon P., himself. Alford's father, Emerson, had a varied career as both manufacturer and farmer. As manufacturer, he was Superintendent of the Collins Axe Company, Collinsville, Connecticut, and as farmer, he was one of that state's first tobacco growers. He also served in Connecticut's House of Representatives from 1886 to 1887 as a representative from Hartford County. The death of Leon Alford's mother left his sister, Clara, in charge and, in later years, with almost filial devotion, he expressed his deep gratitude for his sister's efforts on his behalf.

Alford used to take a great deal of pride in relating that, as a consequence of his mother's death, he had since the age of ten been self-supporting. During his vacation periods, while at both high school and college, he learned the trade of house carpenter. Evidently he also gained some experience in the machine and blacksmith shops and engine rooms in the area, for he was fond of "comparing notes," many years later, with Charles W. Lytle, his colleague on the faculty of New York University, who had started work in a foundry.

It was undoubtedly early in his youth that Alford developed

the quiet and reserved nature that he displayed throughout his life, for the yearbook of his graduating class at Worcester Polytechnic Institute, which he attended from 1893 to 1896—after attendance at grammar school between 1884 and 1890 and Plainville, Connecticut, High School between 1890 and 1893 —commented on his seriousness of purpose even at that time. Remarking about his physical size, five feet ten, 165 pounds at the age of nineteen, his classmates also noted an early cynicism. However, they did admit that scholastically, as far as they were concerned, he was "out of sight," particularly in Calculus and Civil Government. His shopwork, judging from records of his performance in the Washburn Shops during his Junior year (September 13, 1894, to January 19, 1895), was graded around 90. As a matter of fact, his record at WPI can best be judged by a letter written by Charles M. Allen, Professor of Hydraulic Engineering at the Institute, to Roe, on April 22, 1942, soon after Alford's death:

In looking up his record, I found that he had a high scholastic one. I had him as a student and I recall distinctly that he had a wonderful attitude toward his work. We were the best of friends for the rest of his life.

Six months before his twentieth birthday he graduated, in June, 1896, with the degree of Bachelor of Science in Electrical Engineering. He immediately started working at the McKay Metallic Fastening Association in Winchester, Massachusetts. Here he increased his familiarity with shop practice and obtained valuable drafting room experience.

Miss Mabel Allen, the daughter of his drafting room supervisor, Charles Allen, relates that Alford, while working here, roomed at her parents' home, a large house on Stevens Street in Somerville, Massachusetts. It was here, too, that he met and married Miss Grace Agnes Hutchins, a sister of Minnie Allen, Miss Allen's mother.

The Alford wedding took place on January 1, 1900. (Despite the blizzard that took place earlier in the day, Alford used to insist that the date was an excellent one, for it made it easy for him to remember wedding anniversaries.) Mrs. Alford came from nearby Templeton, graduated from the State Normal School at Worcester, in 1893, and taught school for about six and a half years in her home town, in Gardner, and in Somerville. After their marriage, the couple lived in the Allen house, where they had a downstairs parlor and an upstairs bedroom, and according to Alford had their meals in the vicinity for $3.50 per person per week.

Slightly older than her husband—Mrs. Alford was born on September 23, 1872—she survived him by little more than ten years. Throughout his life Alford was keenly devoted to her.[2]

The year 1900 was memorable, as far as Alford was concerned, for another reason: it was at this time that he became a junior member of the ASME. And so, too, began another lifelong association to which he dedicated his professional life. He moved to full membership in 1908, to vice-presidency in 1920, to fellow in 1936, and finally, in 1941, just a few months before his death, to one of the Society's most prized positions, honorary membership.

During his service with the McKay firm, the company went through a period of reorganization and consolidation, and Alford progressed along with it. In 1897, the firm became the McKay-Bigelow Heeling Association, and in 1899, by that time it was known as the McKay Shoe Machinery Company, he had served as assistant machine shop foreman, general foreman, assistant superintendent, and production superintendent, his post when the plant became a part of the United Shoe Machinery Company.

In April, 1902, Alford was primarily concerned with engineering work for the company, where he now took on duties as division engineer. In this capacity, he was sent to the Boston headquarters, where he assisted in the development of the company's new plant at Beverly.

Rooming at the Gould house in West Somerville, where Mrs.

---

[2] Mrs. Alford greatly prized a copy of the *Cost and Production Handbook* on whose flyleaf Alford had handwritten a dedication to her "in recognition of your definite, measured assistance, and your equally unmeasurable devotion."

Alford had once lived during a part of her teaching career, Alford began his work to help develop the new Beverly factory which, at the time, achieved much renown for housing the world's largest reinforced-concrete machine shop. Some notes in the Alford files indicate his work in this connection. Not only did Alford play a major role in the development of the general details of the buildings—which Alford described as "the first application in the United States of reinforced concrete to super-structure work"—but he made the first installation of machinery in such a building, and he was, consequently, the patentee of a device to attach fixtures to concrete ceilings.

When the plant was completed, he and his wife moved to Beverly, first to a rooming house on Railroad Avenue, then to an old "mansion" on Rantoul Street, and finally rented half of a two-family house on Federal Street. Here their son Ralph was born in 1904. Here, too, they took in school teachers as roomers.

In the new plant, Alford was assigned to the Mechanical Engineering Department; in 1906, he became its departmental head. With the experience he had gained he was able, the previous year, to fulfill the requirements for the degree of Mechanical Engineer at Worcester. His thesis was "Power Problems in Connection With the Development of Plans for a Manufacturing Plant." This, incidentally, was not the last degree that WPI gave him; twenty-seven years later, Worcester, in recognition of his work in and for the profession, presented him with the degree of Doctor of Engineering (*honoris causa*).[3]

Not only did his experience in the shoe machinery shops serve him well in later years—the development of shoe man-

---

[3] Although he was exceedingly proud of his doctor's degree, his paternal pride would frequently cause him to remark that it was his son, Ralph, who was the "real doctor." In this connection, indicative of Alford's great devotion to engineering, Harold Coes, whose sons also found success outside the engineering profession, tells of the time when Alford first "confided" that Ralph was planning to study medicine rather than engineering. Coes' remark at the time is still meaningful to anyone who is aware of Alford's devotion to engineering. "Come now, Leon," he said, "after all, engineering is not the *only* profession." It is interesting, however, to note that Alford still influenced his son's life work despite his choice of another profession; because of his father's suffering from hay fever, the son became a successful allergy specialist.

ufacture is referred to by him in many of his later papers and works—but it was here that he began to take interest in many subjects that he subsequently pursued with great success. Here he began to learn the lessons of standardization, not only as an aid to the solution of engineering problems but also as a help to economic ones: he soon became convinced that such a program could effect savings from 100 to 400 per cent; he was always proud of the fact that his efforts in connection with the standardization of screw machine parts of the shoe machines at the United plant cut production costs by $150,000 per year—a considerable sum in those days.

Although throughout his life Alford was always an excellent provider, it may be difficult for the younger generation of today, brought up in the prosperity following World War II, to realize that wages in those early days of the century were never so great that one could neglect any opportunity to make some extra money. (Alford's starting pay at McKay was $20.00 per week, and it became $24.00 on his marriage.) Alford was no exception, and, from time to time, he would contribute articles to technical periodicals. He told Erik Sellman that he was at Kitty Hawk in 1903, and he wrote a report of the exploits of the Wright brothers.

Such articles, particularly those sent to the *American Machinist,* soon led him to establish permanent connections with this magazine, edited by F. A. Halsey and owned by John A. Hill. Apparently Hill had great plans in store for Alford when he hired him, in 1907, as associate editor.

Alford's life at the magazine was not without difficulties. Naturally quiet and reserved, with no interest in either tobacco or alcohol, he was considered hostile and antisocial. Furthermore, his college training gave him the reputation of being highly theoretical and out of place among the practical men whose training came essentially from the shop. Indeed, the rapid rise of this young man, who became engineering editor in 1908 and editor in chief in 1911, replacing Halsey, could not have enhanced his popularity among those who had been with the magazine much longer than he.

While on the *American Machinist,* he learned a great deal from his daily chores. He cultivated the writing and editing ability for which he later justly became famous. He came in contact with matters that were appearing on the contemporary engineering scene, varying from a trip to Newfoundland to report on Alexander Graham Bell's experiments with different forms of cellular wings or airfoils [4] to less spectacular happenings in ordinary machine shops. But primarily, according to Colvin, he learned to handle people and became increasingly aware of the importance of the personnel problem.

When on April 1, 1907, he left New England to take his place in the offices of the *American Machinist* in New York, he actually expected to stay only three years: the lure of the factory was great. He first came to New York as a sort of pathfinder for the rest of his family, and his wife and baby joined him in the autumn. A furnished apartment on West 110th Street and then a railroad flat on West 106th Street, the parents agreed, were not conducive to the raising of their child. Their final choice was Montclair, which was to achieve some fame as the residence of the early leaders of the scientific management movement. After living on Irving Street for about ten years, the Alfords finally moved to 9 North Mountain Avenue, not far from "Oakleigh," the residence on Hoburg Place of Gantt, the man who became Alford's ideal.

Alford's presence in New York gave him greater opportunities to take part in the affairs of ASME. He must have made an impression, for he was invited to deliver a paper at a meeting abroad that ASME was then holding with its British counterpart.

The first paper a young man presents at a meeting of a technical society usually carries a greater significance for the author than for the society. This is an observation that is made with due deference to the admitted importance attached to the recognition of new viewpoints and to the encouragement of younger people. However, in the case of Alford, despite the unquestioned importance such an occasion might have had for

4 Colvin, *Sixty Years With Men and Machines,* p. 173.

School attended by Leon P. Alford, West Simsbury, Conn.

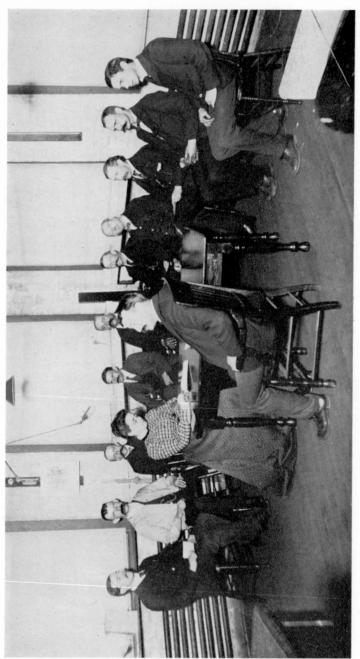

United Shoe Machinery Company (ca. 1903).

one of such seriousness of purpose, this initial work was of benefit to both ASME and Alford.

For ASME, it was the beginning of almost thirty years of continued service that Alford gave unstintingly, unselfishly, and dutifully. For Alford, despite the fact that some twenty years later he referred tersely but proudly in his private papers to "the first paper I wrote for a professional technical society," this introduction was important for reasons other than the supposedly obvious ones. In 1910, he was not a young man whose writing talents and messages were about to be recognized for the first time. At the age of thirty-three, he had already had in addition to his eight years of shop experience some three years of writing recognition with the *American Machinist*.

THE JOINT ASME-IME MEETING

Thus it seems that the ASME invitation was more a recognition of his work than a means of fostering an immature member of the society. This recognition is even more convincing when one realizes that he was chosen as one of three young engineers to represent ASME at its joint meeting with Britain's Institution of Mechanical Engineers at Birmingham, England, on July 27, 1910. Furthermore, his paper, which dealt with the "Development of High-Speed Drilling-Machines," was based on data that had been presented in the periodical for which he was engineering editor.

Also of great importance was the fact that this was the first time he had heard Taylor speak. It would not be correct to say—or at least there is no evidence to indicate—that Alford, on hearing Taylor, was quickly converted to the "movement." There is no reason to doubt the recording secretary who reproduced Taylor's "Discussion" of the papers by the Englishman and the three young Americans. He reported that the British engineer "replied" but that neither Alford nor his two colleagues made any retort. To be sure, Alford was in good company, for Frank Gilbreth, who was also present and who was also called on by the chairman, had "nothing to add."

The Gilbreth silence was probably understandable, since the
Taylor discussion included extensive praise of the well-known
bricklaying experiments. However, there are many possible
reasons for Alford's silence. He might justifiably have resented
Taylor's seizure of the occasion to change the subject from
a "technical" phase of engineering under discussion to a
"broader" one. He may even have felt some resentment when
he realized that Taylor had gained the chair's recognition
merely to foster his own doctrines. Again, he may have remained silent in awe or in dutiful respect to a man who was
not only his senior by twenty-one years but who was recognized throughout the world and who had been president of
the society he himself represented. Either or all of these reasons are plausible. Alford's temper was *almost* always restrained.
And his devotion to dutiful reverence was ever present. However, it does not seem likely that he remained quiet only because his two American compatriots did.

THE TENOR OF THE MEETING

The *Excerpt Minutes of the Proceedings of the Joint Meeting
of the Institution of Mechanical Engineers With the American
Society of Mechanical Engineers* of July 27, 1910, were pub-
lished by the British society. Here are recorded the papers of the
three young American representatives: John Calder [5] ("Rapid
Production in Machine Work: Abstract of Data Collected by
ASME"), Luther D. Burlingame ("Data on Manufacturing
Methods With Machine Tools"), and, of course, L. P. Alford.
The papers of these ASME members were preceded by one of
H. I. Brackenbury, a member of IME, who discussed "High
Speed Tools and Machines to Fit Them."

The tenor of the meeting can be surmised upon closer examination of the Alford paper, which was "confined to a brief
abstract of three articles published during the last few months
in the *American Machinist,* describing machines made by five

[5] Lytle relates that Calder was one of the first to have impressed upon Alford
the mutual benefit of the employer-employee relationship.

different firms, and records of their tests." Implying that during
the two preceding years several noteworthy developments in
high-speed drilling machines had taken place and important
results achieved, Alford brought these accomplishments, already
published by the *American Machinist,* to the attention of his
audience.

ALFORD'S REPORT ON DRILLING MACHINES

Alford presented the main facts that had originally been
brought out by F. E. Bocorcelski in his article on "Radial
Drilling-Machines and Records," by H. M. Norris in his treatment of "Tests of a Remarkable High-Speed Radial Drill," and
by the *American Machinist* staff's "High-Power Drilling Machines." [6] Alford described the four Bickford [7] radial drilling
machines, each of which destroyed the six or more 1¼-inch
drills used in the tests where the drill was driven into steel
at a speed of 310 rpm (101.45 feet) and 0.038-inch feed, with
power consumption, for this work, at a minimum of 18 and a
maximum of 21.3 hp. He went into great detail in describing
a fifth high-speed radial drill which, on the basis of the experience gathered from the other machines, was built and exhibited
in June, 1909, for the Atlantic City Convention of the Master
Car Builders. This drilling machine, with a speed ranging from
38 to 519 rpm, had successfully driven a 1¼-inch drill into a
steel block, "stated to be 0.55 per cent carbon, at 425 revolu-
tions per minute, 139 feet, and 0.02-inch feed giving a depth
of hole drilled per minute of 8.5 inches, without the slightest
indication of distress." In addition to details of construction,
figures on feeds, speeds, and depths drilled per minute, Alford
presented a table showing the power consumed per pound of
metal removed in driving a 1¼-inch drill into machinery steel
at various speeds and feeds. Among his conclusions was the fact

---

[6] These are also reproduced in the same IME volume, pp. 479, 910, and 1187,
respectively.
[7] The Bickford Drilling Tool Company, Cincinnati, later became the Cincinnati Bickford Tool Company.

that "the power per pound of metal removed decreases very slowly as the speed is advanced, as compared with the reduction effected through increasing the feed."

He also gave details of tests made by the American Locomotive Company during November, 1909, and February, 1910, on three high-speed radial drills that were built [8] to meet the company's specifications and that were all "capable" of driving to destruction any drill submitted for tests, and produced results "that one cannot fail to look upon as remarkable." Finally, Alford included a report of performances by a "new drilling machine of the upright or pillar type" that the Colburn Machine Tool Company, Franklin, Pennsylvania, had brought out a month or two previously.

It would not be appropriate here to bring out any further details of the machines and tests. However, it is enough to say that these were the details and subject matter in which Alford was, at the time, engrossed. With but a single exception,[9] Alford's attention never wavered or focused on anything but the machine and its performance. The human operator, the managerial aspects, the broad laws of performance—matters with which Alford would, in the remaining half of his life, be deeply concerned—none of these was even remotely apparent in his work at the time. Even the brief exception noted was written by Alford primarily because of its effect on the *machine's* performance.

TAYLOR'S VIEWS

Nor was Alford alone in this adherence to the analysis of the machine's performance. His two American compatriots and his British colleague did the same.

[8] The builders were the Bausch Machine Tool Co., Springfield, Mass., Edwin Harrington Sons Co., Philadelphia, and the Niles-Bement-Pond Co., respectively.

[9] Alford, in his remarks on the drill displayed at the Master Car Builders' Convention, wrote (p. 983): An interesting point is this—a 1¼-inch drill operating at a speed of 100 feet and 0.20-inch feed requires fewer than 24 seconds to pass through a 2-inch plate. The importance of having a drilling machine that can be so easily manipulated is high-speed drilling may be lost if too great a length of time is consumed in bringing the head and arm into position for a second hole after the first has been drilled.

In any event, this was the atmosphere in which Taylor rose
to discuss the "papers that had been presented to the meeting."
It must have been very difficult for any of the novitiates to
recognize in Taylor's remarks any "discussion" of the subject at
hand. What is more, he began with remarks that were blunt in
tenor and biting in effect.

These papers, he remarked, were reminiscent of the game of
poker in America. He did not—or at least the recording secretary
did not—use the word familiarly associated with poker to designate a player's action or manner of speech in order to convey,
to his opponent, an impression that his own cards were of high
value. He did, however, very frankly maintain that the young
men who were likely to read the American papers ought to
discount—"cut them in two, or divide by three, or something
of that sort"—the figures given. Not that the contents were not
strictly true, but it was natural to put one's best foot forward,
and, furthermore, "it was best in practice not to do the very
maximum."

As if to keep on the subject and to justify his stand, Taylor
insisted that the proceedings of ASME were already over-
burdened with his own remarks on "high-speed steel and similar
topics." Hence, he

. . . welcomed the opportunity, however, of speaking upon the far
broader subject of which the art of cutting metals and the proper use
of machine tools was but one of the small elements, namely the great
opportunity, as well as the duty, which lay before them as engineers
of taking such steps as would, during the next few years, result in a
very material increase in the output of every man and every machine
in their manufacturing establishments.

As always he offered, as an end result, what every worker
wanted most (namely, higher wages, shorter hours, and better
working conditions), as well as what every employer needed
most (lower labor cost that would allow him to compete more
successfully both at home and abroad).

It has always been Taylor's assertion that the problem of increasing the productive capacity of the workman was twofold.
Here Taylor took the opportunity of "translating" the first

aspect from the American term of "soldiering" to the British "hanging it out." He very pointedly posed the question as to what they, as engineers who were capable of understanding the real effects of such incorrect thinking, were doing to correct this "blighting fallacy." As for the second aspect, the increasing of the workers' output by a "deliberate scientific study of the motions of men, followed by a time study of their motions," he spoke at great length. Using the Gilbreth bricklaying experiments, Taylor painstakingly described them. Not only, he asserted, had motion study been pursued in the United States for the past thirty years, but he ventured to predict "that during the next fifty years a very considerable part of the time of engineers would be spent in the minute motion study of every man in every trade."

Of the day's authors, only Brackenbury replied. He

. . . entirely agreed with the remarks Dr. Taylor had made. Unfortunately the Paper did not deal with that subject, and he would very much have valued any remarks Dr. Taylor might have made on tools and machines of which he had such great experience.

It does not seem likely that Brackenbury, despite his lip service, was fully cognizant of Taylor's message. For, as if to justify that he was aware of the human element, he noted that machine builders had in the past and were in the present studying human motions in order to save such motions and to achieve the resulting saving of time. With that out of the way, he then proceeded to a discussion of the "technical" considerations of his own paper.

ALFORD'S CONCEPTION OF TAYLOR'S PROBLEM

It is difficult to say definitely whether Alford, at this time, was convinced that here was a problem of a *greater* import than the one with which he was presently confronted. Alford undoubtedly realized the significance of the problem that Taylor set before the audience. The columns of his own *American Ma-*

chinist had from time to time been filled with opinions on the "Taylor system." However, Alford's makeup was such that he was ever conscious of the problem *he* had at hand. And to him this problem was the important one, even though he would concede that there were other important problems. As an engineer and as a representative of an engineering periodical he would have felt delinquent in his duty if he felt otherwise. And if there was a controlling factor in his life, it was his devotion to duty.

This devotion was partially the result of his New England upbringing. It was unquestionably the singular mark of his character. Lillian Gilbreth has remarked that Alford's devotion to duty was something that he felt was the earmark of an engineer; and as Lytle, who worked with him for almost twenty years, has asserted, he was proud to be an engineer.

The question may be raised as to Alford's impression of Taylor at the time. It would not be difficult to excuse Alford had he expressed some concern as to the manner in which Taylor seized the spotlight, but nowhere is there any record of any dissatisfaction that he might have expressed. His private papers bear a very brief reference to the incident. Writing some twenty years after the occurrence, Alford merely noted that "during the discussion of these papers, Dr. Frederick W. Taylor referred at some length to scientific management, which was making rapid strides in United States at that time." His only other comment was: "This was the first occasion where I heard Dr. Taylor speak."

Perhaps it may be best to postpone at this time any further analysis of Alford's relations with Taylor. Additional instances will become apparent. However, it might not be amiss to remark that Alford never did become as enthusiastically attached to Taylor as he did to Gantt. In 1931, he referred to Gantt and Gilbreth as "my friends" and acknowledged "their living influence." But he fully realized Taylor's greatness. As Lytle has frequently remarked, Alford always maintained that everything that Taylor did or conceived impinged on the well-being of labor and was performed for and to the worker's benefit.

As for Taylor's personal *diplomacy,* Alford, like many others, was aware of the shortcomings from both first- and secondhand sources.

ALFORD'S *1911 INTERESTS*

It would be extremely difficult, if at all possible, even to attempt to determine Taylor's success in his Birmingham plea, in arousing enthusiasm among the ASME and IME members assembled for "the far broader subject of which the art of cutting metals and the proper use of machine tools was but one of the small elements." However, this is certain: there is no evidence to indicate that Alford's interests were greatly changed.

Alford continued to ferret out and present to the *American Machinist* audiences the technical aspects, problems, and solutions of the work-a-day world of his readers. Not that the periodical was unconcerned with any discussion on scientific management in general or on Taylor in particular, for these were matters of lively interest to shop people as well as others. But Alford's interests never changed from those he had had before he first heard Taylor speak.

A fairly good indication of Alford's current interests may be found in the fact that, in August, 1911, just one year after he presented his paper on drilling machines, his book on *Bearings and Their Lubrication* appeared. Published by the *American Machinist,* the McGraw-Hill Book Company acted as the sole selling agents for the test.

The book had a dual purpose. On the one hand, it attempted to set forth the fundamental principles underlying the design of machinery bearings. On the other, it tried to present the current practices with the types that had achieved commercial importance. As Alford remarked with no little pride, "it is believed to be the first treatment of this subject ever put in book form."

The significance of the book goes beyond its subject matter. It is probably the most typical of all his works before 1912, of his manner of presentation, and of the prospective contributions that eventually materialized during his life.

THE ALFORD PATTERN

There can be little doubt that Hill, during the years Alford served under him, exerted a great influence on his editor's concept of the publishing business. The greatest lesson that Alford learned here came from the Hill creed that was expressed somewhat tersely but highly significantly in a sign that was kept in the publisher's Pearl Street office: READERS FIRST. Consequently, in everything Alford wrote or edited, he was ever mindful of this motto. Thus when Alford felt that the industrial world could use the highly desirable but not too well-known technique of preferred numbers, that was his concern. When he felt that standardization might be helpful, that was his text. He was always ready to satisfy a need.

As far as the bearings book was concerned he evidently found that machine design, at that time, was tending toward an increased use of high-speed shafts and spindles and friction-reducing forms of bearings. Consequently, he felt that the time was ripe to present the subjects of bearings and bearing lubrication.

His audience was very wide, as he well knew from his *American Machinist* experience, and it varied from the men at the machines in the shops to those at the drawing boards in the design sections. Since these men had widely varying training, his language and presentation had to have a broad appeal. His magazine writing served him well, and so his text ranged from fairly theoretical discussions of research not generally appearing in American works to a most practical list of "Do's and Don't's" suitable for easy reference at the worker's bench.

As he was wont to do over and over again in his future writings, he relied on two main sources for his data: (1) personal contacts with and (2) published writings of experts in the field. As Roe has remarked he "drew together the experience and knowledge of other people and co-ordinated their work into a completed whole."

What is more, in taking the work of others and dissecting and reassembling it, he would often bring out the true meaning, with the subsequent result that the material was not only more easily assimilated but had a deeper significance, frequently either unexpressed or overlooked by the original author. This ability would have been exceedingly "dangerous" in the hands of less scrupulous men. His ability to select, reword, reassemble, and report was never used maliciously. Not only was every selection checked but, as Coes has remarked, carefully annotated. As a matter of fact, it happened on occasion that Alford's quotation of verse and text found an even "earlier" author— much to the chagrin of the quoted "author." [10]

THE SUBJECT OF BEARINGS

The book bears excellent testimony to Alford's precision and his orderly mind. Beginning with a definition of machinery bearings ("the parts of the bed, frame, or other members that constrain rotating parts, such as shafts or spindles"), he proceeds through a classification of bearings, based on the kind of contact between surfaces and further broken down in accordance with the direction in which the load acts.

Hence, his book is merely a logical expansion of the following (p. 2):

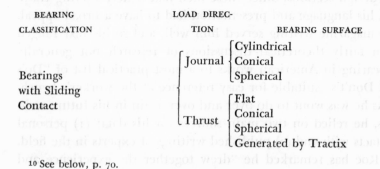

BEARING CLASSIFICATION	LOAD DIRECTION	BEARING SURFACE
Bearings with Sliding Contact	Journal	Cylindrical Conical Spherical
	Thrust	Flat Conical Spherical Generated by Tractix

[10] See below, p. 70.

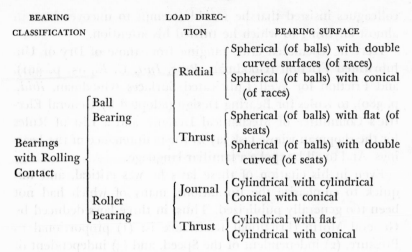

BEARING CLASSIFICATION		LOAD DIRECTION	BEARING SURFACE

Bearings with Rolling Contact

Ball Bearing — Radial — Spherical (of balls) with double curved surfaces (of races) / Spherical (of balls) with conical (of races)

Ball Bearing — Thrust — Spherical (of balls) with flat (of seats) / Spherical (of balls) with double curved (of seats)

Roller Bearing — Journal — Cylindrical with cylindrical / Conical with conical

Roller Bearing — Thrust — Cylindrical with flat / Cylindrical with conical

At one point he asserts (p. 1):

The relative motion of all these constraining members and the members constrained is resisted at their surfaces of contact by a force which is called the force of friction. Thus all kinds of bearings must be designed with particular reference to minimizing this force, and our starting point must be a study of friction.

He then proceeds systematically to discuss pertinent matters concerning material, design, operation, and maintenance of bearings.

FUNDAMENTAL LAWS AND BASIC SIGNIFICANCE

Alford's keen search for fundamental laws is clearly evident here, for the book abounds in presentations of them. Once a subject is treated, he carefully sets down the fundamentals. Of course, in the physical sciences the existence of laws is well known, and it is unquestionably from such a study that in later years he attempted to carry over the "law concept" into the management field. As a matter of fact, so impressed had he become with the importance of such fundamentals that one of his colleagues insisted that he would attempt to uncover laws in almost anything to which he turned his attention.

Here he assembled laws, ranging from those of Dry or Unlubricated Friction (Goodman, *Proc. Inst. C. E., 85,* p. 391), and Friction for Well Lubricated Surfaces (Goodman, *ibid.,* p. 380), to Rules for Bearing Design (adopted by General Electric's Committee of Mechanical Design), and a List of Rules for the shopman whose task lay in the maintenance of the bearings. And to all he spoke a familiar language.

Even in his citation of these laws he was critical, and was quick to emphasize the limitations, many of which had not been too generally publicized. Thus, in three laws deduced by General Morin (Frictional Resistance is: (1) proportional to Pressure, (2) independent of the Speed, and (3) independent of the Extent of the Surfaces), Alford carefully noted that "these laws have frequently been quoted and treated as if they were rigidly true."

However, it was not enough for Alford merely to assert that they were "only approximately true for a very limited range of conditions"; he rather supported his case by referring back to some little-publicized paper or report in which the original author was conscious of such a limitation. In this case, Alford unearthed a letter from Morin to the Institution of Mechanical Engineers to show the awareness of the laws' own discoverer in this connection.

Alford's sources, too, are indicative of the man's breadth. They vary from the classical works (e.g., Coulomb) through his contemporary acquaintances (e.g., Kimball), from foreign associations (e.g., Royal Society) through his own societies (ASME), from practice abroad (British Railways) through American practice (at such places as Westinghouse, Sellers, U.S. War Department).

Even in those relatively early days, Alford was not unaware of the value of pointing out the significance of a subject. Hence he took time in his technical discussions to point out the significance of the three inventions, babbitting, Sellers' bearings (invented by Bancroft), and ring oiling (invented by Sweet), which he considered of greatest importance in the field.

Thus Alford attempted to correct the general notion that the fame of Isaac Babbitt was based on his discovery of the white metal alloy named after him. Alford showed here that the babbitting process had a much greater influence on machinery bearing construction than did the alloy, of which there are "numberless lining metals" in use. Again, he typically substantiated his claim by referring to an original source. This time it was "a little booklet issued by the inventor in 1848" (but not widely known) which, treating the "babbitting process," maintained (p. 139):

Isaac Babbitt would inform the public that it does not consist in the *use* of the soft metal, simply, but in the mode of its *applications and confinement* in boxes prepared for that purpose.

SOME CONCLUSIONS

In brief, the *Bearings* text not only shows that Alford's main 1911 interests were still in the machine tool line, but it is a clear indication of his manner of thinking, his mode of work, and his means of expression, matters that set the pattern for the writings that followed.

In the first place, it highlights the work he did best: selecting, appraising, editing, and presenting even more clearly the work that had been and was being done throughout the world. This characteristic of being able to give a more searching and meaningful form to the works of others is probably most characteristic of Alford.

Secondly, the book shows the many-sided audience for whom he could write, from the theoretical- to the practical-minded. And more than this, it demonstrates how he could blend these diverse interests within a single medium and maintain the interests of all.

Thirdly, Alford's preciseness, his partiality for classifications, and his earnest attempt to establish a fundamental understanding of a subject, so clearly demonstrated here, were to serve him time and time again in all fields from his technical editorship through his classroom teaching.

Alford's love for laws and rules is already established. Despite his attempt to use this method at the "least provocation," as some of his associates have claimed, this was necessary, for Alford, in order to have a clear understanding of a subject. Furthermore, he found it necessary to strip a subject down to its bare essentials not only for clear presentation but also to assure logical correctness.

Once these fundamental laws were set up, biased opinion could no longer do much damage. Coes insists that when on a job it was always with a good deal of assured relief that he would turn to Alford's Laws of Management in order to find points of weakness and strength.

Yet despite his fondness for such laws, Alford was ever-watchful and critical in his understanding of their limits of application. And so, despite his reliance on his wide affiliation and acquaintance with individuals, firms, institutions, and organizations, Alford had a keen ability to appraise their works.

Finally, the man had a keen appreciation of the needs of the times, whether a book, a discussion or a new index. For service was the dominating force in his life, throughout which he served willingly wherever he felt he could enrich his chosen profession of engineering.

"It was the easiest thing in the world," according to Clarence Davies, "whenever we had a job to do, to pick up a telephone, call L. P., tell him what was needed and that he was the one who could do the job, and then rest, knowing it was done."

Alford's humor should indeed be mentioned here. For with the exception of his *Bearings,* it was almost the first time in about a third of a century that there was the slightest evidence of humor in such writings. No doubt he used it more to impress the need for proper bearing maintenance on the shopmen than to display his original witticisms. On page 166, among his rules on the care of bearings, he wrote:

> Squirt oil into the oil holes and not onto the floor—in the latter place it may lubricate your shoes but it does not help the bearing.

Alford's sense of humor was not limited. Almost all his acquaintances still remark about his love of humor, recalling his kindly, smiling face. As Lytle recollects from frequent luncheons at the University Heights Faculty Club, it was not unusual for Alford to write down particularly apt bits of humor so that he could reproduce them on the appropriate occasion—usually the opening of an informal lecture.

On the whole, however, Alford's written works are essentially serious. Fundamentally, engineering was, as far as Alford was concerned, a very serious business, and his works treated it accordingly. Yet, even were it not, it would be extremely difficult to imagine him dealing flippantly with any subject, no matter how trivial. All his actions were deliberate, thoughtful, and planned. Perhaps Cozzens, in reminiscing about Alford, best sized up the situation. "Everything he did he did with a good deal of thought—whether he was trying to decide the next card to play in a game of bridge or attempting to arrive at some important management decision."

Chapter II

THE 1912 REPORT

TAYLOR'S "PRINCIPLES" AND THE ASME

It is hardly necessary to refer to Copley's monumental biography to realize the stormy petrel that Taylor had become, in as well as out of engineering circles. Enough people, engineers and nonengineers, and enough writings, engineering and nonengineering, testify to the facts. However, if any manifestation of Taylor's position were to be considered, the circumstances surrounding the publication of Taylor's *Principles of Scientific Management* might well be used to illustrate the situation.

For a reader who might innocently turn to Taylor's own Introduction to the edition that Harper and Brothers brought out in 1911, it would be difficult to realize what, if anything, had taken place. A single sentence in the last paragraph of a three-and-one-half-page introduction is Taylor's only reference to the affair: "This paper was originally prepared for presentation to the American Society of Mechanical Engineers." The remainder of the paragraph merely pointed out that the illustrations were, consequently, chosen because of the assumption that they would appeal to engineers and managers. Nevertheless, it was felt that the principles were equally applicable to home, farm, church, university, and philanthropic institutions.

Consequently, for such a reader, unless he were particularly intuitive or had a suspicious turn of mind, there would be no further investigation of whether these papers, "originally prepared for presentation," actually were presented to engineering men and their societies.

Person, some thirty-six years later, was somewhat more revealing in his Foreword to the Harper reissue, in a one-volume edition, of Taylor's *Shop Management, Principles of Scientific Management,* and *Testimony Before the Special Committee of the House of Representatives to Investigate the Taylor and Other Systems of Shop Management Under Authority of House Resolution 90.* He pointed out that in 1903, when Taylor presented his paper on "Shop Management" at the Saratoga meeting of ASME, the emphasis was on the mechanistic aspects because the Society "was particular that all papers should be concise and free from what it then conceived to be extraneous matter." [1]

What is more, this emphasis on technique, with only passing interest displayed in principles or in social significance, was probably also in keeping with Taylor's own ideas at the time. Taylor, it must be remembered, was a very practical man—one who believed that management, if it could be taught at all, must be "lived" in the shop and not "read" in a classroom. Furthermore, his audience consisted mainly of engineers and executives who in their industrial lives maintained positions of authority, so that his ideas when once grasped could be adopted, developed, and co-ordinated.

As time passed and as the techniques were thoroughly discussed, questions on principles were raised, and the field of "scientific management" became "controversial."

Just how controversial the matter had become is evident from a series of letters that Taylor wrote to Alford in 1912. Suffice to say for the moment that they bear testimony to the fact that few of the executives—all of whom had received great benefits from Taylor's free services—were willing to allow their names to be associated publicly with Taylor's ideas.

These, then, were the times when Taylor decided, probably as much to clear the atmosphere of misunderstandings as for

[1] P. vi.

any other reason, to present a paper defining and expanding principles rather than techniques. According to Taylor's own files, "this paper was originally presented by the writer to the American Society of Mechanical Engineers during the month of January, 1910, and has been in the hands of the Meetings Committee for nearly a year."

During this period the much publicized Eastern Rate Case Hearings were before the Interstate Commerce Commission.[2] The term "scientific management," used by Taylor in a very limited sense as early as 1903, had been adopted by a group of engineers whom Brandeis called into conference late in 1910.[3] Emerson had captured popular attention by his assertion that "an economy of . . . not less than $1,000,000 a day" could be effected by the railroads "by the introduction of proper efficiency system or scientific management." [4] Numerous articles on the movement and interviews with Taylor appeared. As Taylor wrote, on January 6, 1911, "The general interest invoked during the last few months in scientific management has caused the editors of a number of monthly magazines to visit the writer for the purpose of obtaining material upon scientific management to be presented in the various publications."

It was at this time that Taylor withdrew his paper from the ASME and, at his own expense, brought out a "special edition

2 The U.S. railroads, operating east of the Mississippi and north of the Ohio and Potomac rivers, filed their new tariffs about June, 1910. The Brandeis brief was filed on January 3, 1911. (See Preface, unpaged, by C. B. G. (evidently C. B. Going, Editor of the *Engineering Magazine*) to *Scientific Management and the Railroads* by L. D. Brandeis. See also *Interstate Commerce Commission Reports,* 20, 245 ff.; *Evidence Taken by the Interstate Commerce Commission in the Matter of Proposed Advances in Freight Rates by Carriers,* 61st Congress, 3rd Session, Senate Document No. 725, 2620 ff., November 21 (1910).)

3 The meeting took place in Gantt's apartment. Frank Gilbreth was present, but Taylor was absent. See Drury, *Scientific Management,* pp. 35-39. See also Person, "The Origin and Nature of Scientific Management," in the Taylor Society's *Scientific Management in American Industry,* p. 2.

4 See Brandeis, *op. cit.,* p. 83; *Record,* p. 3533; *Evidence,* p. 2620. In a privately prepared life of *Harrington Emerson* by the Emerson Engineers: "Compiling statistics for this appearance, Harrington Emerson easily found wastes and losses totalling $3,000,000 a day. He remarked that he would be executed by the railroad executives if he used that figure and decided to testify to a $1,000,000 a day waste."

published in February 1911 for Confidential Circulation among the members of the American Society of Mechanical Engineers with the Compliments of the Author." The term "Confidential Circulation" is particularly interesting because Taylor immediately thereafter authorized Harper and Brothers, who published the private edition, to bring out an edition for the general public.

Taylor justified his action by asserting

Inasmuch as the American Society of Mechanical Engineers has received and published in the past all of the early articles which appeared on this subject, it seems appropriate that this paper which attempts to set forth the underlying principles of this management, should go before the members of the Society before being given to the general public.

This object can now be attained only by printing this special edition of the paper, because the time remaining before the publication of the magazine articles referred to is so short as to preclude the possibility of printing the paper in the Journal of the Society. The writer has, therefore, been reluctantly obliged to withdraw his paper from the hands of the Meetings Committee of the American Society of Mechanical Engineers and present it to the membership of the Society with the hope that many of our members will find it of interest.

SCIENTIFIC MANAGEMENT AND THE ASME

It is fitting to examine the factors that have caused this situation. In the first place, the question may be raised whether or not the general subject was an improper one for a society devoted to mechanical engineering. Then, as now, regrettably, there are those who envision engineering as solely concerned with the physical application of technical problems. This is particularly disturbing, since Tredgold's famous definition of 1822 that embraced the social aspects.

Officially, the ASME was from its inception dedicated to problems beyond the limited physical aspects. The Society's first president, R. H. Thurston,[5] in his Inaugural Address asserted that, among the "Objects of the Society,"

> The Society will have much work to do as a union of citizens having important interests confided to them, and its promise will lie no less in the field of social economy than in that which has reference only to the individual interests of its members.

H. R. Towne's paper, "The Engineer as Economist," presented at the 1886 meeting of the ASME, once again brought up the question. After alluding to the development of engineering which "of late years has subdivided itself into numerous and distinct divisions, one of which is that of mechanical engineering," Towne [6] asserted:

> It will probably not be disputed that the matter of shop management is of equal importance with that of engineering, as affecting the successful conduct of most, if not all of our great industrial establishments, and that the *management of works* has become a matter of such great and far-reaching importance as perhaps to justify its classification as one of the modern arts.

He bemoaned the lack of ready availability of the already "vast amount of accumulated experience in the art of workshop management" and added:

> Surely this condition of things is wrong and should be remedied. But the remedy must not be looked for from those who are "businessmen" or clerks or accountants only; it should come from those whose training and experience have given them an understanding of both sides (viz.: the mechanical and the clerical) of the important questions involved. It should originate, therefore, from those who are also engineers, and for the reasons above indicated, particularly from mechanical engineers. Granting this, why should it not originate from, and be promoted by, The American Society of Mechanical Engineers?

Later, in the same year, December 2, 1886, Towne, performing the duties of the acting president owing to the illness of the

---

[5] Thurston, "President's Inaugural Address," *Trans. ASME, 1,* 14-29 (1880) (p. 3, first edition; p. 15, second edition).

[6] Towne, "The Engineer as Economist," *Trans. ASME, 7,* 428-432 (1886).

president, Coleman Sellers, and chairing a session at Stevens
Institute during the Seventh Annual Meeting of ASME, again
referred to his previous paper

. . . in which I modestly ventured to suggest that the Society might
annex another subject to its discussions, bringing in industrial or
economic questions. I had no thought then that such a proposition
would be entertained except as a side issue, a matter which those
of the members who took interest in such things could promote by
attending a supplemental session. The proposition was received
favorably in one sense and unfavorably in another. The idea of
introducing such matters in our discussions was accepted. The idea
of relegating them to an annex or subsection was negatived em-
phatically, and it was voted that such subjects should be introduced
and made part of our regular transactions.

Finally, as if to lay full claim to these matters to the exclusion
of the other two engineering societies then in existence, he said:

I may add that it is more appropriate for this Society to consider
such matters than any other of the engineering societies. We have
in our membership, much more than have the Civil Engineers or
Mining Engineers, men who are managers of labor, who are either
owners or representatives of owners, and who therefore control
capital. There are fewer purely professional men and men having
no direct responsibility for the management of others, in this Society
than in either of the other engineering societies. These economic
questions come nearer to us, therefore, and to a larger number of
our members, and in my judgment they can be most properly considered, to a reasonable extent, germane to the interests and duties
of a large proportion of our membership.

It is appropriate to note at this time that an even fuller
realization of these matters came on January 24, 1920. At that
time, according to the personal files of the secretary of the
Society, C. E. Davies, the Council approved and adopted the
Final Report of the Committee on Aims and Organization.
This committee, which was chaired by L. C. Marburg but which
had among its members and, according to many of those in

authoritative ASME positions, as its "dominating force" L. P. Alford, had presented its Preliminary Report at the 1919 Spring Meeting. Among its recommendations adopted was:

> . . . that Industrial Engineering is a major subject for consideration by the Society and shall be placed on a par with all major technical subjects.

Thus it was probably because of this heritage that the ASME became the center of those interested in the problems of management.[7] However, the discussions here, according to Person, were concerned with individual problems more than with the integrated one. Taylor's temperament was such as to become impatient with such a procedure. He had started at Midvale with a premise that insisted that a "fair day's work" be understood and measured, and with that beginning he had built his "system." Why, then, should that not be everyone's procedure?

Assuming that he was correct in this idea, the psychological approach he took to win converts was hardly valid. In the first place, few ideas, even in the realm of science, are accepted rapidly, even though they are propounded by persons sincere in their beliefs and armed with laboratory data sheets. As if impatience were not enough, Taylor proceeded to present a paper [8] with the intent of dealing with his wage payment ideas but actually dealing mainly with the need for performance measurement as a basis of wage payments. Much to Taylor's chagrin, his wage plan was attacked and—more important—his appeal for an understanding of a fair day's work was ignored. In 1903 he made another attempt. This time he was more forth-

---

[7] Person, "The Origin of Scientific Management," in the Taylor Society's *Scientific Management in American Industry*, p. 6, believes the ASME became the early forum of management mainly because there were no other management, manufacturers', or businessmen's organizations at the time. However, it seems plausible that if the need arose such associations would have arisen. Thus, the National Association of Manufacturers was established in 1895 and the National Metal Trades Association in 1899.

[8] "A Piece Rate System," in *Trans. ASME, 16*, 856-903 (1895).

right in his "Shop Management." [9] Again there was no sympathetic interest in the idea of measuring a fair day's work.

However, Taylor's Presidential Address in 1906, "On the Art of Cutting Metals," [10] brought no such disinterest, for here was a subject that could be viewed with less emotion. However, when Taylor decided to present *principles* of management, a stalemate was reached.

Of course, there is the question as to whether Taylor's *Principles* was or was not an adequate presentation. Person thinks it was not, basically because Taylor's "inacademic mind" was not particularly suited to thinking in terms of generalizations. However, the only real generalizations of which Taylor was capable did not appear until the winter of 1911-12, when his abilities in this direction were brought out in his testimony before the House Committee.

Taylor himself must have been conscious of the power of his testimony for, as revealed in a letter written to Alford on August 15, 1912, Taylor attempted to answer Alford's questions by quoting from it.[11]

In the notes that William Stewart Ayars "wrote up" from the lectures delivered at the First Summer School of Scientific Management, conducted by Frank Gilbreth and his associates at 256 Meeting Street, Providence, Rhode Island, in the period between August 4 and September 1, 1913, there are, of course, numerous matters of great interest concerning the early days of the movement. Two of these bear examination at this point.

The first is directly concerned with some occurrences that took place after Taylor had privately printed his *Principles*. Portions of this work appeared in the *American Magazine* to

9 "Shop Management," in *Trans. ASME, 24,* 1337-1456 (1903).

10 "On the Art of Cutting Metals," in *Trans. ASME, 28,* 30-279 (1907).

11 Taylor's private papers seem to indicate his own realization of the weakness of his writing. In connection with this letter, he emphasized: "I would call your attention to the fact that this testimony has been given orally, and in a great hurry, and it should have been completely revised before being published but there was no time to make a thorough revision." Again, in his draft of his discussion of Alford's "The Present State of the Art of Management," Taylor wrote the following note, evidently to his secretary: "Improve the English."

which, according to the Ayars report of the eleventh session,
August 9,

. . . letters began to pile in from all over the country. These were
turned over to G. for an article; G. wrote his "primer of Scientific
Management" in answer, & the Am. Magazine would not publish
it, lest they offend their subscribers! Van Nostrand then took it up,
G. taking no royalty, & pub. the book cheaply for popular circulation.

Once again indicative of the situation surrounding Taylor.

The second concerns a fact of which few people today are
aware: Taylor attempted to apply scientific management principles to at least the publishing aspects of the ASME. As a matter of fact, the seventh session of the Gilbreth series was conducted by Whittaker, who actually worked on the installation
of scientific management at the Society's offices. This took place
during Taylor's presidency. Taylor began by appointing a standardization committee, and Calvin Rice came in, during June,
1906, first as acting secretary and then, in December, as secretary. Cooke, whose job it was to make the installation, came
the same time as Rice.

Interesting as these points may be, of greater concern at the
moment is the fact that the incidents surrounding and emanating from the *Principles* are sufficient indication of the storm
surrounding Taylor.

ASME'S REQUEST FOR AN INVESTIGATION

The storm's fury was violent enough not only to be observed
in and out of the profession but disturbing enough within
ASME for the Society to take some steps toward discovering
the damage and calming the waters.

Although few then—or now—realized it, the job fell entirely
on Alford. Seemingly he accepted and completed the task as
much because it was assigned to him as a task in his daily employment as for any other reason.

It was early in the summer of 1912 when Hill, president of

The Hill Publishing Company, owners and publishers of the *American Machinist*,[12] and referred to by Alford as "my boss," was visited by James Mapes Dodge. Hill called Alford to his office to meet his visitor because, as Alford noted some nineteen years later, "Dodge had a bit of work that they both would like to have me do."

Alford maintained later that the task was particularly caused by Taylor's withdrawal and private publication of his *Principles* after the Meetings and Program Committee of ASME had held it for nine months. Alford, never given to overemphasis, merely noted factually: "The affair created some ill feeling." Consequently, Dodge was chosen chairman of a special committee "to investigate the matter of Scientific Management and report to the Society."

This, then, was the "bit of work." As to why Alford was chosen, it seems likely that the choice was a natural consequence of the realization that the *American Machinist* had for so long already been a forum for such discussions, particularly on the practical level. Alford, it must be remembered, had assumed the post of editor in chief the year before and, in that capacity, he must have had more than a passing acquaintance with the situation in and out of the ASME. As a matter of fact, in April of that very year, he had investigated the plants of the Link-Belt Company [13] which, as he expressed it, were "frequently referred to as best examples of machine shops using the Taylor System of Scientific Management." He had been particularly interested in examining here the "three objections commonly urged against scientific management": (1) inflexibility, (2) re-

---

[12] It is of interest to note, in this connection, that the *American Machinist* was once before directly concerned with the ASME. According to J. E. Sweet, who served as president in 1882, the Society's beginnings go back to the time "when the *American Machinist* was being published in a small office at 96 Fulton Street, New York, and when," in order to foster closer relationships between the publishers and the contributors, "the notion came to my mind to get as many of them together as well we could" with the eventual idea "that it might lead to an organization." (See Paper No. 1274, "Dedication of Memorial Tablet to Robert Henry Thurston," particularly "Dr. Thurston's Connection With the Society" by John E. Sweet, *Trans. ASME, 32,* 52-54 (1910).)

[13] Alford, "Scientific Management in Use," *American Machinist, 36,* 548-550, April 4 (1912).

pression of the worker's initiative, and (3) "unstabilizing of the working force." He found these "unfounded in fact" at the Link-Belt plants, for the system had been modified and improved, and it was responsible for the increased profits, the elimination of labor difficulties, and the efficient satisfaction of customers' orders.

The Dodge choice certainly was a satisfactory one, for Alford was a conscientious, tireless, thorough, and devoted worker. Alone he conducted the investigation and wrote the report.[14] The committee met but once, and that meeting took place after the report had already been written. Because all the members except one, M. H. Vaughan, signed the report, it was issued as a Majority Report. According to the Alford files, the only modification that the committee suggested, on hearing it read at the single meeting, was that an attempt be made to "soften here and there some of my vigorous language."

THE ASME SUBCOMMITTEE

The Dodge Committee, an offshoot of the Meetings Committee, was officially known as the "Sub-Committee on Economic Administration of Industrial Establishments of the American Society of Mechanical Engineers." Its members, in addition to Dodge (chairman) and Alford (secretary), included D. M. Bates, H. A. Evans, Wilfred Lewis, W. B. Tardy, H. R. Towne, and, of course, Vaughan. Even at the outset, this committee can hardly be said to have been hostile to Taylor. Both its chairman and Dodge were included by Copley among the "most distinguished and open of his [i.e., Taylor's] supporters," particularly at a time when few willingly espoused Taylor's thinking as a matter of public record.[15] As further evidence of the friendliness with which at least the majority of the committee's members held Taylor, it might be wise to take cognizance of the following analysis.

14 Alford's private papers reveal this. As for public recognition of this fact, see Thompson, *The Theory and Practice of Scientific Management*, p. 24: "I believe the actual writer of the report is Mr. L. P. Alford."

15 Copley, *Taylor*, Vol. 2, p. 364.

Dodge, writing for ASME publication in a paper entitled "A History of the Introduction of a System of Shop Management," described his experiences with "the system of shop management, identified with the name of Mr. Fred W. Taylor," was certainly complimentary. He asserted: [16]

The Taylor System is not a method of pay, a specific ruling of account books, nor the use of high-speed steel. It is simply an honest, intelligent effort to arrive at the absolute control of every department, to let tabulated and unimpeachable fact take the place of individual opinion, to develop team play to its highest possibility.

During the testimony before the Special House Committee,[17] Taylor on at least two occasions referred to "my friend, Wilfred Lewis." Lewis, president of the Tabor Manufacturing Company of Philadelphia, had been similarly endearing and wrote of "my good friend, Taylor," in "An Object Lesson in Efficiency." [18] Here he also wrote of the great street railway strike in Philadelphia in 1910, which was accompanied by many sympathy strikes throughout the city; he credited the Taylor System as the bulwark by which only one man in his company's 150 joined the strike. Citing other instances of the effectiveness of the system, Lewis concluded that in his company, at least, "we have firmly established a successful business upon the principles of scientific management as laid down by Mr. Taylor."

As far as Towne was concerned, one need hardly be reminded that Taylor, during his second year of ASME membership, was greatly influenced by a Towne paper. As a matter of fact, according to Person [19]

a convenient milestone to mark the beginning of this movement was Henry R. Towne's classic paper, "The Engineer as Economist,"

[16] *Trans. ASME, 27,* 720-725 (1906).

[17] Taylor's *Testimony,* p. 279 in Harper's reprint. See also Original Public Document, Vol. 3, pp. 1377 ff. Taylor owned 120 shares in the Tabor Company, "all of which I bought as a matter of trying to help out my friend . . . when he was in dire straits."

[18] Lewis, "An Object Lesson in Efficiency," p. 241 in *Scientific Management* by Thompson. See also Lewis, *Technology and Industrial Efficiency,* pp. 173 ff.

[19] Taylor Society, *Scientific Management in American Industry,* p. 5.

presented at a meeting of the American Society of Mechanical Engineers in 1886.

Furthermore, Towne had written, in his Foreword (page 5) [20] to Taylor's *Shop Management:*

As a fellow-worker with Dr. Taylor, in the field of industrial management, I have followed the development of his work, almost from its commencement with constantly increasing admiration for the exceptional talent he has brought to this new field of investigation, and with constantly increasing realization of the fundamental importance of the methods which he had initiated. The substitution of machinery for unaided human labor was the great industrial achievement of the nineteenth century. The new achievement to which Dr. Taylor points the way consists of elevating human labor itself to a higher plane of efficiency and earning power.

Tardy, too, was no stranger to the movement. Two of his papers on the subject were "Scientific Management and Efficiency in the United States Navy" [21] and "A Plea for a Standard Organization of the Engineer Division Aboard Ship, and for a Uniform Method of Management of the Engineer Department With a Section Devoted to the Application of Scientific Management." [22]

As for Evans, he not only wrote on what may be called instances of scientific management in operation but he did this in Alford's own periodical, the *American Machinist:* "Detailed Instructions for Machine Shop Methods," [23] "Do Taylor's Methods Increase Production?" [24] "General Instructions for Machine Shop Method," [25] "Output Under Scientific Management," [26]

[20] For additional tributes to Taylor by Towne, Dodge, and Lewis, see "Tributes to Frederick W. Taylor," *Trans. ASME, 37,* 1459-1496 (1915), collated and edited by H. K. Hathaway, for comments at the Memorial Meeting which took place on December 19, 1915, during the one hour suspension of business at the Annual Meeting for this purpose.

[21] *Engineering Magazine, 41,* 545 ff.

[22] *Journal of American Society of Naval Engineers, 23,* 681 ff.

[23] *American Machinist, 31,* 645-649, April 23 (1908).

[24] *Ibid., 34,* 1133-1134, June 15 (1911).

[25] *Ibid., 31,* 610-614, April 16 (1908).

[26] *Ibid., 34,* 1202, 1203, June 29 (1911).

"Reduction of Cost in Navy Yard Work," [27] and "Effect of the Taylor System: What Is to Become of the Mechanic?" [28]

Clearly, then, a majority of the members of the ASME's Subcommittee on Administration had openly expressed approval of a system which, fortunately or otherwise, could not be completely separated from either Taylor or his personality. What of Alford? Where did he stand?

ALFORD ON TAYLOR

In this analysis, two facts must not be forgotten: (1) Taylor had become so closely identified with the system that it had become just that—the Taylor System—and, in the eyes of many, the two were inseparable.[29] (2) The Alford study was a direct result of the bitterness that surrounded Taylor.

With these two thoughts in mind, it might be wise to examine Alford's writings on the subject between the period that opened with Birmingham ASME-IME Meeting and closed with the New York University days when Alford privately and informally expressed to Lytle the opinion that Taylor's work was for the benefit of the worker and when, just one year before his death, Alford in his text, *Principles of Industrial Management*,[30] insisted that, of Taylor, Gantt, Gilbreth, and Emerson,

[27] *Ibid., 33*, 1200-1202, June 30 (1910).

[28] *Ibid., 33*, 1095, December 15 (1910).

[29] The first question the chairman, William B. Wilson, who later became Secretary of Labor, asked Taylor when he appeared on Thursday, January 25, 1912, before the Special House Committee, related, of course, to his name and address. The second was: "Mr. Taylor, are you the author or compiler of the system of shop management generally known as the 'Taylor System'?" The witness replied: "I have had a very great deal to do with the development of the system of management which has come to be called by certain people the 'Taylor System' but I am only one of the many men who have been instrumental in the development of this system. I wish to state, however, that at no time have I personally called the system the 'Taylor System' nor have I ever advocated the desirability of calling it by that name. I have constantly protested against it being branded with my name or the name of any man's name. I think that it should be properly called by some generic term which could be and ought to be acceptable to the whole country."

[30] P. 61.

> The outstanding personality of this group of four is Tay-
> lor who is continually and properly referred to as the
> "Father of Scientific Management."

The significance of that statement can only be realized when
Alford's keen devotion to Gantt is understood.[31]

Basically, the most pertinent of Alford's views on the *subject*
were expressed in the "Principles of Management," [32] an article
which he wrote with A. H. Church. The article, which Church
admitted was largely written by Alford, was an outgrowth of
an earlier article by Church alone, "Has Scientific Management
Science?" [33]

Without going into the details discussed elsewhere in this
study, Church answered his own question—after alluding to certain extracts from Taylor's writings—in the negative. But, in
the Alford-Church study, Alford enumerated the "principles of
management" and then showed where the "Taylor System"
fitted. Hence, on this basis at least, Alford had before the ASME
Report on 1912 already expressed beliefs as to some inade-
quacies of the "system" (if not the man, Taylor) even though
he found Link-Belt in a good condition.

A further attempt at fathoming Alford's notions at the time
might possibly be made based on a study of the magazine he
edited. In this case, the *American Machinist* had forthrightly
presented articles on both sides of the question.

Among the better known of the critical articles was that of
Dexter Kimball, who at the time was Professor of Machine Design and Construction at Sibley College, Cornell. In his paper,
"Another Side of Efficiency Engineering," [34] Kimball briefly
pointed out some of the social and economic implications of
the movement but was particularly disturbed by the absence of

[31] In 1939-42, Alford was on a Special Committee of the ASME Council on a
Frederick W. Taylor Memorial. This was an unsuccessful attempt to establish
a plaque for Taylor at the Society's offices.

[32] *American Machinist, 36,* 857-862, May 30 (1912).

[33] *Ibid., 35,* 108-112, July 20 (1911).

[34] *American Machinist, 35,* 263-265, August 10 (1911). Kimball's views were
reiterated in his *Principles of Industrial Organization* (McGraw-Hill Book Co.,
1913), which acknowledged Alford's aid in the book's writing.

a treatment of "what we need most . . . [namely] . . . scientific distribution."

Other views even less favorable appeared. Illustrative of the tenor of some of these was one by Frank C. Hudson, which attempted to give "The Machinists' Side of Taylorism." [35] Boasting of his prowess as a machinist, Hudson "sympathized with the opposition," i.e., those who opposed Taylor, which was "bound to be misunderstood by men like Mr. Taylor whose idea of class distinction belongs to the Middle Ages, as is clearly shown in his latest book [36] on the subject." Hudson fought for his fellow workers, denied that "we are a set of loafers," and asserted that the removal of responsibility meant removal of ambition and co-operation and was, in the long run, definitely uneconomical.

Of course, to have inspired such impassioned comments, there must have been some equally fervid articles on the other side. The Evans articles, already referred to, are indicative of these "partisan" viewpoints.

Then, too, there were the middle-of-the-road advocates. James R. Johnson, a manager, insisted that his company, for example, was being successfully operated and suggested that well enough be left alone.[37] C. J. Morrison, of the Department of Effective Organization of Suffern & Company, New York consultants, deplored the criticisms appearing in the magazine which, he felt, gave the impression that "scientific management and the Taylor System are the same thing." [38]

The magazine was rich in articles that showed the operation of the various aspects of the "new management." Many, taking their cue from Taylor, warned of dangers lurking in a haphazard, careless introduction of the system in a plant; even these were matched by the "opposing" camp which included

[35] *American Machinist, 34,* 773.

[36] The Hudson article appeared in the April 27, 1911, issue, and the Taylor book referred to was the *Principles of Scientific Management,* which was published by Harper earlier in the year.

[37] "A Manager's View of the Taylor System," in *American Machinist, 34,* 885-886, May 11 (1911).

[38] Letter appearing in *American Machinist, 34,* 1181, June 22 (1911).

one which, in a decidedly humorous vein, suggested "how not to do it." [39]

Of course, the fact that the *American Machinist* printed an article—be it pro or con—did not necessarily mean that either the magazine or its editors had taken that particular point of view. The attempt to associate the articles of individual authors with the periodical and its editors was evidently made many years ago, when it reached such alarming proportions that the magazine itself took cognizance of it. Here, too, it was the subject of Taylor that brought the matter into print.

THE "AMERICAN MACHINIST" AND TAYLOR

On July 14, 1910, there appeared an editorial [40] titled "What the *American Machinist* Stands For," in which the editors felt that, "judging from letters we occasionally receive from our friends, some of them do not seem to clearly understand the function of a technical paper." Asserting that there was a mistaken impression "that the paper indorses, or 'stands for,' everything that appears in its columns," the editors maintained that this obviously could not be the case considering the fact that some subjects discussed showed such divergent views that "it would be impossible for us to stand for them all." It was felt that the magazine had a duty to report as much information as possible throughout the country, and some of the articles might leave much to be desired. Furthermore, the articles that did appear "are not all approved by the Editors."

Because the example given is pertinent, it may be best to quote, in full, the following:

Because one man writes of his failures to secure good results with high-speed steel, a few seem to think that the *American Machinist* has taken a "stand" against that extremely useful product. Or if some one should criticize any of the numerous shop systems, we are accused of being opposed to all systems.

[39] "Echoes of the Oil Country," in *American Machinist, 34,* 1036-1037, June 1 (1911).

[40] *American Machinist, 33,* 85, July 14 (1910).

If the columns of the *American Machinist* were not open to both sides of any shop problem, it could rightfully be called narrow and one-sided. And whatever its faults, it does not intend to be guilty of that.

Only what appears on the editorial pages can be called the "stand" or attitude of the paper. And whether the ideas advanced in this way meet your views or not, we trust that you will try to believe that they represent what the editors feel to be for the best interests of the industry as a whole.

Since, then, the editorials may speak for the editors and since Alford was engineering editor before 1911 and editor in chief for six years thereafter, it is entirely possible, but hardly likely, that the editorials that appeared during this time did not warrant his attention [41] or meet with his approval.

At the time of the Eastern Rate Hearings, the magazine printed "special correspondence" covering the case.[42] Whether the author, whoever he was, *expressed* the *opinions of the editors* in this very "favorable" article is not known. However, there can be no doubt concerning another article that appeared in the same issue of December 15, 1910: this was an editorial.[43]

The editorial pointed out that these hearings emphasized "an important point that might well be considered by every manager in any manufacturing industry." Without attempting to "instruct the railroads how to run their business," the editors called attention to the "doubtful expedient of meeting every new expenditure by a raise in rates, instead of an attempt to effect economies of operations, which would ultimately work for the good of the service." The argument further attested to the fact that, for too many managers,

---

[41] Robert Mawson, who was with the *American Machinist* as associate editor from 1912 to 1917, in a letter dated May 9, 1942, to Roe, in the ASME files, admits having "worked very closely with Mr. Alford," who "was an engineer anxious at all times to assist the associate and assistant editors who worked with him, in presenting their findings in the best possible manner for the readers of the *American Machinist* magazine."

[42] See "Shop Efficiency and Railroad Rates," in *American Machinist*, *33*, 1097-1098, December 15 (1910), which reported the testimony of November 21, 22, and 23, 1910.

[43] "Increasing Rates and Reducing Costs," *American Machinist*, *33*, 1127.

. . . there are but two [44] ways of increasing profits, or of maintaining them in the face of an advance in material costs. These are the advancing of the selling price, or the reduction of wages. But among the most progressive managers we know, neither of these is considered until after every legitimate means of reducing the cost of manufacture has been gone over.

By "efficient shop organization and hearty co-operation between the different departments," new methods can effect "surprising savings," especially since the amounts saved by wage reduction are "comparatively small."

Clearly, then, the objectives of Taylor and his followers were approved by Alford and his staff. What of Taylor and some of his associates?

It is difficult to conclude that the editors' sentiment was on the side of the Taylor personalities merely because the editorial took the railroads to task. The editorial bemoaned the fact that the railroads here had "grown up with the idea that they were a law unto themselves and they have conducted themselves without regard as to what has been done in other industries in the way of effecting economy." As for their resentment against persons "not connected with railroads that may save thousands of dollars a day," that was natural, but the "real reason for resentment is very likely to be the knowledge that part, at least, of this criticism is true."

However, in the issue of March 9, 1911, of the *American Machinist*, there appeared an editorial [45] that clearly showed the opinion of Alford's staff on Taylor. Of course, it cannot be positively stated that this was in agreement, either totally or partially, with Alford's views, but the editorial was so pointed, terse, and forthright that any member of the staff—particularly the man who assumed the chief position—would have dissented in an accompanying article, if he had objected.

The editorial, "F. W. Taylor and the Steel Mills," was based on two articles that had been published in the March 4, 1911,

[44] Today's maxim evidently has been reduced to only one possibility. Because of the growth of unions, wage reductions are not easily effected.
[45] *34*, 463-464.

issue of the *American Magazine:* "The Principles of Scientific Management" by Taylor and "Old Age at Forty" by John A. Fitch. Citing an almost "perfect case of mutually destructive criticism," the editors studied both articles, which "draw their illustrations from the same source," the steel industry:

Mr. Taylor's article tells a doleful story of the deliberate slothfulness of the American workingman, while Mr. Fitch gives an equally doleful account of the heartless manner in which he is overworked. Mr. Taylor details with elaborate care the hopeless incapacity of the older system of factory management, while Mr. Fitch details with equally elaborate care the manner in which that system has become one of "speeding, unceasing and relentless, seldom equaled in any industry at any time."

Taylor insisted that the shop was "really run by the workmen and not by the boss," and he maintained that soldiering, so prevalent that it limited the accomplishment to "about one third of a good day's work," coupled with natural inefficiency, ignorance, and wastefulness, was indicative of the "deplorable state [in which] modern industry finds itself." Fitch, on the other hand, in referring to almost a year (1907-8) that he spent "among the Pittsburgh steelworkers," claimed that the working hours were "shockingly long," speedups added "overstrain to overtime," and, most horrible of all, the system of repression stifled initiative and healthy citizenship. Steel production had increased, Fitch admitted, not because of American engineering but by virtue of "pushers," overtime, "foolish rivalries," the "buying of men's better judgment in the bonus system," and "the cutting of the tonnage rates" on knowing the relation between the "human element and the tables of statistics."

Did the Alford staff attempt to explain this "anomaly"? They did! Did they take sides? They did!

In the first place, the editors insisted that, although Taylor had probably correctly described conditions that prevailed at the Midvale Steel Works thirty years before, the time now was 1911. As to the "go-as-you-please" environment, with which he admittedly was familiar, he assumed that these conditions

were "both universal and perpetual." Admitting little firsthand
knowledge of conditions in the steel mills either in the 1880's
or in 1911, the editorial staff hastily brought the argument
down to the machine shops of 1911, a topic on which the Alford associates could speak more authoritatively. These, the editorial insisted, no longer provided "a place for peaceful medi-
tation and abode of silence." Perhaps even more devastating are
the closing two paragraphs:

To the movement toward intensive production, Mr. Taylor has
been a leading contributor through his invention of high-speed
steel, but not otherwise. As a reformer of factory management, it
is in the machine shop that he is best known, it is to the machine
shop that he has particularly addressed himself, and it is precisely
in the machine shop that he has made but little progress, and that
his methods are looked upon with suspicion and distrust. The movement toward intensive production has been nationwide. Except always by his invention of high-speed steel, Mr. Taylor has contributed but little.

The demonstration of the unsoundness of his theories and the
fallacy of his argument is complete in the showing by Mr. Fitch
that, under the old system of management, which Mr. Taylor con-
demns as incapable of good results, the pace, in an entire and vast
industry, has been quickened even to the pace that kills.

It is not necessary to veer from the discussion at hand to consider the comments that such an editorial might have brought.
It might be said in all justice that the editors certainly were
so intent on looking for differences that they failed to look for
similarities. Both Taylor and Fitch were on common ground:
they both believed that the old system was of little value. Again,
the point that the worker is fatigued and exhausted was no
assurance that this could have come from overwork. However,
it seems very likely that any discussion of Taylor was one that
seldom could be indulged in with a minimum of passion. It
was probably his personality that many could not divorce either
from himself or from his work. Probably the kindest comment
that could be made about Taylor was made by one who had

been personally acquainted with him: "Diplomacy was never one of Mr. Taylor's prime characteristics." [46]

ALFORD'S SOURCES FOR THE REPORT

It is obvious that the conditions surrounding Taylor had become disrupting and troublesome. When Alford set himself the task of obtaining information for the ASME report, he, of course, not only examined the literature but also attempted to get firsthand information from the men familiar with the "system."

Alford was not too successful in obtaining such information for the very simple reason that few such people were willing to stand up and be counted as either associates of Taylor or adherents of his system. Copley [47] maintains that, of the many executives who were influenced by Taylor, few had any "missionary zeal" for his cause even though most had an interest that was "practically confined to the benefits they could derive from it for their own business."

Of course, Alford also communicated with Taylor directly. The ensuing correspondence, from Taylor's personal files, is of great interest not only because it throws light on Alford's difficulties but also because it shows Taylor's own appraisal of the situation. Furthermore, it also throws light on Taylor the man.

On July 16, 1912, Alford wrote, on behalf of the committee, what appeared to be a "form letter." The two-page letter that Taylor received referred to the committee's task in "preparing a report to be presented at the forthcoming annual meeting in December" and "that this report may be accurate and comprehensive I am addressing you, among others, for information."

Although only a few weeks had passed since he had been given the assignment, Alford, in the methodical fashion so many

---

[46] There is in print, too, a similar comment made by C. H. Stilson, who in a "Letter on Scientific Management," in the *American Machinist*, 35, 175-176, July 27 (1911), referred to Taylor's "unfortunate and tactless statements."

[47] Copley, *Taylor,* Vol. 2, pp. 364 ff.

of his associates still call typical of him, had already laid out the broad outline of his work and the facts needed to complete his study. Alford declared that the report would be developed "under four principal heads": "the first two dealing particularly with the new element in the Art of Management." The four divisions were:

The definition of the new element in the art of management.
The rise of this new element.
The regulative principles of management.
The present status of the art of management with a review of the accomplishments of the past five years.

As for specific information concerning "independent plants where you have installed management systems," Alford asserted that "we would be pleased to have" the following facts: "total number," "line of manufacture," "number of employees affected by changes," "period" of installation, permanence of the installation, "results," and "cost factor of the entire work of installation." Alford also asked for a list of papers and books written by his correspondent.

As if all this were not enough, Alford asked, "if such a course will be without embarrassment to you," for a list of "some or all of these plants" so that they could be written to in the same general way that we are writing to you." Finally, as if realizing the pertinency of the information for which he asked, Alford assured his correspondent that the information would be "confidential" and that the report would be written in an impersonal manner so as not to mention "the name of anyone who furnished the information."

It is interesting to note even in these "enlightened days," about forty years later, how effective such a search for information would be. Nevertheless, it must be remembered that such a search for facts was typical of Alford.

Little wonder, then, that H. V. Coes, former president of ASME, who served on many committees with Alford, told the present author: "Leon always aimed at getting facts and sorting out the opinions. He felt that if one differentiated between facts and opinions, he would never have any trouble. There can be no differing with facts. Leon got facts and let the chips fall where they would. If people didn't agree, then they didn't have the facts. And in all this, no one could ever accuse him of slanting or distorting facts to fit a preconceived conclusion." But how did Taylor react?

Up to July 24, Alford had received no reply from Taylor, but he had heard from Dodge. Dodge had visited Taylor, who at the time was staying at Plymouth, Massachusetts. The Taylors had shortly before returned from a trip abroad, and Mrs. Taylor had been ill.

At Dodge's suggestion, Alford wrote once more to Taylor on July 24. This time the letter was shorter and more personal but still formal. He mentioned Dodge's suggestion and presumed that Taylor had been told that "the burden of collecting the material and writing the report is on my shoulders." Furthermore, he asserted that both he and the committee would "be grateful for suggestions from you" concerning the method of obtaining the desired information. Alford concluded with a prediction:

> If we are successful in getting this information and preparing an adequate report, I believe that it would be the most important contribution to the Society's literature that has been presented for a number of years.

The next day Taylor dictated his eight-page reply, which was mailed out on July 26. Taylor referred to Dodge's visit and doubted "very much whether you will meet with success in getting those people who have introduced our system in their work to write you one way or the other about our management." Taylor felt that "9 out of 10 companies," after paying for expert assistance, look upon the installed system as one of their assets, even going so far as to rename the system, once it is in, with the name of the "manager of the establishment." "This is done in some cases through the personal pride of the owners or managers who do not wish to bear the brand of anyone's system, and more frequently as a matter of settled policy, so that their competitors may not get a hold of the same thing."

As if this were not discouraging enough, Taylor insisted:

In many of these companies, of course, if a man not connected with any of their competitors were to come to see them, they would be shown the details of the system and very probably told frankly that it was a good thing, but even this would not be the case unless they became convinced that the man inquiring had no possible connection with any of their competitors.

Taylor illustrated this assertion by sending Alford a copy of a letter sent to him by Bird, one of the two partners of the Plimpton Press (printers of Taylor's *Principles*). It concerned Hollis Godfrey and the work he did there. (Taylor commented: "It may be remarked, however, that all the time Godfrey was working for Bird, I think for some 4 or 5 months, I paid his salary out of my own pocket, and they gave him nothing. I asked this for the purpose of educating Godfrey, that is giving him the chance to have practical experience in introducing our system of management, so that Bird could hardly do less than write the letter which he did.") Furthermore, any "outsider" unarmed with "a letter of introduction from Cooke, Godfrey or Hathaway" is told that everything "is working very well indeed." If the person is "in the printing business" he is "advised to go slowly and to wait a while yet." Of course, "if Mr. Cooke brings a man there why then it is impossible for them to do anything else but come out frankly with the facts."

Although Taylor insisted that he was "telling you this to illustrate the attitude which is taken by almost all people about the system," he felt that the facts at the Plimpton Press could be obtained from "Mr. Barter, the General Superintendent, who was Mr. Cooke's right-hand man" there. As for the results, the company was using seventy-five less men who were "getting out an enormously large volume of books, keeping almost all their promises instead of breaking them, and getting out their orders in, I believe, one-half the time they used to take."

Taylor wrote that "a typical example of what you can expect from men who have introduced our system is found in the case of Mr. T. J. Wallis, the Master Mechanic of the Pennsylvania Lines east of Pittsburgh," who "came to see me about his work a number of times and was most enthusiastic." However, when "the Congressional Committee wanted to get him to testify as to what he had done in the matter, he told me that if they forced him to come before them, he would be compelled to give them no information whatever." After he was subpoenaed, he appeared and "denied that he had ever done anything in the line of scientific management whatever." He "justified" his action to Taylor by telling him that, otherwise, "in the first place the people in his own railroad would have jumped on him; second that lots of lines friendly to the Penna. lines would have complained that their master mechanic acknowledged that there was good in scientific management; and third —and most important of all—that the unions in P.R.R. would have been apt to antagonize him." In short, he insisted that "it would take three years to recover from the harm that I could have done to my work by my testimony." Nevertheless Mr. Wallis asserted that his next move "would be to systematize the roundhouses and the care and running of the locomotives, and attack the whole problem along the lines of scientific management." Yet, in all this, "he did not dare give this work the name of scientific management, nor in any way identify it with it."

However, Taylor did also tell of the successes that his system afforded the German-American Button Company of Syracuse, the Packard Motor Car Company of Detroit, and the Panhard Company of Paris. He was particularly proud of the latter installation which, because of the workers' appreciation of their new treatment and their receipt of premiums, converted what was "formerly a hotbed of unionism and full of labor troubles" into a plant where labor relations were fairly amicable.

Finally, Taylor related an incident that had occurred on his trip "some two months ago" to Paris, where the Renaud Works were introducing "our system as fast as they can get it in":

I met Mr. Henri le Chatelier and a number of his friends who told me that Renaud was everywhere trying to give the impression that the system in his works was a great failure. He said that no one in France believed Renaud, and the very fact that he was spreading this news broadcast led them all to believe that it was a great success.

Finally, in the last sentence, Taylor asked if Alford wanted a reply to his original two questions, "that is, as to wherein lies the novelty of our system, etc."

On August 13, 1912, Alford replied that he would "be very glad if you will make an answer to the first two questions," and he again asked Taylor for "statistical data in regards to the work you have done."

Two days later, Taylor answered "the first two questions in your letter of July 16," by referring Alford to designated sections in his testimony before the Congressional Committee. Taylor was disturbed by persons who insisted that there was nothing new in the "mental attitude" and that it had been used before:

I think, however, that the combination is new, of having a mental attitude which is unusual in companies, namely that there is no conflict of interest between the two sides, that their interests are truly identical, and furthermore the recognition on the part of both the workman and the management that all other elements relating to the work done by every employee in the company should be the subject of scientific investigation and experiment, and not to be decided and adopted in accordance with some man's opinion or judgment, whether it be the opinion or judgment of a man on the management side or on the side of the worker.

Another troublesome matter to which Taylor addressed himself at this time concerned the "enemies of scientific management," among whom he included some of the "labor leaders," particularly O'Connell, who headed the Machinist's Union of the United States and who had, in Volume 2 of the *Testimony*, asserted that Taylor insisted on "individual agreement" instead of "collected bargaining" and that "men under scientific management are reduced to virtual slavery." Taylor felt it "very difficult to print statistics refuting statements of this sort," owing to the fact that plants using scientific management "object to having their affairs made public." However, he referred to Hollis Godfrey (*Testimony*, Vol. 3, p. 1846), who spent a year at the Tabor Company where, with approximately the same number of men and machines, production had been tripled, wages were 73 per cent higher, the selling price of machines had been reduced 25 per cent, profits rather than losses appeared, and there now prevailed the "friendliest of feelings between management, workmen, and outsiders."

Moreover "to give some definite refutation to those rumors which are so continuously abroad," Taylor sent Alford a letter from Cooke and allowed him to "look through this letter without making a copy of it, and then return it to me, as you will note that Mr. Cooke asks that it shall be held in the strictest confidence."

Finally, Taylor regretted being "unable to give you the names and data concerning the various companies which I myself systematized," because "in four out of five companies" it was "part of signed agreement not to mention the systematizing of the company."

Six days later, on August 21, Taylor again wrote to Alford: this time about "one of the most frequent criticisms." This concerned his insistence on the use of "details," "red tape," and "system." He denied making a " 'fetish' of details" or considering "this red tape as sacred" and "jamming it into every company." Taylor asserted that whenever he was called to a company he made "absolutely sure that the owners of the company *wanted* scientific management and *wanted it very badly*." Before starting on a job, Taylor would explain that no two companies could have the "same Mechanisms and details" and he invariably "made a clear-cut bargain" that "wherever there was a conflict of opinion" it was necessary that "my decision must be final." For, he maintained, "these men had no notion of the fact that the greater the number of elements the greater the need for harmony."

To prove his point, Taylor gave the analogy of a man going to the Packard people and saying, "I should like to have one of your automobiles, but I already have a Pierce-Arrow, many of the parts of which suit me exactly; will you not therefore kindly use the parts of the Pierce-Arrow car which I shall point out for you in furnishing me with a Packard." Obviously, Packard would reply, "If we are to be responsible for the working of our car, we must have the final say as to just what parts are put in the car." Hence, Taylor insisted that his must be the final decision since he had the responsibility.

In his reply, on August 24, Alford acknowledged Taylor's "refutation of the criticism," [48] returned, "without having copied" the Cooke letter, but still asked, "in regard to the statistical data," for "an impersonal statement."

Nevertheless, in the report Alford, probably more out of courtesy than candor, acknowledged the "response" as being "generous." However, he carefully added the modification, "in the main." Evidently he was adverse to admitting to what would have seemed a serious impediment to the extent of the study he had made. In the appendix he did list fifty-three industries in which the management movement under investigation had to some extent been installed. Yet at the close of the report he did complain about the existence of this "secretive stage."

He tried to explain the reluctance of people to receive public acknowledgment by claiming that, first, many still considered these matters as "trade secrets," which, like machines or processes, ought to be kept from competitors, and second, there seemed to be a feeling that the use of outside experts cast aspersions on a plant's own executives.

Finally, nowhere in the sixty-three paragraphs that comprise the main body of the report, even when he quotes from pub-

---

[48] Taylor's resentment to criticism can best be illustrated by an incident still currently recounted among those who knew him. During an ASME "Discussion" session, Taylor, who had spoken previously, was "criticized" by James Newton Gunn. At lunch, at the Engineers' Club, Taylor reprimanded Gunn. Taylor concluded his rebuke with words to the effect: "Newton, I don't think you know anything about management. I don't think you know anything about the principles of management. I don't think that you even know the first principle of management." "Oh, yes, I do," replied Gunn, "the first principle is: 'Thou shalt have no other gods before me.'"

lished writings, is there mentioned the name of one individual known to be connected with the "new" management. The single exception was the footnote reference to the *Principles of Management* that Alford wrote with Church. All other references to authors—and these were limited to ASME papers—were grouped in the appendix.

Thus the man who, in later years, Alford had conceded as being "properly" called the "Father of Scientific Management" went unmentioned in the body of the report. Taylor's name does appear in Appendix II: twice, as the author of two papers, and once as part of the complete title of Barth's paper on his slide rules.

It should again be stressed that this was not done out of any enmity toward Taylor. The name of Gantt, to whom Alford on numerous occasions, both public and private, acknowledged his devotion, was treated similarly. It was done, as he had previously informed Taylor, in order to keep the entire matter impersonal. Of course it did have a distinct advantage: it drew away unnecessary attention from associating the movement with the man who had become such a storm center in and out of ASME circles. Admittedly this was no easy task, for much of the work was associated with Taylor. And Alford was not entirely unconscious of the man's pioneering in the movement.

THE STATUS OF MANAGEMENT

The Alford report called attention to the more important of the "striking phenomena" of which even the "most superficial" of observers must have been aware:

1. The popular interest aroused by the Eastern Rate Hearings, which emphasized the fact that the "application of newly discovered principles of management" were capable of effecting economies of $1,000,000 in the railroads and could possibly be effective, too, "in every form of business activity."

2. The great number of professional lectures, papers, and reports on the subject by employers and business executives in many lines of endeavor.

3. The opposition of the labor unions to these methods, as evidenced by strikes and the legal prohibition that limited its use.

4. Governmental recognition of these methods and their application was evidenced by:

   a. Appointment by the House of Representatives of a special committee to investigate systems of management in federal arsenals and shops. (Reported March, 1912.)
   b. Report of a civilian board by the Secretary of the Navy to investigate management in the navy yards. (Reported July, 1911.)
   c. Senate Bill (S. 1672) which was, at the time of the ASME investigation, in committee and which prohibited time study and premium (or bonus) payments on government work.

5. The great increase in management literature as evidenced by the fact that a directory of books on business management listed 500 titles (approximately 375 of which were written between 1907 and 1912).

6. The formation of two societies in the field.[49]

7. The formation of two camps, one of vigorous supporters and the other of strong opponents, of the "new element in management."

8. The most striking phenomenon, the unquestionable evidence that the application of management principles was capable of effecting advances in unskilled work (e.g., shoveling) and in ancient trades (e.g., bricklaying).

MANAGEMENT "PRINCIPLES"

The report did not undertake to explain what was meant by *principles*—especially to distinguish the term from *laws*, as was later done in the development of management—but used the term, as Taylor and others had, in its ordinary day-to-day use. Consequently, under the subheading, "The Principles of Manufacture," it reviewed the beginnings of modern industry, a cus-

---

49 Evidently the Taylor Society and the Efficiency Society.

tom that almost every text on management has since followed, in order to give "a historical setting from which the present can be more truly judged." Included is:

1. The development of laborsaving machinery, introducing the change from handicraft to manufacture.

2. The contention of Adam Smith [50] and the British economists that the principle of division of labor was the basis of manufacture (because of increased dexterity of the workers, saving of time lost in passing from "one species of work to another," and machines that allow one man to do the work of many).

3. The addition by Charles Babbage,[51] the English mathematician and mechanician, of the principle that, by dividing the work, the master manufacturer can "purchase the precise quantity" of skill and force instead of being compelled to hire one person capable of performing the most difficult and the most laborious tasks.

4. The basic principle in the rise of industry, namely, transference of skill (from the inventor to the power-driven mechanism).[52]

5. The development of analysis methods and operation recordings, as particularly evidenced by Smith's listing of the operations in manufacture, Babbage's table of operations, time, operator cost, and tool and material expense in pin manufacture in England and France, Babbage's "comments on the use of the watch to time operations," and the experience of Coulomb, the noted French physicist, in time study.[53]

---

[50] *An Inquiry into the Nature and Causes of the Wealth of Nations*, 1776.

[51] *Economy of Machinery and Manufacture*, 1832.

[52] So great was Alford's belief in the importance of this principle that he carefully illustrated it by discussing Henry Maudsley's invention of the lathe slide, John Nasmyth's invention of the steam hammer, and (indicative of the reality of Alford's influence in the preparation and writing of the report) the shoe machinery of the United Shoe Machinery Company where Alford once worked.

[53] Both Babbage and Coulomb (1736-1806) had suggested timing workmen unaware that they were being observed. Evidently, this idea was also adopted by Taylor who later rejected it (Taylor, *Shop Management*, p. 153). One warning that Coulomb gave, however, is still valid: "We cannot be too well warned of the danger of self-deception in computing either the speed or effective time of work through an observation of a few minutes."

6. The basic application of the principle of transference of skill (together with an early appreciation of the value of detailed study operations to make the transference more complete) on the basis of the machine as the point of focus. (Babbage had pointed out that the great lack was that of scientific principles and applications, and he had suggested, as important additions to the machinery factor, accurate drawings and careful regulation of the "domestic economy of the factory.")

7. The lack of change in the basic principles discovered and applied in industry during the half century or so following Babbage, but the extension of these principles particularly to the drawing room, i.e., the art of machine design: more complex machines that further the transference of skill to the machine.

8. The fundamental organization of the industrial plant of these fifty years, with two basic aspects, design and production.[54]

MANAGEMENT TRENDS

The report brought the progress up to date—i.e., through the twenty-five years following the half century after Babbage. It called attention, it must be admitted, to changes that had not been universally adopted:

1. More attention was being focused on the worker who by profit sharing, bonus, and premium systems was now being rewarded for increased effort and output. Then, too, there were the tendencies, fostered and initiated by employers, in the direction of industrial accident prevention, improvements in work conditions, as well as welfare work, etc.

2. There was an improvement of employer-employee relations, including the use of the results of experimental psychology.

---

[54] Usually the head of each of the activities, design and production, reported to a manager. Work in the design activity had made rapid strides, become highly specialized, and its workers were fairly well paid. Often the chief executive devoted much of his time to this aspect of the business. As for production, however, only rarely was an attempt made to transfer the skill of the management to the production department. Little attention was paid to the worker here as a producing unit other than to give him the tools and machines designed

3. The most important and comprehensive change, however, was the change in mental attitude toward production problems. As Alford wrote: [55]

> The tendency is toward an attitude of questioning, of research, of careful investigation, of everything affecting the problems in hand, of seeking exact knowledge and then shaping action on the discovered facts.

The report pointed out the use of motion and time study as instruments [56] of such investigations, the planning department as the means by which the investigation is put into practice, and wage plans as the method of stimulating co-operation.[57] In short, "the drawing room is the planning department of design, and the planning department is the drawing room of production."

THE "NEW" ELEMENT IN MANAGEMENT

Alford's request for a "definition of the new element in the art of management" brought such diverse views as: "I am not aware that a *new* element in the art of management has been discovered . . ."; "the term 'scientific management' is a catchword which assumes that industrial institutions have not been scientifically managed—which is not the case . . ."; "there is hardly any part of it that has not been practiced by managers for the past 100 years . . ."; "the best designation of the new element I believe to be 'scientific management' . . . (which) . . . carries . . . the fundamental idea that the management

---

by the drawing department and fully expecting him, with no additional aid other than his own skill, to produce work of the desired quality and quantity.

[55] Note carefully this quotation which, many may say, is what is known as the "scientific attitude." This may or may not be true. However, Alford's failure to use such an appellation was in line with his belief, at the time at least, that management had not yet become "scientific."

[56] This view has also been claimed elsewhere. E.g., Hoxie, "Scientific Management and Labor Welfare," in the *Journal of Political Economy, 24,* 838, called motion and time study "the chief cornerstone of scientific management."

[57] These views are in agreement with those expressed by Alford's friends and associates. See Hathaway, "The Planning Department," in *Industrial Engineering, 12,* 7 ff., and Roe and Lytle, "Wage Payment Plans," p. 915, in *Management's Handbook.*

of labor is a process requiring thorough analytical treatment
and involving scientific as opposed to 'rule-of-thumb' methods
. . ."; ". . . the new element briefly. . . . The critical observation, accurate description, analysis, and classification of all
industrial and business phenomena of a recurring nature, including all forms of co-operative human effort and the systematic application of the resulting records to secure the most economical and efficient production and regulation of future
phenomena . . ."; ". . . the Taylor System is not a method
of pay, a specific ruling of account books, not the use of high-
speed steel. It is simply an honest, intelligent effort to arrive
at absolute control in every department, to let tabulated and
unimpeachable fact take the place of individual opinion; to
develop 'team play' to its highest possibility . . ."; ". . . management engineering . . . seems more fully to cover its scope
than science. . . ."

Alford attempted to summarize these views and contended
that they imply an impartial study of facts, which can then be
systematically applied to worker training and departmental
control. He asserted as the fundamental element:

> The mental attitude that consciously applies to the trans-
> ference of skill to all the activities of industry.

He insisted on *all*,[58] because he regretted the former restriction
of this transfer to machines only.

[58] Despite his use of "all," Alford admittedly excluded accounting works in
listing the sixteen ASME papers, in the period 1886 to 1908, that exemplify
"the rise of this mental attitude." These papers, together with their ASME
Transaction numbers, regrouped for convenience, include: Towne's "The En-
gineer as Economist" (207); Kent's "A Problem in Profit Sharing" (256); Towne's
"Gain Sharing" (341); Halsey's "The Premium Plan of Paying Labor" (449);
Robinson's "The Relation of the Drawing Office to the Shop in Manufacturing"
(596); Taylor's "A Piece Rate System" (647); Richard's "Gift Proposition for
Paying Workmen" (965); Gantt's "A Bonus System for Rewarding Labor" (928);
Richard's "Is Anything the Matter With Piece Work?" (1012); Taylor's "Shop
Management" (1003); Day's "The Machine Shop Problem" (1001); Gantt's "A
Graphical Daily Balance in Manufacture" (1002); Barth's "Slide Rules for the
Machine Shop as a Part of the Taylor System of Management" (1010); Gantt's
"Modifying Systems of Management" (1011); Dodge's "A History of the Intro-
duction of a System of Shop Management" (1115); and Gantt's "Training Work-
men in Habits of Industry and Cooperation" (1221). The first of these papers,
since recognized as the "beginning" of the movement, treats management "as a

CORRECTING CONTEMPORARY VIEWS ON MANAGEMENT

Alford candidly expressed his own views on the "scientific" nature of "scientific management" when he deplored the term as being incorrectly interpreted by many to mean that "there is a science rather than an art of management." The term should, on the other hand, more properly imply the use of methods "taken largely from the sciences of physics and psychology." Feeling that a more meaningful term was "laborsaving management," he advocated the use of this term to designate the mental attitude and "industrial management" to denote the subject.

He was troubled by the inaccurate thinking and muddled expression especially evident in the many statements of "the so-called principles." He believed that these could, at the time, be classified into two categories, "personal characteristics of managers and mechanical means of applying," neither of which was effective.

TRANSFERENCE OF SKILL

Alford insisted that the transference of skill, the basic and fundamental principle whose application made modern industry possible, was "put into effect on the management side of all industrial activities" by means of three regulative principles that he himself had expressed earlier (May 30, 1912) in the *American Machinist* (36, p. 857): [59] (1) "systematic use of experience," (2) "economic control of effort," and (3) "promo-

modern art" and maintains that executives ought to be able to "observe, record, analyze and compare essential facts. . . ." The next eight deal with worker payments and illustrate the attention that had been begun to be paid to the employee. The tenth, Taylor's "Shop Management," Alford recognized as "the first complete presentation of the subject" and, with subsequent works by Taylor, became "the only comprehensive outline of industrial management" up to 1912. Some of its features were illustrated and amplified in the next five papers. The last paper discusses "tested methods" that were capable of fostering "the all-important transference of skill."

[59] Church and Alford, *The Principles of Management*.

tion of personal effectiveness." In brief, these three principles implied "accumulation and use of records and the setting up of standards," [60] "the previous application of skill by the executives," [61] and "the most thorough comprehension of the human being." [62]

In actual practice "laborsaving management" must be installed slowly and carefully. It must be remembered that a mental attitude is implied here that must be acquired and understood by the executives themselves before it can be applied. As Alford expressed it, "they must acquire knowledge and skill before they can transfer it."

Alford really expressed a view that Taylor and Gantt and the other leaders held when he insisted that the basic cause of "most so-called failures" was traceable to a lack of complete understanding and a hasty application of the concepts. Furthermore, with the necessary knowledge, adequate standards, correct environment, and tactful and patient understanding and proper training of workmen, the resulting co-operation would assure the success of the methods.

Alford's assertion that the practice of management, although built on fixed procedures and standards, was not as "rigid and inflexible" as has been alleged can be best interpreted by analogy. Just as laborsaving machinery had many details that allowed wide application in varied plants and industries, so too were the details of laborsaving management capable of diverse application. Thus it is possible to understand better his idea that

> There can be nothing fixed in such human endeavor except the underlying principle.

There was, however, a difference in the use of "scientific" methods in the physical, chemical, and biological laboratories

[60] Used by executives of traditional knowledge; personal experience; and the results of scientific studies.

[61] Dividing and co-ordinating executive and productive labor; planning, testing, and comparing tasks; and training workers.

[62] Allotting responsibility and encouraging and rewarding executive and productive labor; developing contented workers; and the promotion of workers' physical and mental health.

as compared with their use in industry. In the former, the goal
was the discovery and statement of facts. In the latter, the management investigator must limit his laboratory's use to the discovery of pragmatic facts capable of immediate use. Hence, in
management,

> It is therefore unwise and in fact detrimental to carry any
> investigation to an extreme. Enough facts must be observed
> to shape intelligent action.

THE CONTEMPORARY "EXPERTS"

The report, as might be expected, did not remain silent on
"one of the most unfortunate features of this great movement,"
the "systematizers." These were the "alleged experts" who, if
allowed to install their systems in a plant, promised "extravagant results." Because of their unquestioned damage to the
profession it might be wise to list some of their unfortunate
characteristics:

1. They published statistics implying almost unbelievable
gains but disregarding the original deplorable conditions of
the plant.

2. They disregarded the investors' interests and regarded
the plant as a laboratory for obtaining interesting but ex-
pensive experience.

3. They refused to admit that the application of past solutions to new and different conditions was merely an experiment.

4. They wasted time and money on nonrecurring problems.

5. They undervalued management leadership and, consequently, seldom achieved permanent results.

6. They overvalued the "system," thereby removing individual responsibility for results.

7. They assumed that all problems of similar plants were
capable of the same treatment.

8. They neglected a proper appraisal of the value of internal
good will in a going concern.

9. They analyzed improperly and appreciated inadequately the human factor in industry.

As opposed to these "systematizers," the real expert studies facts, draws on his own analytical, co-ordinating, and responsible experience and, by scientific methods, effects a solution suited to the human and material factors involved. He does little of the actual installation but much of the training and direction of those who become the permanent managers. In this way, a true process of skill transference is obtained.

Broadly speaking, successful laborsaving management results in lower product cost, more prompt delivery, and increased worker output with higher wages. Alford cited, as proof of its ability to promote contentment among workers, instances where attempts to organize strikes in plants (only some of whose employees were under the "new" conditions) resulted in a walkout of only those who were *not* subjected to these "new" procedures. Nevertheless, the report admitted at least one shortcoming of laborsaving management. This was an admission that, as yet, the cost of product to the consumer had not been decreased. Hopefully, Alford believed that the third member of the employer-employee-consumer trio would, as the result of "increased production," eventually be as fortunate as the other two.

THE MINORITY REPORT

Before engaging in any further analysis of the Alford report and the significance and influence of his ideas, it might be interesting to examine the Minority Report, especially its reason for existence.

Vaughan's explanation, if taken at face value, is relatively simple: he was unable to sign the Majority Report because of his inability to agree completely with all its findings. Perhaps there were other factors also involved.

He admittedly admired the "thoroughness" of preparation as well as the great interest of the Majority Report. He was not too sure, but he got the "impression" that

In its general tenor, it distinctly implies the desirability of what is termed labor-saving management, involving the planning department, functional organization, and the bonus system.

Were these undesirable? Vaughan did not say, but he felt that, even though the "art of management is developing into a science," any one of these methods, regardless of individual merit, "is no panacea for all our suffering." But most of all, he was disturbed by the claims made by the advocates—particularly the $1,000,000-a-day figure reported at the ICC Hearings and which the Majority Report mentioned. He consequently concluded that

. . . labor-saving management is not any particular system but will always remain the art of selecting and applying the most appropriate methods furnished by the science of management, the science that records what these methods are and the results obtained from them.

Fundamentally it seems that the Minority Report was not in basic disagreement with the Majority Report. When it was presented to ASME, Gantt was quick to observe:

. . . a careful reading seems to indicate that the writer is fundamentally in accord with the majority except that he wishes to take a shot at the statement that the railroads were losing one million dollars a day . . .[63]

Gantt had been acquainted with Vaughan and, with Dodge and Day,[64] whose consulting office was located in Philadelphia, had done some work for Vaughan, who was connected with the railroads. It is of no matter that Gantt had reported that the Vaughan company was "one of the most progressive and best managed on the continent." What is important is this illustration of how disturbing the movement had become.

[63] Gantt at first believed that the Emerson statement was a trifle "extravagant" but in later years he felt it to be "conservative." This agrees with the report recently issued by the Emerson Engineers.

[64] Charles Day, with Gantt and Emerson, in 1911 served on a committee organized by George von L. Meyer, President Taft's Secretary of the Navy, to study the organization and management of the navy yards.

SOME MANAGEMENT LEADERS ON THE REPORT

Of course, in the discussions at ASME following the reports, Alford's identity as the author of the Majority Report was lost. It could not have been otherwise. However, Taylor, for example, who had been contacted mainly by Alford and no other member of the committee, must have been aware that it was to Alford that he was paying homage when he praised the "careful research," "close analysis," and "new and original viewpoint."

Gantt felt that the Majority Report had caught the spirit of the movement and pointed to thirteen paragraphs which, he believed, presented "an excellent résumé" of the subject. Church, Hathaway, and Taylor were even more selective: they felt that, in a single statement, the basic concept of the entire movement had been captured. Taylor said:

Most writers upon this subject have emphasized the necessity of reducing to a science the knowledge which in the past has been in the heads of the workmen. The change from rule-of-thumb has been largely dwelt upon, and its importance pointed out. The thought of the committee, however, centers mainly about transferring this knowledge to the workman after it has been acquired by the management; and from this viewpoint scientific management is very properly summarized as "the mental attitude that consciously applies the transference of skill to all of the activities of industry."

Taylor was also impressed by the attention given to the mental attitude which, even according to those who testified before the House Committee, was the *sine qua non* of the movement.

Hathaway, too, was greatly impressed and asserted that "the novelty of the new management lies in this transference of skill from the management to the workman." He wondered if, as he expressed it, "the older descriptions of the essence of scientific management may not have been wrong." In the last analysis, he felt that the Majority Report had, in a single sentence, implied what the earlier writers had called "the four principles of scientific management."

A closer examination of the Hathaway contention is of interest from two standpoints. First, it demonstrates Alford's keen insight, thorough analysis, and meaningful language. Second, it calls attention to a view that too many texts, even now, some forty years later, fail to recognize. The earlier writings dwell at great length upon the gathering and systematizing of information, the development of a science, and the replacing of rule-of-thumb concepts. The Majority Report did not stress these, because they are obvious precedents to management's readiness to transfer skill. The earlier writers' treatment of the selection and training of workmen is also implied in the basic phrase, "transference of skill." The older authors' "bringing the science and the scientifically selected and trained workmen together" is more forcefully expressed in the committee's "mental attitude that consciously applies the transference of skill." Finally, the "almost equal division of work and responsibility between the management and the worker" is the result of the first three "principles" and must, consequently, have also been implied in the committee's report. Unfortunately today's texts, too frequently reflecting notions expressed in books of the immediate past, accumulate the original ideas expressed by the writers during the days of immaturity. Re-examination and re-evaluation would be indeed beneficial.

A most practical affirmation of the Alford view was presented by John G. Aldrich, manager of the New England Butt Company. He pointed to the experiments at his plant, pertaining to micro-motion study, which furnished evidence of not only "transference of skill from man to machine" but also "transference of experience from a man who has it to one who has never had it."

Of course, A. H. Church might be expected to be particularly favorable to Alford's assertion that more attention had been paid to design of the machine than to its use. He was an advocate of an "exhaustive study" of machine capacities and limitations and felt that he had, in his studies of industrial accounting, attempted to assign to the machine its true position as a productive factor. The Majority Report made even more evident the reasons why indifferent handling made the machine inefficient.

In his comments, Church might have been expected to applaud the inclusion of the three principles of management that had first been expressed in the paper he wrote with Alford. Of them, he said: "The credit for the formulation of these principles belongs in a larger degree to Mr. Alford than to me."

He did, however, enlarge on the Majority Report's mention of the "habit stage," for he felt that the adoption of good and harmonious habits was a proper goal for all levels of production. For him, the "new ideals of management engineering" could be summed up with: [65]

> Take nothing for granted.
> See that every habit is adapted to its purpose.
> Cultivate habit.

Although many felt that the origin of industrial management's "new spirit" lay in the realization of social responsibility, its source was, if Church's views may be analyzed, the result of man's natural development from a state of "natural innocence" to one of "awakened self-consciousness."

SOME CRITICISMS OF THE REPORT

As would be expected, the Majority Report did not receive unanimous acceptance even among the members of ASME. For the most part, however, most of the criticism was the result of individuals' feeling that this or that concept, so important to one person or another, had been omitted. Thus, for example, C. B. Thompson [66] deplored the failure to treat

[65] A study of Church's beliefs will show that he felt that, first, experience must be drawn upon; second, the resulting effort must be intelligently adopted to the purpose in view; and third, this intelligent effort must become habitual. For him, time study, the new and precise accounting methods, etc., were not causes but consequences of the new stage of self-consciousness.

[66] Thompson was a lawyer and lecturer on Manufacturing at Harvard. He is probably best known for his collection of articles on the "Taylor System."

the labor aspects, for the committee could have supplied a sorely needed "education" role: the worker had "a right to be shown," for example, that time study was not, as the "propagandists" declared, "slave-driving" or "unfair" and that systematic planning was not an "outright destruction of initiative."

However, it must be remembered that Alford had attempted to be brief and impersonal. Consequently, not all aspects could have been covered.

Some five years later, Thompson, in *The Theory and Practice of Scientific Management* (p. 40), took issue with Alford's list of industries which included applications of this new concept of management. The report listed fifty-two industries under fifteen headings (including "Miscellaneous"), while Thompson listed one hundred industries. Of course, the importance of the discrepancies may be overemphasized, especially since one used over-all headings and the other did not. Thompson also objected to the fact that Alford listed some industries where the "new" management methods did not eventually materialize as well as industries in which Thompson failed to find evidence of the use of the methods. Again, Thompson's failure was not an indication of Alford's inability.

What disturbed Gantt more than anything else was the Majority Report's description of the improvement of employer-employee relations as "another tendency, less pronounced in character." Gantt also regretted the limitation of the bibliography to ASME works.

The first of these criticisms was probably justified, as Alford had not yet been *too strongly* concerned with the "human element." This aspect of Alford's development did not publicly manifest itself until after World War I, when Alford was asked by the Meetings and Program Committee of ASME to prepare a study, similar to the 1912 Report, of industrial conditions, particularly in industrial relations, brought about by the war. Of course, the full impetus of the Gantt mission was still to come. However, there were others, too, who much earlier had begun to impress Alford with the importance of the human element. Lytle believes that Calder, Alford's associate at the ASME–IME meeting in Birmingham in 1910, was one of these. *The Human Element in Scientific Management* is indicative of Calder's views on the problem. Fred H. Colvin, Alford's associate on the *American Machinist,* was another; in a letter to the author of this study, Colvin asserted, "I assume that some of my ideas did have an influence on him."

Furthermore, it is doubtful whether, at this time, the movement itself had felt its importance even as a function of management. Nevertheless Gantt's objection to the report's listing of only ASME works was mainly due to his belief that two books, not mentioned, were particularly indicative of the expression of the "democratic as opposed to the autocratic spirit in industry," *Modern Organization* by C. de L. Hine and *The New Industrial Day* by W. C. Redfield.

Taylor felt, however, that some points in the Majority Report were "misleading." Among these was a statement from Adam Smith. A comparison of the quotation and the fifth paragraph of the first chapter ("Of the Division of Labor") of the first book ("Of the Causes of Improvement in the Productive Powers of Labour, and of the Order according to Which its Produce is naturally Distributed among the Different Ranks of the People") of *The Wealth of Nations* [67] proves Alford to be correct. Nor is Taylor's disagreement with Alford's quotations from Babbage entirely justified.[68]

But Taylor was particularly annoyed by references to the history of time study. Since a table was reproduced listing the operations, times, costs, etc., of pin manufacture in France in 1760 (from Babbage) and a reference to Coulomb in 1830, Taylor deemed it "desirable to make a statement as to the beginning of 'time study,' " and insisted that "time study was

[67] Smith, *The Wealth of Nations,* Vol. 1, p. 7.

[68] The data on pin manufacture are reproduced from Babbage. Even Person, "The Genius of Frederick W. Taylor," in *Advanced Management, 10,* 4, January-March (1945), refers to "over-all time studies of the major operations involved" by M. Perronet, who was a French pin manufacturer and whose studies Babbage reproduced.

begun in the machine shop of the Midvale Steel Company in 1881." This, of course, was not strictly correct. As a matter of fact Urwick and Brech [69] assigned "time observation to Coulomb." According to Lytle, Taylor's own stopwatch experience can be traced to his (Taylor's) classroom work under the tutelage of Wentworth, the American textbook writer, at Phillips Exeter Academy in New Hampshire.

However, once Taylor brought the matter up, he himself was quick to maintain that what he meant was not merely watching, analyzing, and timing men's movement, which he conceded were in use before the rise of "scientific management." He meant the beginning of the "profession of time study," and he insisted that E. H. Miller "was the first man to make 'time study' his profession." This was at Midvale in 1883. Taylor, of course, was correct.

Thus, general aspects of the report were for the most part acceptable, and the "idea of transference of skill" clarified management thinking. Consequently, from the viewpoint of both ASME and the movement, it was effective. For Alford it did more than merely start a cycle of ten-year histories. It opened the doors for many of the channels of management, and as a result, Alford explored and enriched a great number of them.

SOME SIDELIGHTS ON THE REPORT

The private files of Taylor further reveal Taylor and the times. On November 7, Alford wrote to Taylor, informing him that the report had been published "in the November number of the Journal, beginning on page 1601." He enclosed a reprint and, inviting Taylor to partake in the discussion, asked if he would reply orally or in writing.

Evidently, General William Crozier had seen a copy of the report and was somewhat perturbed about it. To make sure that Taylor had not missed it, he sent Taylor a copy. Crozier's own indignation, however, can be explained by a careful perusal of the November 12 letter he wrote Taylor:

[69] Urwick and Brech, *The Making of Scientific Management,* Vol. 1, p. 25.

The report dealing with the introduction of scientific management has so little to do with the only serious attempt that has been made to introduce scientific management into the government establishments, and places on so nearly an equal level the Navy Department, which has avowedly turned the subject down, and the Ordnance Department, which has, I believe, finally established it in the government service, that I do not feel inclined to do anything about it.

He concluded by assuring Taylor that, in his own estimation, he could "not see that it adds anything" of value that Taylor had not "already given the industrial world on this subject."

Two days later, Taylor replied. Perhaps it would be best to give the full text so as not to distort the matter:

I agree with you entirely as to the nature of the report on the present state of the art of industrial management, which is to be submitted to the A.S.M.E. early in December. It is so colorless and insipid that it seems hardly worth discussing. It would seem as if the whole object of the writers of the report were to point out the fact that, after all, one thing is about as good as another, and if there is any good in anything, the same thing was done two or three hundred years ago. There are lots of men who take exactly this stand in life, who have no enthusiasm for anything, and whose only object seems to be to show that it doesn't make any difference what you do—it's all about alike.

They have asked me to discuss their report, and I hardly know what to say. Of course, it would be rather rude on my part to write them the criticism that I am writing you, and yet that is all that I could say about it.

It is surely disgusting to have them place the Navy Yard management on a level with yours. If there are any two things in the government service that offer marked contrast in every way, they are the respective managements of these two sets of establishments.

However, I do not believe that a report of this sort will carry much if any weight one way or the other.

Then, as if to change the subject, Taylor referred to Wilson's recent election, and "for the first time in my life I voted for a Democratic president."

One week later, on November 19, in a letter that bore the rubber-stamped notation "DICTATED BY F.W.T. BUT NOT REVISED," Taylor informed Alford that he would not only discuss the report but that he would send a written copy of his remarks.

Taylor's files contain fourteen typewritten pages of discussion, treated above, in addition to four pages that bore the notation "I thought it best to omit this." [70] Of course, the files also contain the eleven-page final copy, as presented and dated December 6. Evidently he sent his discussion to Hathaway, for on the stationery of the Tabor Manufacturing Company, Hathaway, on December 3, wrote:

I have read with much interest your discussion of the paper entitled, The Present State of the Art of Management, which I am returning herewith. I think that what you have said hits the nail on the head admirably.

Hathaway signed the letter, which contained the notation, "Dic but not read."

Perhaps the best indication of the success of the report is the letter that Taylor wrote to Alford on December 11. It is difficult to imagine that this is the same person who barely a month before had written to Crozier criticizing the report and predicting for it such a doleful future. For Taylor now wrote:

Please let me congratulate you, first upon the very fine report which you made, and second upon the success of the A.S.M.E. meeting. I do not recall in the course of my experience with the A.S.M.E., any single subject which brought the same amount of interesting discussions. And in addition to the subject matter which came before the meeting, it seems to me that you conducted the meeting's whole session with remarkable success.

Taylor's enthusiasm must have been genuine, for a letter in his files from Sanford E. Thompson, on December 16, revealed:

[70] Although it also is noted: "Part of the material which was originally included in my criticism of the paper on the Present State of the Art of Industrial Management, which have been left out." The material here coincides exactly with Hathaway's discussion, *Trans. ASME, 33,* 1218 (1912).

I agree with you that the meeting last Saturday was a great success. I could not but contrast the remarks made then with what would actually have been made at a meeting five years ago.

Evidently Alford's report was now considered as a vindication of Taylor, at least as far as Thompson was concerned. For he added:

The opposition did fail to make out a case against scientific management. The remarks of Mr. Vaughan, it seems to me, would cause an unbiased reader to entirely discount the Minority Report. It struck me that his remarks were really an endorsement of scientific management because showing out so clearly the defects of the old-fashioned management.

Finally, if additional verification of Taylor's attitude were needed, it could be obtained from two requests made by Miss Grace Darrack, Taylor's secretary, to Calvin Rice, ASME Secretary, on March 24 and April 11, 1913. These asked for twenty-one copies of the Alford Report and Discussion. Ten were to be sent directly to Taylor at Chestnut Hill, while eleven were to be sent to designated persons in England, Japan, Russia, France, Mexico, and other places. The latter copies were to be accompanied by a "memorandum with each of these shipments, stating that they are sent with the compliments of Fred W. Taylor."

The receipted bills, indicating Taylor's prompt payment, are still to be found in Taylor's private files.

Chapter III

THE WORLD WAR I PERIOD

THE PREWAR PERIOD

The success of the 1912 Report did much to establish Alford in ASME circles. Still serving as secretary to the Administration Subcommittee, he was appointed to a two-year term on one of the standing committees, Meetings. The latter appointment would have been indeed important to Alford even had it not started him on a steady succession of committee appointments at ASME, for Gantt served on the Meetings Committee with him. (In practically no single year from 1912 until his death thirty years later was Alford without an appointment of one kind or another at the ASME.)

In the early summer of 1913, Alford, in the company of the leaders of scientific management, went to Germany as a representative of ASME to the Verein Deutscher Ingenieure. Clearly, Alford was becoming increasingly at home in management circles.

Nevertheless, this was no indication that he was neglecting his earlier interests. His articles in the *American Machinist* in 1914 testify to this: "Respeeding of Lathes" (*41*, No. 23, pp. 973-977, December 3, 1914), "Respeeding of Machine Tools" (*41*, No. 24, pp. 1017-1021, December 10, 1914), "Standardizing Lathe Tool Posts" (*41*, No. 25, p. 1062, December 17, 1914), "Standard Taper Sockets and Shanks" (*41*, No. 26, pp. 1112-1115, December 24, 1914), and "Standard Boring-Bar Cutters, Gibs and Keys" (*41*, No. 27, p. 1148, December 31, 1914). However, even here he was beginning to point out matters

75

that were more than mere technical details, for they emphasized standardization in general and Barth's work in particular.

WORLD WAR I

Soon after the events at Sarajevo, machine shops and munition works were called upon to supply their products to the belligerents, and it is interesting to note how effectively this call was answered. Despite the fact that only two years previously there were, at most, three government arsenals in England, by the winter of 1916-17 more than four thousand English industrial plants were being run as government factories and thousands more, while remaining under private control, were also engaged in war work. Obviously, such a program called for a mammoth program of industrial organization and education. Of course, to greater and lesser degrees, similar organization and education were taking place in Germany, Italy, France, Japan, and even Russia.

INDUSTRIAL PREPARATION

Since the United States did not officially enter the war as a belligerent until the spring of 1917, it may be assumed that our machine shops and munition plants had, at this time, little or no occasion for war production. This, however, was not the case. For at least two years prior to our official entry, our plants received orders from foreign governments for war products. And, during this period, it became clear to conscientious observers that here was a "new" art, one with which we, at least, had had little contact and one in which our workmen were, for the most part, unskilled.

In 1905, the value of machine tools exported from the United States was $4,332,665. It reached $9,369,056 by 1907, only to drop back to $3,640,034 in 1909. By 1913, it had increased to $16,097,315, but it fell in 1914 to $14,011,359. In 1915 it practically doubled to $28,162,968, and by 1916 it more than doubled again to $61,315,032. As impressive as these values may sound, they were comparatively small in relation to the total value of munition contracts placed in this country—approximately $1.6 billion—in the fall of 1916.

To satisfy these demands, the existing machine shops were no longer adequate, and many firms—firms that had, before this time, never built such machinery—entered the field. To give just one instance, there were at least thirty firms which, with no previous experience, began to build lathes.

THE NEED FOR THE AMMUNITION MANUFACTURES TEXT

The need for developing machines for munition manufacture became evident, and Alford,[1] as editor in chief of the *American Machinist,* was mindful of these demands. The columns of the magazine during 1915 and 1916 were filled with information concerning special grinders for shell bodies and bases, millers for shell bases, drilling machines for face parts, special machinery for rifle manufacture, semiautomatic and automatic machinery for fuse-making, etc. But, more than this, Alford set down for his readers a much broader and a more fundamental concept: he showed them how to apply what they already knew in one field to what they were studying in another. Without going into the psychologists' beliefs in the transfer of learning, few can argue with one of the basic problems of engineering education, the development of the ability of transferring ideas from the solution of one set of problems to an attack on a totally different set of problems. And at this Alford was a master.

Factually, Alford had a dual purpose: (1) service in muni-

[1] Alford also brought up America's war needs at the ASME. For example, during a discussion of De Leeuw's paper (No. 1589, "A Foundation for Machine Tool Design and Construction," *Trans. ASME, 39,* 185-198 (1917)), Alford, on behalf of the Research Committee, asked what could be done to help the country at war. A subcommittee had suggested a study of the action of cutting tools and the cause of chip formation. It was this year that he became chairman of the Research Committee's Subcommittee on Cutting Action of Machine Tools. He was particularly anxious for aid from Jenkins and Poliakoff, especially the latter who had considerable experience in Russian rifle research (*Trans. ASME, 39,* 206-207 (1917)).

tion manufacture and (2) furthering of machine-shop practice. The realization that the store of information already printed by the magazine had to be presented in a more coherent and permanent form, resulted in *Manufacture of Artillery Ammunition* in the early months of 1917.

Published by McGraw-Hill Book Company, publishers of books for the *American Machinist* and eleven other technical magazines, the book lists as the authors "Members of the Editorial Staff of the *American Machinist:* L. P. Alford (Editor in Chief), F. H. Colvin, E. A. Suverkrop, Robert Mawson, and John H. Van Deventer." Of these colleagues of Alford, Van Deventer was managing editor, the others were associate editors. Each of these five men contributed at least one chapter. In addition, it includes the work of R. Trautschold, J. P. Brophy (Vice-President and General Manager of the Cleveland Automatic Machine Company), P. E. Barbour (New York Engineers of the National Guard) and J. H. Moore.

AMMUNITION MANUFACTURES

The book is divided into four sections: [2] "Shrapnel," "High Explosive Shells," "Cartridge Cases," and "Fuses and Primers," and an Appendix. Although more than one person contributed to each section, one of each of Alford's colleagues whose names

---

[2] The "Shrapnel" section first explained what a shrapnel was and what it did. It then expounded on the forging of shrapnel blanks, the manufacture of the 18-pound British shrapnel with its powder cups, discs, sockets, and plugs, as well as the making of the 3-inch and 12-inch Russian shrapnel.

The "High-Explosive Shells" section treats the making of shells with regular shop equipment and discusses the high-explosive shell, the forging of blanks for such shells, and the manufacture of British (18-pound; 4.5-inch; 8-inch) and Russian (1-pound; 3-inch) high-explosive shells, the French 120-millimeter explosive shell, and the Serbian 120-millimeter shell, as well as the operation of the British 9.2-inch, Mark IX, and the 12-inch Mark IV howitzer shells.

The section dealing with "Cartridge Cases" explains the manufacture and rolling of cartridge brass and the making of the 1-pound, 18-pound, and 4.5-inch howitzer cartridge cases.

The section on "Fuses and Primers" explains the making of the British Detonator Fuse Mark 100 and the Time Fuse Mark 80-44, as well as the manufacture of primers for cartridge cases. In all cases the treatment is thorough, explaining the sequence of operations, the machines, special fixtures, tools, and gages used, complete specifications and drawings, etc.

appear on the title page is given credit for each section. As
for Alford's contribution, it consisted of the over-all editing as
well as an article, "Machine Tools for Munition Manufacture,"
which appeared in the Appendix.

ALFORD'S CONTRIBUTION

Although not of great length (pages 729 through 734), Alford's
contribution raised the level of the book from that of a mere
text on munition manufacture, important as that might be, to
a blueprint that the country's machine tool industry might
follow if and when the United States went to war. If anywhere
in his writings, it is here that the depth of Alford's thinking
and analysis are clearly shown.

Not that the book without Alford's article would not have
satisfied the need for a text dealing with the manufacture of
army and navy materials. It still would have complied with
Point Two of the Three-Point Program of the Naval Consulting Board of the United States: [3] (1) an inventory of the
manufacturing resources of the country; (2) the training and
education of these resources for national services in both war
and peace; and (3) an attempt to build up a reserve of the
country's skilled laborers so that they might remain in industry and not be "lost" to the fighting army. But with the Alford contribution the book became even more valuable.

Although Coffin did pay special homage to Alford's work on
the book, he seemed to particularly stress his patriotic effort.
Again, Alford's keen adherence to duty and his acceptance of
the responsibilities of an engineer are evident. However, he
could not have done otherwise. Here was a problem, and Alford attacked it in his customary rigorous fashion—and with
the usual engineering approach. He examined American ma-

[3] Harold E. Coffin, who wrote the Foreword to the book, was a member of
this board. A vice-president of the Hudson Motor Car Company, he was chairman of the Naval Consulting Board's Committee on Industrial Preparedness,
where he served with W. L. Saunders, T. Robins, L. Addicks, W. L. Emmet,
B. G. Lamme, and B. B. Thayer. The work of this committee was later turned
over to the Council of National Defense, a body created by the government.

chine-shop practice and its role of fulfilling foreign contracts, he analyzed the necessary machine program, he examined manufacturing methods both here and abroad, he studied purchasing policies, and, finally, as would be expected, he laid down some principles for the standardization and procurement of machine tools in organizing for American industrial preparedness.

The original article, written in October, 1916, based its analyses and conclusions on an examination of "broader events" and data of the preceding twenty-six months. Despite scattered buying, the majority of American machine tools during this period was being exported to Great Britain, France, and Russia. Some tools were also going to Holland, Italy, and the Scandinavian countries, but exports to Germany and Austria had been cut off. Consequently, little was known concerning the details of Germany's industrialization program, but a great amount of information was available regarding the methods used in Great Britain and France. It was, therefore, on the procedures in these two countries that Alford attempted to formulate "the principles of action to govern the design, purchase, production, and distribution of machine tools in preparing for a national emergency of war."

ALFORD'S PLAN FOR PREPAREDNESS IN THE MACHINE TOOL INDUSTRY

Alford broke down the types of machine tools exported into three general classes:

1. Plain machines that were either a manufacturer's "standard" before the war or built thereafter to satisfy the increased foreign demand.

2. Regular machines of a higher grade (particularly semiautomatic) of a manufacturer's prewar "standard" type.

3. Specialized machinery for some particular detail of munition manufacture.

The early British, French, and Russian orders were placed originally by the same European machine tool agents who had regularly handled American products. During the first year of the European war, however, these dealers' contracts were supplemented by orders originating from special agents or commissions sent here by their governments. So heavy was the ensuing demand that our shops were operating at their full limits. Hence, these foreign governments were compelled to deal with shops—other than actual machine tool shops—that made high-grade machinery for the printing, woodworking, and other industries. Alford felt that the purchasing methods and procedures of the government commissions were most capable and that these bodies were better managed than those representatives sent by private dealers.

The private dealers were so intent on buying what amounted to one type of machine at a time that it is actually possible to divide their buying methods into three distinct periods in accordance with their purchases: first, simple lathes and turret machines; second, grinders, millers, and drilling machines; and last, planers, shapers, and toolroom machinery. Only through experience was it learned that the toolroom machinery should have been bought first, for these were necessary for the production of fixtures, jigs, and gages needed at the outset.

Alford believed that, in the event of a war in which the United States was involved, not only would our manufactures possibly be inadequate but we would be compelled to import machine tools. If this was the case, he felt that our purchasing abroad should be done by an American counterpart of the British Ministry of Munitions together with its subcommittees whose results he admired.

For example, England had been faced with speculative buying and selling, a wide and unsystematic variety of machine tools purchased abroad, and an improper distribution of machine tools with its resulting effects on the quantity and quality of production. The British Ministry of Munitions met this situation by prohibiting the importation of machine tools without a license from this body: the result was a more efficient control. In Germany, the Ministry of War prepared a list of articles that would be of value to the enemy and banned their export.

As the war continued, the Ministry established a War Raw Materials Committee and an Industrial Committee, which controlled the machine tool industry as well as others, directed what machines should be bought and where they should be built, handled the raw materials supply program, and arranged for the distribution of machines. France, too, early mobilized the nation's machine tool industry.

After analyzing what Europe—including Germany (!)—could send us in the event that the United States went to war, Alford came to the conclusion that the stock of machine tools in the hands of European manufacturers and distributors not only was small but was insignificant in relation to our needs. Hence, he concluded, there were two alternatives open to us: (1) buy standard machines regularly manufactured abroad or (2) order machines specially adapted to our requirements. He felt that the latter action would be preferable and based his timetable for production on this assumption.

It may be wise here, however, to set down from his study (page 734) his "principles for the standardization and procurement of machine tools in organizing for American industrial preparedness": [4]

1. Organize at once in skeleton form an industrial committee of the Council of National Defense to control the standardization, design, and preparation of machine tools for the production of American munitions.

2. Through joint action of this committee, the American Society of Mechanical Engineers and the National Machine Tool Builders Association standardize the details of regular machine tools and design whatever additional special machine tools may be necessary for the rapid and economical production of American munitions.

3. Immediately on the outbreak of war prohibit the exportation of any machine tools from the United States.

4. Immediately on the outbreak of war prohibit the importation of any machine tools in the United States except under license and control of the committee mentioned under 1.

[4] Alford had also sired these principles previously at the ASME. *Trans. ASME*, *38*, 62 (1916).

5. Order all machines abroad through this committee or its representatives in the capitals of Europe and intrust these men with the responsibility of securing the desired deliveries and quality.

6. Order no machine tools abroad except to standardized American designs either for the complete machine or the essential details, as the committees may determine.

It is interesting to note in this analysis the engineering approach with which Alford tackled this problem—a pattern that he would use over and over again in attacking other problems: gather as many pertinent data as are needed, study and analyze these, and finally set forth in a clear and concise fashion a set of principles to be followed.

ALFORD'S ANALYSIS

Some questions as to the details may, of course, be raised. For example, it was evident when he wrote that we could not expect to import machine tools from Germany after war came. Yet why did he include Germany as a possible source? In the first place, there was no clear-cut belief that we would, if the war actually came, be opposed to Germany. Sentiment here, in the main, was mixed in the early years. However, be that as it may, Alford was compiling a maximum from which we could draw, and his final conclusion was, basically, that there was not enough to draw from, even if the whole of Europe could serve as our supply.

Again, could we count on Europe's machine shops and munition works if Europe was the actual scene of the fighting war? It must be remembered that this was 1916, a time when wholesale bombings were not the accepted order.

In general, however, it is Alford's general analysis that concerns this study. Unquestionably it was the engineering method carried to its limit. Compared to the actual details of the other authors of the book, *Manufacturing Artillery Ammunition*, the scope was indicative of Alford's depth and breadth of thought. He was concerned with the over-all problem and not with the manufacture of this item or that.

As for the importance of his contribution here, there were at least two aspects that should be mentioned. Both of these cropped up again and again in his life. It gave him an increased incentive in his pleas for standardization which resulted, as will be seen, in his work in this field. And also, it displayed the effectiveness of engineering analysis when applied to national problems, a field that he eventually served faithfully and well.

SCIENTIFIC MANAGEMENT PUBLICATIONS

The literature by means of which the story of "scientific management" was told is a diverse one, and it is made up of many facts. It includes a few books written by the pioneers of the movement, a great many descriptions of the workings of scientific management by the managers of the plants in which the "system" was being installed, some legal proceedings (commission, committee, etc.) arising out of the "system," and lastly some discussions relating to management, labor, and human relations.

In a few instances, the medium of the published book was used. In more cases, the forum afforded by the professional societies was utilized. However, at all times the columns of the periodicals were filled and the presses of their printers were at work. Consequently, any treatment of the growth of scientific management must make some mention of the periodicals that played such a great part.

Even some of the "popular"—or, perhaps, the nontechnical—magazines did their share. It must be remembered that the development of the movement was due in great part to the publicity it received, sometimes even in the Sunday supplements. However, a fair share of articles could be found in such periodicals as *American Magazine, Nation, Harper's, Review of Reviews, Outlook, Living Age*. As a further instance of the wide scope, there were discussions and statements in the *Journal of the Society of Naval Engineers, American Gas Light Journal, Electric Railway Journal, Journal of Political Economy, Journal of Home Economics*, to mention but a few.

Perhaps, in this connection, outside the various societies' publications, more attention should be paid to those magazines some of which, in one form or another, have come down to us today and which we still associate with management men's reading.

Among those which, after playing an important role, disappeared from the scene was the short-lived *Industrial Engineering,* a publication devoted particularly to the Taylor group, and *Efficiency* which, before it finally was abandoned, was known as *One Hundred Percent.*

As for those that are in some form still with us today, there were *Factory, System, Machinery,* names that will come up again in the ensuing discussion. Probably most important because of the number and importance of its publications was an organization owned by John Dunlap called The Engineering Magazine Company. Under the editorship of Charles B. Going, who himself was the author of a widely known text, *Principles of Industrial Engineering,* it published not only as articles but also in book form the writings of Gantt, Emerson, Church, Knoeppel, Day, Carpenter, Shepard, and many others identified with the management movement.

However, in 1917 Dunlap was in search of a new editor. Charles E. Funk, who had taken on Going's job, had decided to leave. Dunlap was no doubt contemplating more than merely filling an editor's job, for he came to the offices of *Machinery* in an attempt to find someone who might help in bolstering the sale of his books. Erik Sellman was recommended for this job. As for the other position, his inquiries concerning the availability of Alford must have borne fruit. Alford was given the editor's job on Gantt's recommendation.

At the time, Alford was still at the *American Machinist,* in his seventh year as editor in chief. Although, as his own notes show, the magazine under his guidance earned a net profit of $200,000 that year, he had not been completely contented since the death of Hill in 1916. Hill's successor was Arthur J. Baldwin, with whom Alford could not always see eye to eye. Evidently Alford felt that many of the ideas promulgated by Hill in the old offices on Pearl Street were being abandoned in the new building at West 36th Street and Tenth Avenue, New York.

In April, 1917, Alford came to the Dunlap magazine (originally established in 1891, the magazine had been renamed *Industrial Management* under Funk) to assume the post of editor. Here began Alford's friendship with Sellman, an association that lasted throughout Alford's life.

Although the Dunlap magazine was in new quarters at 6 East 39th Street, New York, the magazine itself was not in too healthy a state. An indication of affairs are evident from the fact that, according to Sellman, it at this time had a subscription list of 7,253, of which about two thirds of its subscribers' accounts were delinquent. Nevertheless, as a result of Alford's policy and work, in a little over a year its circulation climbed to 18,750. Among Alford's private papers is his own notation that he had come to a magazine that was "practically bankrupt" and that "in 1920 the net profit was some $70,000 after all obligations had been paid off."

How was this done?

Alford's prowess as an editor and a writer was more than helpful. He could dictate copy that needed little, if any, revision. Even in later years, Miss Dora Albert, his secretary at NYU, has frequently commented on the manner in which he wrote his texts: unlike many authors who would painstakingly prepare a written manuscript with numerous corrections for typing, Alford would sit at his desk with a few notes and dictate, stopping only occasionally to make a page reference to a book from which he might quote. What is more, he handled just as easily the works of other authors whose contributions he was editing.

Equally important was Alford's appreciation of the need for healthy promotion, a matter in which he was aided by Sellman. Fundamentally, Alford was responsible for that very important technique, the "serialized article." Although it had been used in connection with fiction, Alford applied it to the technical magazine with astounding success: Harrison's series, "Cost Accounting to Aid Production," was typical. It might be noted that not only did the series idea allow an extensive treatment of a subject, but it was also used for promotional purposes. Frequently the series appeared later as an individual publication.

Another example of the Alford use of the series was that written by Merrick. When Alford was still at the *American Machinist,* he felt that articles by one of Taylor's own time study men would be helpful to the readers. This series was dropped when he left the magazine. However, in his new post his prophetic insight in the management field led him to the belief that the time study story ought to be told, and he was successful in obtaining a new series.

Alford had a keen sense of anticipating future trends in the management field. However, it was not the sole result of intuition: his keen analysis indeed contributed. Thus, as pointed out below, his feeling that costs would assume a role that up to this time had been held by production led him to a greater emphasis on control of costs. Even in these early days, he assigned to quality control a role far more important than the narrow limits of inspection to which it was then currently confined.

Mention might also be made, at this time, of another matter that the engineering world now accepts as a matter of course but that was brought to its full maturity by Alford: *The Engineering Index.* Originally it was essentially a set of clippings from periodicals both here and abroad. Supervised by a Miss Kingsley, it had been an idea associated with the Dunlap firm. It seems that Miss Kingsley would mark all articles that she thought of interest; these would be clipped by George Piper. The clippings would then be filed and sent to subscribers on request until the supply ran out. It was, however, due to the efforts of Alford that it was properly classified, annotated, developed, and finally sold to the ASME. Nevertheless, even after the sale it continued to be run as a feature of *Industrial Management.* Later, of course, Hannum, who was associated with Alford, worked on the *Index.*

Clearly Alford had become firmly established in the publication field in general, and in the industrial management branch in particular.

Little wonder that he was again chosen by ASME to record the progress and status of scientific management.

Chapter IV

THE POSTWAR PERIOD

THE MANAGEMENT HISTORY REPORTS

The 1912 Report was followed, ten years later, by another that attempted to treat the intervening "ten years' progress in management," and that second report, in turn, was followed by a third "ten years' progress" report in 1932. However, before the "custom" was established, Alford presented a report in 1919 to ASME.

This report, like its 1912 predecessor, had been "requested" and, as revealed by his private papers some eighteen years later, was the result of conditions that had come about. This time the conditions were industrial ones, caused not by any single personality but rather by the "activity and requirements" of World War I, which "gave a strong impetus to personnel or employment management."

The request was made by the ASME's Meetings and Program Committee, which suggested a "report after the manner of the one of 1912, which should bring in review the changes and progress of the seven intervening years, and, in particular, should deal with the development of industrial relations."

The paper, under his own authorship, was "The Status of Industrial Relations," and was presented at the ASME's Detroit Meeting in June, 1919.[1]

[1] *Trans. ASME, 41,* 163-186 (1919).

THE "NEW" APPROACH

Evidently, Gantt's criticism of the 1912 Report concerning the minor role Alford had cast for the "human" problem had not gone unheeded. For Alford, who hoped that the 1919 Report would be looked upon as a continuation of the earlier report and as a study of what had occurred during the seven years that had passed since he examined "the broad aspects of the management problem as it then existed in the industries of the country," had since matured. He had come to realize the importance of the human element.

ASME itself noted that, in connection with the study Alford made in 1919, "the question has been studied from many different angles and has come to be viewed in quite a different light from that in which it was regarded when the original report was prepared."

The transition from a minor to a major role was more or less complete when Alford, in the last years of his life, wrote his text, *Principles of Industrial Management*,[2] where he not only recognized Gantt's "greatest single contribution . . . to industrial administration and management," his 1908 paper on "Training Workmen in Habits of Industry and Cooperation," [3] but gave room to a comment made by William Kent, who had considered the Gantt paper as one "which I regard as the most important ever to appear in the Transactions of the Society." Yet in 1912 Alford had not fully recognized its major importance.

ALFORD'S REALIZATION OF THE
IMPORTANCE OF THE "HUMAN PROBLEM"

Of course, personal contact with Gantt, Calder, Colvin, and others had influenced Alford in this matter. But he himself had discovered a "remarkable statement of the responsibility of en-

2 Pp. 450-451.
3 *Trans. ASME, 30,* 1036-1049 (1908).

gineers in solving the problems involved in the relations of employers and employees." He found the following in the presidential address of Robert H. Thurston before ASME: [4]

In singular and discreditable contrast with all the gains in recent and current practice in engineering, stands one feature of our work which has more importance to us and to the world, and which has a more direct and controlling influence upon the material prosperity and happiness of the nation than any modern invention or than any discovery of science. I refer to the relations of the employers to the working classes and to the mutual interest of labor and capital. It is from us, if from any body of men, that the world should expect a complete and satisfactory practical solution of the so-called "Labor problem." More is expected of us than even of our legislators. And how little has been accomplished.

If Alford had not realized its importance before, he took cognizance of it then, for it involved a call that he never failed to heed: the responsibility of the engineer. This was, as Lillian Gilbreth, L. W. Wallace, Ralph Flanders, and others have asserted, a directing force in his life.

Alford looked upon Thurston's contention as a challenge that thirty-five years later was still unanswered. In fact, Alford would be the last to deny that anything had been done on the matter during the next third of a century. He would, however, be among the first to admit that the problem still lacked a complete solution.

INDUSTRIAL RELATIONS

In his treatment, Alford realized the complexity of the problem and, of necessity, limited his discussion to a study of "industrial relations" from the Civil War period whence America's industrial might may be traced. In gathering his data, he again leaned heavily on personal contacts as well as on the published

[4] "The Mechanical Engineer—His Work and His Policy," The President's Annual Address, *Trans. ASME, 4,* 87-105 (1883).

writings of those who witnessed the development of the problem.

In true scientific and logical fashion, Alford began with a definition. It may be wise to examine it not only because it limited the material of his treatment but also because it presented his view:

> Industrial relations comprise that body of principles, practice and law growing out of the interacting human rights, needs and aspirations of all who are engaged in or dependent upon productive industry.

Alford evidently excluded "feelings" of unrest, per se, but included their actual manifestations, which appeared as strikes and lockouts. His classification under "principles, practice and law" [5] was more than an assertion of a concept that was soon to occupy his attention, for it served the very utilitarian purpose of assigning the problem as being properly in the domain of ASME whose function it was to enlighten its membership on production and manufacturing matters.

It is of great interest to note the "timelessness" of the problem that made the report necessary:

> At the present time we are witnessing the payment of higher wages than were ever before known in this country, there is a general feeling of uneasiness and unrest throughout our entire industry, labor is making many demands, and strikes are so frequent and widespread that it is doubtful if a single member of this Society has not at least been inconvenienced during the present year by

[5] In later years, Alford omitted the *law* aspects and treated only the *principles* and *practices* (see *Principles of Industrial Management*, p. 450). It is also of interest to note that, as late as 1930, he used the terms *personnel management* and *employment management* interchangeably. In the last book he wrote he has one chapter, entitled "Employer-Employee Relations," in which he insisted that popular usage had negated any distinction, although it might still be possible to make one in connection with *employer-employee relations, industrial relations,* and *labor management,* all of which may be used to designate the broad subject, while limiting the use of *labor maintenance* and *personnel administration* to worker hiring, training, placement, and grievance adjustment. Historically, it may be noted that in 1909 Tolman, in his *Social Engineering,* dealt with what we now call *personnel management.* In 1917, Drury, in his "Scientific Management and Progress," *Bulletin of the Taylor Society, 3,* 9 ff., February (1917), used the term *human engineering* in the same sense.

the temporary cessation of some function of industry upon which he is in some degree dependent.

Then as now labor unrest begot a more intensified study in an attempt to understand and relieve the situation.

In the 1880's the remedies essentially set forth were profit sharing and wage incentives, while in 1919 they were, Alford maintained, the shop-committee system and profit sharing. Of course there can be no doubt as to the extensive use of profit sharing; it began as early as 1868 [6] and probably reached its height during the depression that preceded World War II. However, it is difficult to understand why Alford did not include incentives in the 1919 period.

Alford considered the true beginnings of industrial relations to have taken place in the United States in the 1880's, but he felt that the problem did not become acute until 1905, when the "evils" of the "absentee" directorate of large corporations came into prominence. Alford was particularly concerned with the system of management and control that the owners, as a result of consolidations, had set up in the major cities away from the plants situated at various places throughout the country.

EMPLOYEE-EMPLOYER VS. LABOR-MANAGEMENT

It is surprising that Alford failed to take true cognizance of the fact that the problem had become one of management–labor and not employer–employee: he did not make any clear distinction between the manager and the owner. Thus, when he spoke of a partial reason for the necessity of exploring industrial relations, he assigned it to "the factory system wherein all personal contact is lost between the owner or manager and the worker." [7] His interest was in the absentee directorate, whether

[6] The Pennsylvania Railroad had a type of profit sharing in connection with a material waste program (see Lytle, *Wage Incentive Methods,* p. 201). Of course, Towne used a modification of profit sharing in 1886.

[7] For a clearer distinction, see Juran, "Transition in Corporation Controls," in *Advanced Management, 13,* No. 3, 126-130, September (1948).

in the guise of manager or owner. He also assigned a great part
of the clash between the employer class and the worker class
to "losses in fitness of control." These he felt were caused by
the loss of the old relationship that once existed between master
and workman and apprentice, the disappearance of the managers' personal knowledge of the work, the tools, and the conservation of materials and human effort, the withdrawal of the
managers' families from productive work, and difference in
living conditions between the families of the managers and the
workers.

Of course, some of these details may be questioned. For example, motion study had begun to become aware of the waste
of human effort. However, what Alford basically was attempting to set forth was that the community of interest between
master and worker no longer existed—with the result that there
was no assurance that the one was any longer aware of the
other's interests. This cessation of contact, according to Alford,
necessitated the development of "a body of principles, practice,
and law" which would meet this situation.

HISTORICAL "SOLUTIONS" OF THE EMPLOYEE-EMPLOYER PROBLEM

An attempt toward a solution was made along many lines.
Probably because of "their actual or promised permanence and
widespread acceptance and application," Alford expanded on
six of these.

The first was profit sharing. Despite the impressive array of
thirty firms that had installed some form of profit sharing before 1889 (as listed by Boyd Fisher and by N. D. Gilman in
the book, *Profit Sharing Between Employer and Employee,* published in 1889), "it has never had widespread adoption." Alford
felt that its failure was due to the fact that its payment was not
immediate, that business hazards influence the workers' share,
which cannot be proportional to his efforts,[8] that the amount

8 Emerson, too, did not take kindly to profit sharing, because it "repudiated
individuality" and made "business a kind of providence that rains on the just
and unjust alike."

distributed shows up only as a very small amount compared to the workers' hourly wage, and that there were discrepancies between the amount shared by the owners and managers and that by the workers.

The second line along which an attempt was made to improve relations between employer and employee (so far as division of earnings and profit was concerned) came with the incentive plans that developed during the rise of "the science and practice of management." [9] Beginning with Towne's appeal that, because he "essentially affects the economy," the engineer must become an "economist" (1886) and his own gain-sharing plan (1889), as well as many plans, including those of Halsey and Taylor, were set forth. The relationship between these wage plans and "labor unrest" is well illustrated by a letter that Halsey wrote to Alford on March 31, 1919, for this report. Recalling the "epidemic of strikes" effected by the Knights of Labor and the methods of wage payments at the time, Halsey wrote:

My A.S.M.E. paper read at the Providence meeting of 1891 analyzes these methods, points out their inadequacy and compares the premium plan with them. I have recently had occasion to reread my old paper, and I must say that it strikes me now as a very adequate summary.

The more I reflect on it the more I feel that the premium plan offers the best solution yet suggested for the condition of labor unrest. It assures increased wages and cheaper output simultaneously and one as the outcome of the other. What more can you ask?

The Halsey plan was looked upon as a "considerable achievement" [10] and it won, for Halsey, an ASME gold medal in 1923.

The third direction taken in attempts to bring about labor peace involved the reduction of industrial hazards and the mitigation of the effects of occupational diseases and injuries. Its full realization came about 1910 when juries in the American courts began to award fairly large amounts to individuals for

[9] Note that, in this report, Alford actually referred to the subject as a "science."

[10] Lytle, *Wage Incentive Methods,* p. 202.

industry-connected injuries. It was then that industry turned
to liability insurance companies on the one hand and to a
"safety first" campaign on the other. Alford maintained that
from the beginning this was a "young man's movement" and
that it was fostered by people in companies having plants west
of Pittsburgh but main offices in New York.

Judging by a letter to Alford by John L. Henning, chief
engineer for a Louisiana sulphur-mining plant, the year 1904
marks the beginning of the payment of accident compensation
in this industry:

About 1902 . . . with . . . personal injury cases . . . laws in existence . . . attempted to divide the responsibility solely between
employer and employees and the basis . . . was simply whether employer or employee was the proximate cause of the injury.

. . . It appeared unjust . . . but every plan was "unconstitu-
tional."

. . . The common practice was to "try" these cases in the "offices" of the employer, and if . . . the employer was the proximate
cause . . . an effort would be made to get out from under by mul-
tifarious methods; likewise the injured was induced by a certain
type of lawyer to try to get as much as possible. The result was that
neither . . . was getting a square deal. . . .

I proposed . . . and installed a system that provided 100 percent remuneration while the injured person was off duty, and paid
. . . other expenses until . . . able to resume work.

. . . In cases of permanent disability . . . a liberal estimate was
made. . . . As evidence of the success of this plan . . . in 15 years
. . . I had only two cases reach court . . . before a jury and I won
both. . . . Each of these . . . afterwards stated . . . they were induced . . . by their lawyers . . . against their own inclination.

I think it was about 1905-1906 that the Bureau of Mines undertook to standardize the methods . . . in the various states. I proposed . . . a state compulsory compensation law with a division of
the cost . . . 50 percent directly to the industry, 25 percent to the
public at large through state aid, and 25 percent to be borne by the
injured employee . . .

The fundamental reason for a distribution of the cost to the
three elements of society is that all will take more interest in safety

methods to prevent the enormous toll of life that at present exists in industry.

In the enactment of state compensation laws the old "master and servant" concept was no longer the basis. In its stead the responsibility for industrial accidents was placed upon industry, and commissions were set up to assure the employee of his just due. The first of the laws came in July 4, 1911, in New Jersey, during the administration of Governor Wilson.

However, the growth of safety engineering, improvement of working conditions, and industrial welfare plans have been equally important. Alford stressed the influence exerted by ASME in general and its safety codes in particular.

As far as Alford himself was concerned, this phase of the industrial relations problem soon led him to other fields. Thus, it was his interest in safety problems that indirectly led him to his kmh analysis,[11] for a good part of that study had its beginnings in his analysis of the production and man-hour data gathered by American Engineering Council for the Safety and Production Study in 1926.

A fourth development to improve employer-employee relations came into prominence around 1916 under the guise of "a new profession in industry, that of employment management." It included all policies and work connected with personnel, including hiring, firing, welfare, etc. Alford assigned to the B. F. Goodrich Company the distinction of an early, if not the earliest, organized employment department (about 1900). As long ago as 1907, H. F. J. Porter (before ASME)[12] and in 1914, M. W. Alexander (before the National Machine Tool Builders' Association) warned of the heavy cost of labor turnover. It was this problem that gave impetus to the organization of the Boston Employment Managers' Association in 1910. A prime reason for the growth of the establishment of the employment department in a plant has been the need for employees during periods of labor scarcity. Involved, also, was a

11 See below, pp. 166-200.
12 "The Realization of Ideals in Industrial Engineering," in Trans. ASME, 27, 343-356 (1907).

study of the reasons for men leaving a plant. The national government insisted that all plants handling war contracts have such a department and set up six weeks' training courses in employment management.

The fifth trend was the declaration as well as the enforcement, particularly during the war, of "three rights of workers, namely collective bargaining, restricted hours of labor, and the living wage." These were officially the work of the National War Labor Board created by President Wilson. What is more, the Treaty of Versailles also recognized these and other rights and principles (e.g., labor not a commodity, the eight-hour day, forty-eight-hour week, abolition of child labor, equal remuneration for equal work regardless of sex, etc.).

Finally, systems have been developed that allow mutual or joint control by employers and employees. Alford was fearful of the view stating that labor unrest was fundamentally a "struggle for control." He saw at one extreme a "confession" on the part of the owners and the managers "that they have already lost some of their control." (Probably a current manifestation of this is the "Mitbestimmungsrecht" or "Codetermination" of recent years.) On the other side, Alford saw the concept of an "industrial democracy." (The slogan, "No taxation without representation," was reworded, "No control without representation.") The "shop committee," which is found in our modern "Bottom Up Management," "Multiple Management," etc., was the method most commonly used.[13] The oldest form of shop committee was at the Pittsburgh Plant of the Nernst Lamp Company, where it was installed by H. F. J. Porter.[14] The success of the shop committee in broader fields was predicted by Cameron[15] who had used it in connection with safety problems.

[13] This was a departure from Taylor, who was "adamant against such ideas of industrial democracy as labor-management committees or shop committees" (Lepawsky, *Administration*, p. 121).

[14] Porter, "The Higher Law in the Industrial World," in *Engineering Magazine, 29*, 641-655, August (1905).

[15] Cameron, "The Attitude of the Employer Toward Accident Prevention and Workmen's Compensation," *Trans. ASME, 37*, 899-906 (1915).

Alford believed that an important element was missing from these six lines of development, preventing them from exerting their great force in solving labor difficulties: they did not remove the fear of unemployment. In fact, Alford asserted exactly what Roper, about a quarter of a century later, in *Fortune's* poll, was to discover.[16]

Alford questioned the motives of industry in setting up its plans for settling industrial difficulties. He was particularly suspicious of the altruistic concepts that prompted many industrialists to set up welfare plans. He correctly asserted the workingman's general contempt for such favors. Although he believed that the employers had translated the safety engineers' moral and economic motives into commercial ones, which in themselves were neither selfish nor paternalistic, he felt their inadequacy toward developing proper industrial relations.

"SERVICE" AND INDUSTRIAL DEMOCRACY

The missing element that he set forth was *service*. Just one month before, *Industrial Management,* the magazine whose editorship he had assumed just two years earlier, published an article by Gantt: [17]

In other words, we have proved in many places that the doctrine of service which has been preached in the churches as religion is not only good economics and eminently practical, but because of the increased production of goods obtained by it, promises to lead us safely through the maze of confusion into which we seem to be headed, and to give us that industrial democracy which alone can afford a basis for industrial peace.[18]

[16] See Lytle, *Job Evaluation Methods,* p. 14.

[17] Gantt, "The Religion of Democracy," in *Industrial Management,* May, 1919. Reprinted in the collection *Organizing for Work,* p. 104.

[18] It is interesting to note that, despite the great admiration that Alford had for Gantt, few of Gantt's articles appeared in the magazines Alford edited, and those that did came after 1918. A Gantt article, "Application of Scientific Management to the Labor Problem," appeared in the *American Machinist* in 1904 (Volume 27), but this was before Alford was on the staff. It was not until 1918 (May) that a Gantt paper was printed by an Alford periodical: this was "Passing the Buck." The next was "Efficiency and Idleness" in the November issue of the same year.

Evidently, Gantt had finally influenced Alford! How complete this influence was is manifest in the tendencies that Alford set down as marking the way for the continued growth of industrial relations: (1) the service motive, (2) to build *morale* or *spirit of the organization,* consideration must be given to the workers as a group, and (3) joint control as an expression of democratic ideals.

Although Alford's conclusions concerning service and democratic ideals have borne the test of time, it is questionable whether the concept of group appeal has been as successful. His assertion was made in an attempt to explain why so much had been *said* concerning "co-operation" and so little had been *accomplished.* He felt that the views of the industrial psychologists had not been fully appreciated by the technical engineers and cast his lot with the former. Seemingly, the industrial psychologists did not fully approve their own views, for today they believe that individual treatment must not be overlooked.

An examination of the reception [19] afforded Alford's paper is useful not only as an illumination of the times and their problems but also as a means of taking cognizance of their predictions and expectations.

SOME CRITICISMS

Alford's contention that the worker had a great desire for security was affirmed by C. B. Auel and J. L. Henning. Henning, as a matter of fact, felt that such an assurance would, in dealing with some very real problems of that day, serve as "the greatest single weapon against unrest and Bolshevism." He assigned to the engineer the role of supplying the personal contact that was now missing between the employer and the employee.

Some of the comment inspired by Alford's paper covers problems with which the field of industrial relations is no longer

[19] Alford was not entirely correct when, some twelve years later, in reminiscing, he wrote that "the amount of discussion was generous, of which twenty-two pages were published in Volume 41 of the Transactions." These pages (145-162) also were devoted to a discussion of another paper (No. 1692, "Industrial Personnel Relations" by Arthur H. Young) as well as Alford's paper (No. 1693).

concerned, as well as those still under discussion. In the first category is Auel's dissatisfaction with Alford's neglect of the problem of illiteracy among the workers. In the other category is H. F. J. Porter's concern for Alford's "inadequate" treatment of suggestion systems, benefit plans, etc.

Cyrus McCormick, Jr., Works Manager of the International Harvester Company, objected to Alford's reference to the "struggle for power" among those who employed and those who were employed. McCormick maintained that the real problem in employment management was the removing of "class distinction," a matter that was properly dealt with in his plan for industrial democracy. It is interesting to note that D. T. Farnham maintained that the institution at International Harvester of its industrial democracy was marked by almost immediate demands for wage increases, but on examination of the company's books by the committees the unreasonable demands were withdrawn. Of course, many may question whether these actions would be repeated today. However, Farnham's conclusion is still timely: sincere industrial democracy needs "profits that will survive in the light of public opinion."

A very profound warning was expressed by F. E. Cardullo. If the old concept of competition were to be replaced by a new idea of co-operation—with proper regard to the community's interest—much must be done to do away with the idea that labor itself is free from any obligations. Labor has by necessity up to now fallen into the habit of emphasizing its own "fighting power." The needs are for workers' economic education, their selection of considerate leaders, and their adherence to the fact that efficiency is the basis of economic and national welfare.

Whether Alford "discovered" the human problem early or late is not the point. No one can deny that he was instrumental in focusing the attention of ASME audiences upon it. For, as C. E. Knoeppel insisted, the problem was deserving of the "prominent place" it now had been given, because neither employees nor employers could give it the proper attention; only the engineering world could do that.

THE 1922 REPORT

"Ten years after the report of 1912 on 'The Present State of the Art of Industrial Management,' " Alford noted in his private papers, "I was requested to make another review of the progress of management. This paper entitled 'Ten Years' Progress in Management' was presented at the annual meeting in New York City in December, 1922."

Coming about three years after his report on industrial relations, Alford had by now established himself as the "historian" of the management discussion, and it would have been extremely difficult even to imagine ASME requesting anyone else to bring the subject up to date.

This report [20] certainly did not have the unqualified success of his earlier papers, and Alford himself probably recognized this fact. Some ten or so years later he wrote in his personal papers:

> The discussion was animated, not all of it being favorable.

But he did cull for his own files three statements—one each from Fred J. Miller, Dexter Kimball, and L. W. Wallace—that he called "appreciative comments."

It would have been a herculean feat had he been able to duplicate, much less exceed, his earlier attempt. This time he was writing about what had happened in the brief span of a decade and not about what had occurred in a century and a half after the Industrial Revolution. This time he was writing about the accomplishments of persons whose abilities, though great, were not entirely comparable to those of Taylor ("the pioneer in management"), Gantt ("who humanized the movement"), and Towne ("the earnest, constructive supporter").

What is more, it must be remembered that Alford's great capability lay in his ability to interpret the works of others. His powers were similar to those of the Biblical scholars whose commentary has enriched and made meaningful the funda-

[20] This paper was first presented during Management Week, October 16-22, 1922. It appears in *Trans. ASME, 44,* 1243-1274 (1922).

ments of the basic law. Although Alford's interpretations could and often did rise above the original and cryptic work, the subject matter here was, comparatively speaking, not overly significant.

Hence, Person was fully aware of the comparative meagerness of the data when, commenting on the attempt, he asserted that "Mr. Alford showed a great deal of commendable bravery in tackling this particular subject." Person rightfully maintained that the period covered by the earlier report was a very rich one, marked not only by advances in management but outstanding in the very basic principles of the movement itself.

Furthermore, the developments during the 1912-22 period not only were less ostentatious but they lacked the practical aspects of the earlier period. Person was in full agreement with Miller, who believed that "the most important progress" during the decade covered by the 1922 report "cannot be measured or weighed, for it is manifested mainly in a changed attitude of mind."

Then, too, aside from these facts, the manifestations of growth in this phase of development were not as great as the earlier ones. And the report was indicative of this.

Kimball was similarly concerned with the effectiveness of Alford's dealing with the progress of management. His attitude, however, was that "as time goes on the curve flattens out and it becomes increasingly difficult to see what principle should be next applied to keep the movement progressing."

He made a very quaint analogy. Just as an inspired prophet attempts to teach religious fundaments by means of parables, so too the Taylor work, which served as the reservoir of much of this, dealt with and "described a specific form or piece of mechanism." And, since each disciple might "pin his faith for salvation on an entirely different passage of Scripture," a great many diverse interpretations were the result. It is therefore difficult if at all possible to measure progress in any particular field. But growth in the basic fundamentals can be recognized, even though the measure of the effectiveness of their applications will vary among different men and different industries.

Kimball did "consider Mr. Alford's paper, therefore, a very important one since it presents a clear résumé of the progress made, and interpreting Mr. Taylor's gospel of management."

Alford himself was conscious of the difficulties of writing the history of a period in which "eight of these ten years were abnormal." Although we are by now as accustomed as we shall ever be to the abnormality that has prevailed since 1914, it is interesting to note Alford's reason for calling this fact to the reader's attention. He felt that a great number of the "management changes were of a temporary nature or were mere expedients" for these troublesome times and that it was not an easy task to separate them from the "more permanent developments." Of course, this is characteristic of the true historian, and Alford's cautious and deep insight served him well.

However, his critics—and the Gilbreths were probably the most vociferous—took him to task not so much for his commissions as for his omissions. As a matter of fact, Alford seemed to summarize this attitude when he said that "I feel like taking the same position" as Dodge did when he maintained that "the points of objection which had been raised, on the one hand, by certain speakers, had been adequately answered, on the other hand, by other speakers."

THE BASIS FOR THE 1922 REPORT

Because his 1912 Report "was well received and in a large measure approved," Alford decided to use it as a model for his current report. He, therefore, contacted management and industrial engineers and industrial executives and educators. And from an interpretation of their answers to such basic questions as "What steps have been made in the progress of management since 1912?" and "What (if any) mechanisms of management do you consider as generally accepted (a) in principles, (b) in practice?" plus "certain well-recognized facts, there emerges a group of factors of varying importance which mark the progress of management during the past decade."

Evidently this approach did not meet the approval of either

the Gilbreths or Person. The Gilbreths felt that the method was satisfactory insofar as it afforded a plan of attack but unsatisfactory in that new methods would be either overlooked or improperly emphasized in attempting to keep to the 1912 confines. Thus the Gilbreths, singling out four points from the 1912 Report, looked in vain for further points of discussion on these matters, but they did find "the only strong emphasis noted is on the consideration of the human factor."

Why? Unfortunately, Alford's papers do not yield any direct answer, but it is not improbable that what he meant—and he said this to Person—was that "the methods used in developing these two reports are identical."

As for the other points of the earlier report, he asserted that the three regulative principles, systematic use of experience, economic control of effort, and promotion of personal effectiveness, had since 1912 been given wider interpretation and meaning but they had not been superseded. And he proudly quoted one correspondent who asserted their "nearly universal acceptance."

THE "QUESTIONARY METHOD"

However, was Alford justified in his reliance on opinions gathered from correspondents in answer to his questionnaires? Because his 1912 Report had used this method, in his retort to Person's assertion, "I do not think much of proof based on opinions," he implied that Person could not rightfully accept the method in the earlier report and reject it in the later one.

Aside from Person's insistence that Alford earlier had used only "a very much smaller proportion of the whole," matters were not the same. Previously, Alford had sent his queries to the very persons whose work he was appraising. This time he was appealing to others whose interests were not so vitally direct.

The Gilbreths stated their objections to the "questionary method"—"to whom to send the question" and the "small per cent" of the responses as far as their quantity and quality were concerned. However, the value of the report does not lie in any tally of the results. Alford is at his weakest when he attempts, by the "weight of opinion and fact," based on an "essay of four industries," [21] to give, in the order of "importance of application," the following mechanisms: (1) Balance of Stores, (2) Incentive Wage Plan, (3) Purchase Control, (4) Selection and Placement, (5) Cost Control, (6) Idle Time Analysis, (7) Planning, and (8) Time Study.

But he is in a more positive position when he chooses, from experience, the fields indicative of the progress of management in regard to mechanisms used. That is to say, the value lies not in any statistical calculation but rather in the very "bias" that influenced his selection of the sample.

THE PROGRESS OF MANAGEMENT

Thus it is of little value to know that, of ten opinions submitted, seven indicated progress while three professed little improvement, if not retrogression, during the 1912-22 period. It is, however, infinitely more important to examine Alford's conclusions, grounded to a large extent on his own experience within the field.

In characteristic fashion, he divided the gains into three main groups under which he assembled the points of progress:

1. Mental Attitude
   a. The decline of the old science-versus-art controversy and the emergence of an "increased recognition of the scientific basis of management."
   b. The abatement of the old "opposition and distrust of management and the passionate antagonism to the installation of management methods."
   c. A growing appreciation, on the part of industrial leaders, of management problems. (Alford felt that the federal government itself took cognizance of the need for man-

---

[21] Metal Trades, Printing, Boots and Shoes, and Men's Ready-to-Wear Clothing Manufacture. Alford was personally familiar with at least three of these fields.

agement methods and pointed to the appointment of Herbert Hoover as Secretary of Commerce and Charles Dawes as Director of the Budget.)

   d. A wider acceptance of management principles among engineers, industrial executives, and educators.

2. Application of Management Methods

   a. The extension of the "engineering and scientific method" into the field of industrial cost accounting. (Alford maintained that this phase was evidenced by the development of standard costs, idleness-loss determinations, sales forecasting, budgeting, and uniform costing systems.)

   b. A growing appreciation of the worth of standardization, simplification, and, during the 1920-22 period, elimination of waste.

   c. The insistence upon facts, as a basis for judgment, among almost all good managements, has led to a wider use of specifications and graphics in recording and communicating management knowledge. (The development of the Gantt Chart since 1917 was indicative of the trend.)

   d. The almost universal application of at least some of the management methods in manufacturing and distributing organizations as well as in institutions.

3. Especially Significant Developments

   a. The broadening of management activities beyond those "usually associated with the Taylor System." (Alford listed some seventy-seven items of "management work" under "General": e.g., Locating Unprofitable Lines of Product, Preparing Graphical Statements for Executives, etc.; "Material": e.g., Organization of Material Storage Records and Controls, Establishment of Quality Control, etc.; "Labor": e.g., Installation of Wage Payment Methods, Motion and Time Studies, etc.; "Equipment": Development of Equipment Inventories, Analysis of Equipment Layout, etc.

   b. Whereas, in 1912, only one engineering college (Pennsylvania State) had an established management course, in 1922 Columbia, MIT, NYU, Pennsylvania State, Purdue,

the Universities of Kansas and Pittsburgh, and Yale's
Sheffield Scientific School had management courses, and
at least two (Cornell's Sibley College and the Worcester
Polytechnic Institute) had management courses in their
mechanical engineering course.[22]

c. Among the most striking of all management developments were the "appreciation of the human factor in industry and attempts at its study from a fact basis."

d. The almost universal insistence by "management engineers" that the "service motive must prevail in industry"
and questions involving human relationships must be considered without any feelings of arbitrariness or autoc-
racy.[23]

OTHER ASPECTS OF MANAGEMENT PROGRESS

Although to many, Alford's listing might give a more than
adequate picture of a decade in management's history in the
United States,[24] some leaders in the field felt that he had overemphasized one aspect and underemphasized another. This
was to be expected, for each one, to use Kimball's analogy,
sincerely believed that his own selection among the basic
prophecies was the one most worthy of attention.

Thus, while Alford realized and emphasized the importance
of transference of skill, the Gilbreths felt that there could be
no such transference "until the method of work is recorded
in detail." Not only did they complain of Alford's omission of
this contention, but they ascribed it to the fact that Taylor,
himself, was compelled to discard all time study data that he
and his associates had gathered "when he started planning his
book on time study which was finally written after his death
by Dwight Merrick."

22 See below, pp. 286-302.
23 Alford had first become aware of this development in his 1919 Report to
which, incidentally, he did not refer in this paper.
24 Although Alford did not, in his title, limit this study to the progress of
management in the United States, he completely neglected any mention of foreign developments. Surprisingly none of his critics took him to task for this.

They further listed "some twenty-four advances in management" which, they felt, Alford either omitted or de-emphasized and some of which are the direct result of emphasis on the one best way to do work. Some of the Gilbreths' items were unquestionably important: e.g., realization "that the sixteen elements of a cycle of motions and not the motions are the true fundamental units," process charts, etc. Some were very detailed: e.g., mnemonic classification for information filing, "change order" forms, etc. Some were matters of direct concern to the Gilbreths' work: use of handicapped workers, fatigue study as "a first step in motion study." Many Alford had expressed in different words: the value of psychology in management, the use of labor turnover as a measure of management efficiency, etc.

Of course, it must be realized that the lot of the historian is not entirely similar to that of the observer in the laboratory. The readings of a calibrated meter by two independent observers can be expected to be reasonably close. The views of two persons observing the less quantitive aspects of a current scene can be expected to be further apart. The surprising feature is that these management observers were not really too far apart.

Do the duties of the historian, it may be asked, include only a recording of what has taken place or should they also concern an estimate of the future? Although Alford's task technically was to chart management's progress during a past decade he did not avoid the indication of trends and their potentialities. Some of these future aspects were spelled out definitely, while others were suggested. On occasion, his "statistical" study was instrumental, on the part of critics, in ascribing to him a wrong accentuation of certain facts.

Thus J. P. Jordan, a president of the National Association of Cost Accountants, an organization that, Alford later regretfully admitted, he had not included in a listing of management societies, took issue on the position given cost accounting in a ranking of management mechanisms. Although its position was determined "by the results of 125 questionnaires" and "there is a difference between presenting that which you discover, and that which you would like to discover," it is doubtful whether Alford felt that it was deserving of this low rating. Otherwise would he have included it among the management mechanisms? Would he have listed it in first place among the management applications he mentioned to indicate the progress during the decade? Would the cost aspects have been mentioned so frequently among the "management work" listings?

Be that as it may, the prophecies of Jordan bear reiteration:

It is to be regretted that management has not awakened to the realization of the necessity to "Know Thyself"; that the advisers of management have failed absolutely as a class of recognized cost control *as the control;* that all such things as time study, incentive wage plans, planning, idle time analysis and such are but means to the end of reducing costs; and that management is so blind to the creed that facts and facts only should guide their every action. Then—when facts are known, and known month in and month out, put into operation such necessary adjuncts of management as may be clearly indicated as necessary.

Certainly this is the heritage that became an integral part of the concept promulgated by Somervell, Nourse, Rathe, and Thurston.

THE HUMAN FACTOR IN INDUSTRY

Alford reiterated here the development of the human factor that he first mentioned in 1912 but more strongly emphasized in 1919. He asserted that there was now an awareness that personal problems exist, a realization that their solution is a management responsibility, and a growth of the concept "that job analysis, selection, placement, and training can be put on a scientific basis." Although the Gilbreths insisted that he should have devoted more space to the idea "that training the worker is the real key to industrial relations," Wallace commended Alford for his belief that industrial leaders should "begin to train from the bottom up, instead of the top down." And no greater compliment could have been paid to Alford's idea that

Wallace repeated in connection with the following uncanny observations:

We, as industrial leaders . . . have been too content . . . too complacent, we have sat behind our desks and let our employees get their information regarding the economics of industry from the speaker on the soap box in a street corner . . . we should give them the fundamental information that they need in order to arrive at a fair judgment as to what industry means to them. . . . If industry is to go forward without being hampered by federal and state legislation, it is going to be necessary also for management, in the coming years, to give to the public the fundamentals it should have and is entitled to, regarding industry.

Certainly these are lessons that today's industry could have had by merely glancing back now and then on the pages of history.

MANAGEMENT ASSOCIATIONS

Alford was particularly pleased to report that "management engineers as a group have declared that the service motive must prevail in industry, that everything planned and done must be directed to securing the worthy result of producing useful goods with a minimum expenditure of time, material, and human effort." It must have been with a great deal of pleasure that the views of his friend, Gantt, on "the doctrine of service," expressed in *Organizing for Work* should have been adopted in the preamble to the Constitution of the Federated American Engineering Societies.

As a matter of fact the growth of societies concerned with the practice of management was another manifestation of the decade's progress. By 1922, there were over four thousand memberships (including duplications) in such societies as the ASME's Management Division, The Taylor Society, SIE (Society of Industrial Engineers), and the NPA (National Personnel Association). At this time, NACA (National Association of Cost Accountants) boasted a membership equal to at least three fourths this number.

Of course, the ASME had been in existence for some forty

years, during many of which it was the only forum of management in the country, before the formation of the Professional
Divisions in 1920; [25] the Management Division was organized
in July of that year, and by September, 1922, when Alford
wrote his paper, it numbered 1,740 on its rolls. "Almost from
the start," Alford commented, "the membership of the Management Division has exceeded that of any other Professional
Division." Its program was based on the now famous definition
it gave, in its first annual report:

Management is the art and science of preparing, organizing, and
directing human effort applied to control the forces and to utilize
the materials of nature for the benefit of man.

In view of these facts, the question may properly be raised:
why was a separate management organization formed? To answer this, it may be of interest to examine a brief statement
that was prepared by Person in regard to the formation of the
Taylor Society (originally known as the "Society to Promote
the Science of Management") for the Alford paper.

Person insisted that "the group of young engineers associated
with Mr. Taylor" was alarmed that the enthusiasm that met
the early papers of Towne and Taylor soon waned, that "the
dominant group in the Society" felt that discussions on management subjects should not be engaged in and "put obstacles
in the way of such attention," that there was "hostility to the
Taylor theories and methods," and that "it required a struggle
to get a paper on management before the ASME."

Consequently, Person maintained, this group—Morris L.
Cooke, Robert Kent, Conrad Lauer (representing Charles Day),
Wilfred Lewis, and Frank B. Gilbreth (the host)—met on November 11, 1910, at the New York Athletic Club and informally
organized a society which made possible "a discussion of management problems to an extent warranted by the importance
of the subject and public interest in it." During the next two
years the membership was between twenty-five and thirty, and
the informal meetings, with Dodge as president and Kent as

25 See above, p. 32.

secretary-treasurer, were held about monthly, usually at Keen's Chop House on West 36th Street, New York.

As a result of the great interest stimulated by the Eastern Rate Case Hearings, a more formal society was formed on November 7, 1912, at the Hotel Astor. Named the Society to Promote the Science of Management, the officers of the old organization were elected. Meeting three times annually, in either New York, Philadelphia, or Boston, it began in 1914 to publish the *Bulletin of the Society to Promote the Science of Management.* In 1913 Person was elected president, and he succeeded himself annually until 1919. More than half of its slightly more than one hundred members were "absorbed into the war organization of the United States." After the armistice it was reorganized under the name of the Taylor Society, a title it assumed one year after Taylor's death in 1915. Person became its managing director, and among its presidents were Otterson, Feiss, Cooke, Dennison, Kendall, and others.

The Gilbreths, admittedly hosts on the occasion, asserted that "a most unfortunate and serious error" was contained in the Person account. They insisted that "there was no feeling of criticism" against ASME and "so far as we know, all members of the original group were, always have been, and are at present enthusiastic and loyal members of The American Society of Mechanical Engineers."

The private files of Alford are of great interest in this regard, at least as far as one of the founders is concerned. On September 28, 1920, Alford wrote to Cooke, who was then at Sugar Hill, New Hampshire, acknowledging the receipt of a letter written three days earlier together with a "copy of your paper, 'How About It?'"

The pamphlet, containing forty-eight pages of "comment on the 'absentee management' of the American Society of Mechanical Engineers and the virtual control exerted over the Society by big business, notably by the private utility interests" was written and published by Cooke in August, 1917, "a recent member of the Council." Although it charged the Society with an organization that was "archaic, undemocratic, and inefficient," a council whose operations were "shrouded in secrecy," and a Code of Ethics that "has actually been used to punish a member without trial," its merits or demerits need not be discussed here, for both Cooke and the Society have survived and gone on to even higher levels of service and respectability.

What is important is the fact that, despite the Gilbreths' assertion, not all the founders of the Taylor Society were always enthusiastic supporters of the older Society.

It is of interest in this connection to observe how Alford reacted to the receipt of the pamphlet and its sections marked by Cooke as they "bear on the subject of the organization and administration of the Society." Alford wrote, "I am pleased to renew my memory in regard to what you wrote three years ago," and added:

Incidentally you will receive shortly, if it has not already reached you, an invitation to prepare a paper on the Organization of Administration of the Engineering Society for the spring meeting of the American Society of Mechanical Engineers.

Evidently Cooke's acceptance letter was sent to Greul, for there is a pencil notation to that effect on a letter Alford wrote to Cooke on October 5, 1920, indicating pleasure "that you are willing to undertake the presentation of the paper."

In addition, the *Bulletin of the Taylor Society*, in April, 1930, published an editorial on the "Fiftieth Anniversary of A.S.M.E." It reproduced the text of its filial greetings, signed by its president (Kendall), its managing director (Person), and its two official delegates (Hunt and Cooke). The Taylor Society was "stimulated to say more than could be properly included in a formal greeting," and it expressed its indebtedness "for the helping hand it has from time to time received from A.S.M.E." This included, "through the courtesy of its Secretary, Calvin Rice, personnel . . . equipment . . . and . . . temporary location in one of the large offices of A.S.M.E." It was also appreciative of the older society's position as the sole forum for management development "for nearly twenty-five years." Finally, it ascribed the formation of the Taylor Society to the fact that the "expansion of the content of mechanical engineering . . . compelled that Society about 1907 to give relatively increasing attention to pure engineering and less to management."

Those who lived through these times associate the Taylor Society with the Society of Industrial Engineers. (Later, in February, 1936, both were merged to form SAM, the Society for [the] Advancement of Management.) The SIE was organized one day after the closing of a national convention, held in Chicago in May, 1917, by the Western Efficiency Society, dealing with the theme, "The Importance of the Human Factor in Industry." This society's own initial objective was: "To furnish a vehicle for bringing together in closer relationship persons who are actively engaged in promoting efficiency in business and for making the training and ability of such persons available in the emergency arising out of the present war." Although it was originally founded by request of the Council of National Defense, the SIE in 1919 expanded into the wider concerns of the industrial engineer in general and management in particular. Its founding organization, the Western Efficiency Society, was even older than the Taylor Society, for the SIE's organization was based on that established by the Board of Trustees in July, 1910.

H. J. F. Porter was the founder and executive secretary of the Efficiency Society in 1912. In 1918, this society joined with the National Institute of Efficiency to form the National Efficiency Society, with offices at 119 West 40th Street, New York; the official organ was the *Independent*.[26]

Another society, the National Personnel Association, took over the activities of the National Association of Corporation Training (NACT) and the Industrial Relations Association of America (IRAA). Originally the National Association of Corporation Schools, organized on January 24, 1913, to foster working training, had among its directors people from companies such as New York Edison, Burroughs, Pennsylvania Railroad, Curtis Publishing, Yale & Towne, General Electric, Westing-

[26] See *Industrial Management* 59, No. 1, 84, January (1920).

house, National Cash Register, and New York Consolidated Gas. It expanded in 1917 to include "all of the activities classified as human relations." Faced by rising costs and increasing service, in 1920 it was reorganized, incorporated, and renamed NACT. Between 1910 and 1917 there were several local and, eventually, intercity organizations that discussed employment problems. In 1917 these meetings resulted in the formation of the National Committee of Employment Managers' Associations. The following year a more formal organization, National Association of Employment Managers, was organized. On March 1, 1920, to expand its interests, the name was changed to the IRAA. The business situation of the early 1920's soon had its effects on both NACT and IRAA and, at a joint meeting of the Executives Club of New York and the New York Chapter of NACT, on February 17, 1922, plans were made for the formation of the National Personnel Association, officially incorporated on April 21.

Other organizations also discussed certain aspects of the management field. One of these was the National Association of Cost Accountants which, Alford insisted, "has lived largely within itself" and consequently was "not well known" at the time in the field of management, but which, Alford prophesied, would be of growing importance. Alford's faith was manifested by his eventual membership in NACA.

Outside of a rapid growth of these and other societies, what value could Alford see in their expansion? His forecast was terse and direct. He saw a hope for the development of a management terminology, of a literature classification, of standardization of management graphics, and of methods for management measurement. Alford himself played a great part in bringing this forecast closer to reality.

MANAGEMENT'S RESULTS

Alford felt that, although since 1912 management had to some extent begun to earn its economic justification, it now stood at the threshold of even greater opportunities. By organization it could determine policies; by planning it could determine how, when, and by whom work should be done; and by direction it could set and keep in motion both production and distribution. In brief, it was "a tremendous, hitherto unknown engineering tool" and "the agency by which community, state, and nation shall endure."

His own work during the next twenty years was indicative of this promise.

ALFORD AT RONALD

After spending almost three and a half years with the Dunlap organization, Alford felt that he could better carry out his potentialities elsewhere. His private files are helpful, not only in evaluating his work at *Industrial Management,* but also in indicating that he had finally decided to organize and bring out a periodical of his very own.

On September 5, 1920, G. S. Radford, who did much to bring a new point of view to the problem of quality in manufacture, wrote a letter to Alford: "This is just a note to express my appreciation for your kindness and courtesy in the treatment of 'Control of Quality.' I have received today the September issue of 'Industrial Management' and recognize your handiwork." And he added: "What I am wondering is how 'Industrial Management' is going to get along without you after all you have done for it."

Alford's reply is dated September 15: "Don't fear for *Industrial Management.* You know the old saying, 'The King is dead—long live the King.' It will not be difficult to keep going a magazine that has already arrived."

Despite Alford's modesty, others also showed regret. For example, I. W. Chubb, who was connected with the European and Colonial Edition of the *American Machinist,* wrote on September 6 from London:

I was sorry to see that you had left a position which, it seemed to me and us here, you were doing a large amount of useful work for the world. I have no doubt that you will soon put yourself into another place in which you can continue your good work.

Evidently Chubb was correct, for, as Alford wrote to F. J. Reuter (who under Alford's guidance about six years later was to present one of the earliest accounts of the Break-Even Chart), on October 8, 1920: "With a few friends I am at work on a proposal to start a new engineering magazine with January. The name is *Management Engineering.*"

Alford took his idea to The Ronald Press Company, a publishing organization founded by Hugh Ronald Conyngton, that had begun to establish its reputation in the field of business books in general and accounting in particular. Ronald was anxious to expand its field, for the American Institute of Accountants had decided to publish its own *Journal of Accountancy,* a publication formerly brought out under Ronald's auspices.

The first issue of *Management Engineering* appeared in July, 1921, with Alford as its editor. In June, 1922, Ronald added to the title the subheading *The Journal of Production.* This move was evidently made to broaden its appeal. Ronald, it must be remembered, was essentially a book publishing organization. Consequently, it decided to consolidate its magazines; in 1923, it combined the magazine with *Administration,* another of its periodicals. Because of the relative newness of the field described by the title and because the publishers thought that many potential readers were being frightened away by a title that seemed to indicate it was of concern only to top management, Ronald decided to change the name again. First it was renamed, in 1925, *Management and Administration in the Manufacturing Industries;* finally, in March, 1926, it became *Manufacturing Industries.*

During this period, the Shaw Company in Chicago was publishing magazines in the industrial field, e.g., *Factory and Systems,* eventually sold to McGraw-Hill. F. Ahrens, who was with Shaw, left and established periodicals in the hotel and restaurant management field. By the beginning of 1928, Ronald had decided to leave the periodical field, and it sold *Manufacturing Industries* to Ahrens who, beginning with the March, 1929, issue, began to publish it. Eventually it was merged, at McGraw-Hill, with *Factory and Industrial Management* to form what became the present *Factory Management and Maintenance.*

Soon after Alford came to Ronald, George Hagemann became his assistant. Although Hagemann left Ronald along with *Manufacturing Industries,* he returned to bring out the *Production Handbook* after Alford's death.

Throughout the various phases at Ronald, Alford remained the editor. As a matter of fact, he was also a contributing editor to *Factory and Industrial Management.* However, despite the fact that the magazine had left Ronald, Alford remained with the company. In May, 1925, Alford became a member of Ronald's Board of Directors, a post in which he continued to serve until his death. According to a letter written by F. J. Kenny, Secretary of The Ronald Press Company, on March 30, 1942, to the ASME, Alford also held the posts of editor and vice-president from July, 1926, to May, 1937.

Alford in his private papers has described his work as vice-president very simply by stating that "in this relation, I was concerned with the procurement and publication of books, mainly business books and college texts." However, such a description hardly scratches the surface of his endeavors at The Ronald Press Company.

While on the staff of the Ronald periodicals, Alford maintained his own high ideals and standards along with the great consideration for the readers that Hill had imbued in him. Sometimes his fervent belief in the quantitative approach together with his firm idea of what would be helpful to his readers caused him to bring out a series of articles for which his audience was not fully ready. Sellman, for example, believes that the series of articles by Polakov was in that category. More particularly, as pointed out elsewhere in this volume, he determined to bring the technique of preferred numbers to the attention of production men.

In most instances, however, his keen prophetic sense has been vindicated. For example, the Radford series of articles and the resulting book on the *Control of Quality* formed a new approach to the quality problem, which before this time was simply inspection and gaging. For further evidence, the reader may refer to Shewhart's "Statistical Control in Applied Science" in the *Ten Years' Progress in Management*,[27] the 1942 Report that Alford did not live to write. Here Alford is credited by Shewhart as being an attendant at the creation of statistical quality control, for this new approach was greatly aided by the Shewhart article [28] published by Alford in *Manufacturing Industries*.

Another important instance is the question of the Break-Even Chart, a matter eventually brought to its full importance by Knoeppel and Rautenstrauch. It is interesting to note that Alford, as early as 1926, in his *Manufacturing Industries,* published an article by F. J. Reuter,[29] who related his experience with the Break-Even Chart as early as 1913.

In the interest of his readers, Alford launched out on a program for which he became famous: the handbooks. Although the German *Hütte* books formed a basis for his thought long before he came to Ronald, his position at the publishing company crystallized his thinking on this matter. By 1924 he felt that, although management had developed both as a science and as an art, its data were scattered, and nowhere was there assembled in a single volume a ready reference to its principles and methods. He was particularly concerned with the need for a handbook of treatment and style similar to those of its counterparts in electrical and mechanical engineering. Furthermore, he felt that the time was ripe for a departure from the usual management manuals, which were restricted to techniques that had been publicized in magazine and book articles since Taylor.

Alford was particularly suited for the task. His capacities as

27 *Trans. ASME, 65,* No. 3, 222 (1943).
28 "Finding Causes of Quality Variances," *11,* No. 2, 125-128, February (1926).
29 "The Break-Even Chart as a Management Tool," *11,* No. 4, 290, April (1926).

an editor included not only his ability to write and whip into shape the writing of others but also his keen insight as to what was important and beneficial. Also, Alford himself had been a handbook contributor: "Industrial Motor Applications—Machine Tools" in Frank F. Fowle's *Standard Handbook for Electrical Engineers* [30] and "Machine Tools and Machine-Shop Practice" in Lionel S. Marks's *Mechanical Engineers' Handbook*,[31] both published by McGraw-Hill.

In this work, Alford used a group of specialists: the list of contributors to Alford's *Management's Handbook* reads like a 1924 Who's Who in Management Engineering. It included, to mention but a few, D. B. Porter, W. Clark, L. W. Wallace, C. W. Lytle, J. Roe, D. S. Kimball, H. V. Coes, and G. Hagemann.

The painstaking care with which Alford worked was indeed remarkable. He reworked the contribution of each specialist with astounding precision, neatness, and care. He divided the subject matter into three main groups:

1. General information: fundamentals of mathematics, statistics, etc.

2. Management functions, methods, and mechanisms.

3. Basic industrial data: economic principles, organization concepts, budgetary controls, etc.

Of the thirty-two sections, his name appears as author of "Organization for Operations." Here he brought in not only his concepts of the "principles" and "laws" of management but also measures of "management effectiveness."

In 1933 he thought the time was ripe for a revision of *Management's Handbook*. He called it the *Cost and Production Handbook,* and it appeared in 1934. Whereas *Management's Handbook* attempted to organize information on administration and operation of business and industrial enterprises, the newer book was restricted to manufacturing operations but included more details—in addition, of course, to the new de-

---

[30] Pp. 1184-1201 in the fourth edition (1915) and pp. 1220-1237 in the fifth edition (1922).

[31] Pp. 1396-1466 in the first edition (1916).

velopments that had taken place since 1924. The first handbook used the services of thirty-three contributors (excluding Alford) and the second eighty contributors (again excluding Alford), who were called "Contributing and Consulting Editors." Since they acted as a "board," no personal credit was given to their respective contributions. However, although Alford's editing is visible in many places, it is not difficult to pick out his very own section, "Principles of Industrial Engineering." As for the details of his thinking here, the distinction between "laws" and "principles" was becoming evident.

It was Alford's intention—a matter that he felt would have been needed and therefore proper even if the handbooks had not been successful—to issue a revision of the handbook every ten years. Although it might be thought that the ten-year management reports for ASME gave him the idea, it is more likely that the decennial concept in both cases came from a common belief: ten years comprise a proper and adequate period during which management movements and concepts crystallize and are ready for the printed page.

Hence, just as in 1941, the year before his death, he had according to Lytle been collecting data pertinent to the 1942 Report on management's history, so too had he been working on the handbook. Alford had felt that the new revision of the *Cost and Production Handbook* ought to appear in two volumes, because of the amount of data. Hence he proposed that there be two distinct books and, according to Sellman, Alford had at his death completed about 90 per cent of the *Production* book and had started on the *Cost* text.

The *Production Handbook* appeared in 1944 under the editorship of George E. Hagemann and John R. Bangs. Credited on the title page as well as in the Preface, Alford's structure and foundation are evident. Hagemann, who acted as staff editor, attests to the Alford influence. Although Bangs had been acquainted with Alford, the Hagemann connection was very much more intimate. Hagemann, aside from his own work in materials handling, is almost universally recognized for his assistance to Alford, beginning in the 1920's. Although Hagemann had left Ronald when *Manufacturing Industries* was sold, he had maintained his contact with Alford, and he was definitely the logical person to follow through the details of Alford's work on the *Handbook.*

The cost aspects of Alford's plan was put into effect by Theodore Lang's editorship in the form of the *Cost Accountants' Handbook,* which Ronald published in 1944. Although Alford's name does not appear on the title page, Lang in his Preface pays tribute to Alford's "good work" and "guidance in planning."

In order to appreciate Alford's contributions, it must be remarked that his contributions even in the book field, although unmistakable, have too often been limited to books on the title page of which his name appears. Just as in professional societies his work frequently is shrouded by his committee membership, and just as in the periodical field his contribution is often thrown out of focus by his editorship, so too his work in the book field has publicly not been too widely recognized. Many books bear in their prefaces grateful acknowledgment to his aid. This help varied from simple encouragement to material assistance. A few of these books whose authors gratefully acknowledge at least some aspect of Alford's work include C. E. Knoeppel's *Graphic Production Control* (Engineering Magazine Company); Prior Sinclair's *Budgeting* (Ronald); G. S. Radford's *Control of Quality* (Ronald); Dexter S. Kimball's *Principles of Industrial Organization* (McGraw-Hill); Wallace Clark's *Gantt Chart* (Ronald and Pitman), to mention but a few.

Clearly, it was during these years before 1932 at Ronald that many of Alford's ideas reached full maturity, while many more of his beliefs were still in the conception stage. For example, his ideas on standardization began with his engineering career. In the shops of McKay and United Shoe Machinery, these were limited perhaps to machine-shop practice. However, even there he began to realize their economic effects. On the *American Machinist,* he made a further transition, with Carl Barth, from the shop procedure of machinery speeds to the managerial connotations of these practices. Slowly but surely the ideas began to germinate and develop until he felt that management would be aware of the potentialities of preferred numbers.

Here, too, his ideas on management "laws" began to have some impact. As will be evident, this was a concept that many of his contemporaries declare to be his great achievement, if it is possible to limit him to one. However, even in this field his concepts continued to develop and mature, although he felt that his ideas were ready for presentation on a professional rostrum and on the printed page.

Finally, during these years of exploring management's responsibilities, his search for a "measuring stick" brought him to kmh. He valued this greatly for what it could afford not only management but the country, and it caused him much disappointment. This study attempts to explain its lack of general acceptance, for even today it is considered by some to be built on a basically correct concept although it came a little ahead of its time.

EARLY APPLICATION OF PREFERRED NUMBERS

Although Carl Barth's work in connection with slide rules for practical use in the machine shop is universally known, only those who have examined his efforts are cognizant of the fact that, as he remarked, "years before we ever heard of the term 'preferred numbers,'" he had embodied these principles in the arrangement of feeds and speeds for machine tools. He attempted to standardize the feeds and speeds [32] within the limitations set by the gear mechanisms of a machine, in order to facilitate the setting of rates on machines of a similar size and type.

[32] See Alford, "Respeeding of Machine Tools," in *American Machinist, 41,* No. 24, 1017-1021, December 10 (1914). See also "The Geometric Progression of Feeds and Speeds," an Editorial, in *American Machinist, 41,* No. 23, 1003-1004, December 3 (1914).

Few also are aware of his application of the principle of preferred numbers in analyzing a series of wage rates, and it was indeed long ago that he first set himself to this task.

One of his early employers had given him the idea that as a man's wage increases, the increments that he received from time to time should also increase, for the worker's services were becoming more and more valuable. Barth decided to make use of this concept in 1904 when, as he later wrote for Alford's publication,[33] "I for the first time was put to work by Mr. Taylor to calculate a series of machine hour rates, and these naturally came out in all sorts of odd figures."

Consequently, he proposed "to construct a standard scale or series of machine hour rates, and then select for each machine the nearest standard rate to calculated rate."

Although it may not be pertinent here to go into the minute details of how Barth arrived at what the "increasing factor" might be, or even if it is possible to measure it with any precise accuracy, the point is that he did use a geometric series.

Lest the reader reach the conclusion that the introduction of this concept was easy or that the general idea had universal acceptance, it might be best to relate Barth's further experiences concerning the use of it in his consulting work:

Later I also suggested that a similar series of rates be adopted for the day wage earners. To this the president first raised a rather far-fetched objection, based on certain pet ideas he had cherished for years regarding a man's relative wages. These he later withdrew at the persuasion of the manager, who as a real diplomat had more influence with him than I had, and who agreed with me that those ideas were bosh. . . .

That is all there is to my standard wage scale, the construction of which is so simple that I have never kept a record of it, and hence I always had to reconstruct it for every concern I have cared to persuade to adopt it, probably only a half a dozen all told. It is one of those things, the value of which is at once recognized by

[33] Barth, "The Barth Standard Wage Scale," in *Manufacturing Industries, 10,* No. 6, 357 ff., December (1925).

some individuals, but of which it is too fruitless to try to convince others that life is too short to waste in the attempt.

Of course, it might not be too difficult to realize that American managers then were not completely convinced that wage increments should be other than arithmetic; but even a quarter of a century later the value of the geometric progression was still unappreciated. As a matter of fact, although the development of size standards necessitated a study of the methods for preparing such standards, much of the basic work was performed abroad, particularly in France and Germany. Although the French Standards Committee had laid down its rules on the basis of the "Serie de Renard," [34] it was the German study that was eventually adopted in the United States.

Consequently, in 1925, when few could even see the obvious advantages that preferred numbers could yield to standardization, Alford had already seen even beyond them. As Alford wrote, one year later: "The more the responsibility is recognized of formulating laws in developing management methods, the greater will be our progress."

Hence he opened his journal, *Manufacturing Industries*, which he had been editing since 1923, to Barth for presentation of his experiences with his wage scale. Five months later,[35] on receipt of a letter from Charles D. Demond, a mechanical engineer, Alford featured along with it Barth's reply:

I have read with interest Mr. Demond's letter proposing an alternative to the standard wage scale submitted by me in the December issue of this journal, and I am gratified that somebody has evinced the interest to give the matter some serious consideration.

Demond had suggested that, instead of Barth's use of 1.15 as a basic rate (i.e., a 10 per cent increase), the value $\sqrt[5]{2}$ (approximately 1.1487) be used instead. Not only did it have

[34] Col. Renard was a French Army officer who, in 1870, as head of the Captive Balloon Organization, noted that there were 425 different sizes of mooring cables, with the resulting problems of excess stores and inventory (see Juran, *Quality Control Handbook*, p. 70).

[35] "The Barth Standard Wage Scale: Discussion and Reply," in *Manufacturing Industries, 11*, No. 3, 373, May (1926).

"strong appeal" for Barth, but, "on the whole I think it is a decided improvement on my original scale."

Barth did make this interesting comment:

The rather puzzling fact that I overlooked that the number 1.15 is so close to $\sqrt[5]{2}$ is, no doubt, due to the circumstance that my original article was prepared at the request of a friend, principally in the spirit of a reminiscence, and not in a spirit of seriously advocating a strong wage scale to be generally adopted. For as is well known, I am a strong advocate of the roots of the simple number 2 as against the more complex number 10, as brought out in my discussion of the papers on preferred numbers read before the ASME.[36]

THE LAWS UNDERLYING PREFERRED NUMBERS

Alford's interest in standardization, undoubtedly originating from his shoe machinery shop experience and maturing to a full realization of its importance while at the *American Machinist,* led him to a contemplation of *preferred numbers.* But it was only after he had begun to examine all procedures and techniques in the management field in terms of laws and principles that he set forth as the "underlying principle" of application of preferred numbers the concept that

In manufacturing, the series of greatest economy is the one that will satisfy the conditions with the fewest terms.

He had formulated this fundament on the basis of two observations:

1. The most economic group for manufacturing purposes was that which contained the fewest number of items.

2. The fewest number of items that will satisfy a given set of engineering conditions is that which is contained in a geometric series. Alford was also aware of the psychological foundation of this concept for, in his paper on the "Laws of Man-

[36] The ASME discussions came at the December, 1922, meeting. Incidentally, the reader of the Barth quotation should not take too literally in a mathematical sense his use of the term "the more complex number 10."

agement," [37] which he presented at the ASME meeting in New York in December, 1926, he referred to the "Law of Discrimination" as [38]

Sensations increase in arithmetical progression as the stimuli increase in geometrical progression. (Weber)

As a matter of record, he had referred to it even earlier in *Manufacturing Industries* (in his editorial comments on the Barth article). However, it was only in his book, *Laws of Management Applied to Manufacturing* (1928), that he assigned the "Economy of Series" among the "Laws of Economy," together with "Economic Manufacturing Lot Sizes (ASME)," "Economic Purchase Quantities (Davis)," and "Economy of Labor Saving Equipment (ASME)."

In this connection, two points are of interest. The first pertains to the fact that, although the other three aspects of "Laws of Economy" carry parenthetical notations concerning their origin, the "Economy of Series" does not. This was probably due to the fact that it was not possible to assign any clear-cut authorship to this concept. Secondly, although he referred to a "law" here in his text's treatment of the "underlying fundament of the application of preferred numbers," Alford spoke of the "underlying principle" when he spoke on May 11, 1929, at a technical session of the Institute of Management (since absorbed by the American Management Association) in New York.[39] It is difficult to say whether, in one year's time, Alford had decided that it was a "statement of probability to guide judgment" rather than one "of fact to govern decision." More than likely he was less interested in explaining to his 1929

[37] See below, pp. 134ff.

[38] It is not clear whether, in this statement, Alford meant to subscribe authorship to Weber or to connotate it as Weber's Law, as it is commonly known. However, it is not completely accurate to use Weber's name alone. Weber's findings were less general, and he merely asserted that people notice relative rather than absolute changes in stimuli. It was Weber's colleague, Fechner, author of *Elements of Psychophysics*, who elaborated the original statement and was responsible for the mathematical relationship expressed.

[39] "Preferred Numbers as a Tool of Management Research," Institute of Management Series No. 14.

audience the philosophical basis than he was in focusing his listeners' attention on the technique and the application of preferred numbers.

PREFERRED NUMBERS AS A TOOL OF MANAGEMENT

As Alford in his private papers recalled a year or two later, he had chosen preferred numbers as his topic before the Institute because he felt that the technique was truly a "contribution to the methods used in manufacturing analysis."

At that meeting, Alford's assertions were reinforced by three men with whom he became closely associated—Roe, who was then head of NYU's Industrial Engineering Department; Lytle, who was then NYU's Director of Industrial Co-operation; and Hannum, who was then editor of the *Engineering Index*. Roe reiterated the importance of preferred numbers in standardization and simplification. Lytle felt that preferred numbers were of great assistance in the field of apprenticeship in general, and Western Electric's program (based on performance rating), in particular. Finally Hannum, to stimulate additional interest, appended a bibliography which he, together with F. J. Schlink (of the American Standards Association), had drawn up.

However, to quote Alford's private reminiscence of the meeting, "only a limited amount of discussion was offered." "Perhaps the subject," Alford added, "was too uninteresting." That was the only explanation that he could offer in the face of the importance he attached to the theory and application of preferred numbers in management and engineering practice.

Were he correct, he may be partially responsible for not having made the subject more interesting. But he was not correct. *Preferred numbers* was only one manifestation of Alford's thinking being ahead of the times. Only twenty or so years later the engineers and managers have begun to catch up with this concept. And even now its importance is not too fully realized.

ALFORD'S EARLIER WORK ON PREFERRED NUMBERS

In view of his advanced thinking, it is even more astounding to realize that Alford's attitude on the subject predates 1928. Liberal attention is paid to the subject both in the section on "Mathematics" [40] and the one on "Simplification and Standardization" [41] in his *Management's Handbook* (1924).

Alford's interest in standardization had led him to a chairmanship of a committee of the American Engineering Standards Committee (as the American Standards Association was then known). This committee, officially known as the Working Committee on Preferred Numbers,[42] in addition to its chairman who this time represented the SIE, consisted of L. J. Bedford and W. I. Slichter (members at large), L. A. Hazeltine (IRE), F. T. Llewellyn (ASCE), C. E. Lucke (SPEE), C. T. Myers (SAE), and F. R. Still (ASME).

The Working Committee spent approximately two years studying the various preferred number systems, particularly the French (using three series of $\sqrt[10]{10}$, $\sqrt[20]{10}$, and $\sqrt[40]{10}$), and the German (using five series of $\sqrt[5]{10}$, $\sqrt[10]{10}$, $\sqrt[20]{10}$, $\sqrt[40]{10}$, and $\sqrt[80]{10}$ ratios in developing their series). The German system, it was felt, was of "greater simplicity in detail," and it was unanimously chosen by the committee. This recommendation was duly submitted to the General Committee on Preferred Numbers who, after submitting it to a letter ballot, adopted it by a "nearly unanimous vote" on April 6, 1927.

It was at an Executive Committee meeting on April 14 that

[40] Section 2 by G. W. Greenwood, secretary and treasurer of the Warren Lumber and Supply Company.

[41] Section 17 by Ray M. Hudson, Director of the Division of Simplified Practice of the U.S. Department of Commerce.

[42] This was a subcommittee of the General Committee on Preferred Numbers that was chaired by C. E. Skinner (NEMA) and had as members K. H. Condit, E. R. Hedrick, A. Maxwell, J. A. Mease (members at large), G. M. Barnes (Ordnance Department, U.S.A.), C. S. Gillette (U.S. Navy Department), C. F. Hirshfeld (National Electric Light Association and AIEE), H. W. Miller (U.S. War Department), and A. H. Moore (NEMA).

C. E. Skinner announced the recommendations of the Working Committee and the approval by the General Committee. Finally the matter was brought to the attention of the AESC's Main Committee at its meeting on June 16, when its members voted to give "informal approval to the proposed standard for preferred numbers, recommending to industry that it be used for a period of trial in practice."

The result of the work of Alford's committee was issued by the AESC office (AESC Z 17-1927), but it was incorporated in his Institute of Management paper some two years later. Alford was obviously pleased with this AESC report not only because of the import of the work and the general service he was affording management but because, as his private papers reveal, "In one respect my committee had an unusual record. It never met, all of its work was done by correspondence."

SOME CONCLUSIONS

This was unquestionably a remarkable achievement for any committee. But unfortunately the committee's work in general and Alford's enthusiasm in particular were to remain unappreciated for many years, despite the wide applications he forecast for the use of preferred numbers. He had felt that there was no need to limit the technique to the establishment of physical sizes and realized its value "in determining the prices of articles that are offered in a variety of qualities." Thus, he suggested that women's dresses may be offered in a $15, $30, $60 series. He was particularly hopeful of the possibilities of the electric household refrigerator, which had then begun to appear on the market. He felt that the sizes offered in these appliances had already been set by a geometric series and, since prices varied with cubical content, he believed that they, too, were in proper geometrical sequence. Whether this last observation was justified by the actual planning of the appliance manufacturers or whether it was the result of a happy coincidence is not the point. It was a manifestation of his enthusiasm for a cause that he deemed wise and helpful. More than anything else, the lack of contagion for his idea was caused by his failure to understand that logic and clear thinking, commendable as they are, were not adequate in obtaining converts. As a scientist and engineer, he knew what was "good" for industry, but as a student of human relations he had not yet discovered that people "buy" what they "want" and not what they "need." Unfortunately, it took management many years to realize—assuming it has fully realized the matter even yet—that preferred numbers were not only what it needed but also what it wanted.

Nevertheless, the work went on.

An examination of the records reveals that Alford's Working Committee's report, which the ASA had approved in 1927, had been recommended to industry for a trial practice period. As Alford's private papers reveal,

After four years of this trial period, it appeared desirable to restudy the situation particularly because of the work of a technical committee on preferred numbers organized under the procedure of the International Standards Association. An autonomous committee was therefore organized under the American Standards Association. I was a member of that committee.[43]

It was 1934, however, before the first draft of this committee was published for general comment and criticism, and not until the fall of 1935 when the final (slightly revised) draft was unanimously adopted by this committee. Finally, on April 14, 1936, almost ten years after he addressed the ASME on the "Laws of Management," the ASA authorized the recommendations as a "proposed American Standard."

[43] Others included R. E. Hellmund (chairman), J. Gaillard (secretary), L. F. Adams and F. Thornton (NEMA), D. W. Atwater (IES), E. S. H. Baars (ASRE), K. H. Condit (ASME), S. L. Conner (Ordnance Department), E. W. Ely (National Bureau of Standards), W. Fondiller (Telephone Group), K. Hathaway (Taylor Society), S. Liebowitz (SAE), A. Maxwell (Electric Power and Light Group), A. F. VanDyck (IRE), O. B. Zimmerman and E. R. Hedrick (members at large), and the "Officer in Charge" (Bureau of Engineering, Navy Department). Outside of Alford, who again represented the SIE here, no member of the old Working Committee was on this committee. However, Condit and Hedrick had served with Alford on the old General Committee.

The report [44] itself went into far greater detail than had the earlier one in the matter of standardization of "sizes" (i.e., dimensions of length, area, volume, weight, ratings, capacities, etc.). In view of the work of the international body, which played a larger part in necessitating this further study and remembering that the Basic Preferred Numbers System is an international system, it is not surprising that one important addition made by the Sectional Committee on Preferred Numbers was the inclusion of a Table of a Fractional Series of Basic Preferred Numbers, which would have its greatest application in the countries where the "English System" was firmly established.

In general the 1936 Report attempted at every opportunity to show the benefits afforded by preferred numbers, starting with the desirability for uniformity and ending on the facilitation of calculations and the reduction of costs.

As to the actual and widespread use of preferred numbers, only industry itself has the answer. This, however, is certain: although its use may not be as wide as it ought to be, its continued gains have been slow but sure. Certainly, even Alford could not ask for more.

[44] "American Standard Preferred Numbers" (Approved ASA, April 14, 1936, ASA Z 17.1-1936, American Engineering and Industrial Standards, published by the ASA).

Chapter V

LAWS AND PRINCIPLES

THE MELVILLE MEDAL

Although there is little question of the high esteem in which Alford was held by his colleagues throughout his entire life, and although there can be little doubt of the responsible positions he held in the firms for which he worked and the professional societies to which he gave service, the first material recognition of his achievements came during the evening of December 6, 1927.

His three- or four-sentence notation in his private papers of the events of that date is about as verbose as his modesty would permit in reporting a personal item. It was probably more out of a feeling of grateful pride than boasting praise that he wrote:

On the evening of December 6, 1927 President Charles M. Schwab presented to me the Melville Gold Medal which had previously been awarded by the council of the society. This was the first time that the medal was bestowed.[1]

After the presentation Mrs. Alford and I stood in the receiving line and received the congratulations of many friends.

The Melville Prize Award Medal for Original Work, established in 1914 by a bequest from Rear Admiral George W. Melville, who had served as engineer in chief and chief of the Bureau for the United States Navy as well as a past president and honorary member of ASME, was awarded through the

[1] According to ASME records, funds became available for the design and die of the medal in 1926. See "ASME Honors and Awards," in *Mechanical Engineering, 61,* No. 4, 302-304, April (1939).

Committee on Awards, acting under the Council's supervision, for "an original paper or thesis of exceptional merit presented to the Society for discussion and publication." Evidently the Committee, consisting of I. N. Hollis, A. M. Greene, Jr., H. L. Seward, R. V. Wright, and K. N. Condit, considered Alford's paper, "Laws of Manufacturing Management," presented at the Annual Meeting in December, 1926, in New York, of great importance. For, as Alford's own files show, "it was selected as the paper of 1926 to receive the Melville Award."

GENERAL ACCLAMATION FOR THE ALFORD CODIFICATION

Although the award is undoubtedly the profession's stamp of approval on Alford's efforts, it was preceded and has since been followed by an appreciation of his work in this field.

In 1926 there was an appreciative and sizable group of leading engineers who were aware of the worth of Alford's attempt at codification. Roe, who joined with Alford "in hoping that the Laws of Management may be established as firmly as those of mathematics, physics, and chemistry," felt that "this paper will help toward that end." Wallace Clark considered the Alford work to be "an important step in the development of the science of management." R. G. Wells welcomed the opening of "an interesting and somewhat unexplored field," for "one handicap to the management movement has been the over-emphasis of system and routine rather than underlying principles." Barth thought that Alford deserved "much credit for his bold attempt to formulate a set of laws for the guidance of managers." R. T. Kent called the Alford codification "a milestone in the progress of Scientific Management." H. V. Coes, too, thought that Alford had "advanced the cause of intelligent management" in attempting to get at the fundamentals of "the present nebulous science of management."

Today, more than twenty-five years later, the comments are no less favorable. Leaders in the management field are unanimous in considering the "Laws of Management" as the most important of his many accomplishments.

Coes' views, in 1952, were as favorable as they were in 1926. "In my own work," he told the writer of this book, "I always found Alford's Laws very helpful in both getting things and data arranged. When data were to be found in several places, the Laws helped me in getting these together in one place. The Laws helped me by letting me know that 'this must be done with the data' and 'that must be done with the organization.' Moreover, they were extremely valuable in testing when and where things went bad. One merely looked for violations of Alford's Laws!"

A more recent commentary on the worth of Alford's Laws is that of J. M. Juran, who believed that Alford had a better grasp than, say, Taylor, of the whole managerial process as well as a better balance in his thinking on its manifold activities. Admittedly Taylor did some very necessary pioneering work, but much of it was on a "lower" level and little of it remains in current use. Alford's search for fundamental laws was on a plane altogether different from that of the problem of cutting of metals. What is more, Juran felt that even today the full import of Alford's Laws has not been completely recognized. And it is of interest to note that it was Alford's Laws of Management that attracted Juran's own attention and aided him to a fuller realization of the fact that, if there is a science, there must be a rigid connection between cause and effect.

THE DEVELOPING OF ALFORD'S VIEWS

The success of Alford's presentation of his "Laws" was not accidental. It was not the fruit of a hasty conception, but rather the result of a lengthy, thoughtful study of the problem. In his private papers, Alford reveals that:

After the publication of my *Management's Handbook* in 1924 my mind turned to the possibility of codifying the fundamentals that formed the foundation of modern industrial management. After intermittent work for about eighteen months I completed a professional paper that I titled "Laws of Management." This I presented at the December Meeting in New York City.

However, it is doubtful whether it is at all possible to set so brief a period as a year and a half as the time during which these laws took root and grew even in his own mind. Perhaps the idea of "codifying" was the result of this short period, but the germination of the idea goes back much further. It is probable that he began his thinking on the matter back in the early days of "scientific management" when the familiar science-versus-art controversy raged.

His work for the 1912 Report, for example, must have opened numerous and wide vistas to him. As a matter of fact, reference has already been made to his investigation of conditions at the Link-Belt Company's plants for the *American Machinist,* earlier that year, when he had taken advantage of the opportunity and had expressed his discontent that "a multitude of so-called principles" had been given in the many discussions of shop management: [2]

One writer has given us twelve.[3] This complication has tended to befog a situation that needs to be seen with the greatest possible clearness. There is no mystery in regard to shop management. As shown there are but two underlying principles and these have been recognized for many years. The sooner these are grasped and applied, the sooner will we reach a situation that will be accurately described by the expression "rational shop management."

As for the two principles, Alford then insisted

. . . these are: the subdivision of labor, and the systematizing and use of accumulated data. Neither is new. The principle of subdivision of labor was recognized by the earliest writers who considered manufacturing conditions. The second is fundamental in every human activity.

It is likely that his interest in these matters had been established even earlier—perhaps when Church wrote, in Alford's

[2] *Scientific Management in Use.*
[3] Evidently Emerson's Twelve Principles of Efficiency.

American Machinist, his article titled, "Has Scientific Management Science?" Although this was evidently a review of Taylor's *Scientific Management,* this article, in which Church asserted that "what Mr. Taylor describes is neither a science nor an art but simply a set of ethical propositions and moral aspirations," was not unrelated to the later one, "The Principles of Management," which, though Alford wrote it in the main, was issued publicly under the names of both Alford and Church.

Back in the first years of the twentieth century, Church was not alone in questioning the existence of a science of management. Redfield,[4] probably best remembered as a member of the congressional committee that investigated "the Taylor and other systems," was an industrialist in his own right. He maintained, in view of the lack of uniformity of principles even in the same industry, the existence of labor difficulties, etc., that "if a science were ever needed, it is in this very matter of management." Others were equally strong in their opinions.

Like Church, most were disturbed by the fact that "Mr. Taylor and his associates have been considered (or have allowed themselves to be acclaimed without protest) as the inventors or sponsors of a special system of industrial administration which they term 'scientific management,' implying that all other management is unscientific." Science, Church insisted, was made up "of a long series of ascertained facts" that have stood up under time and criticism: it involved logical proof and not personal authority.

Church and Alford, therefore, wrote their paper that aimed at "the fixing of a systematic basis for a definite art of management." It was not intended to be dogmatic or final, but it was intended as a statement of fundamentals based on logical reasoning rather than an author's authority.

As early as 1912, Alford started on his search for fundamental principles, for, he felt:

---

4 Redfield, "Scientific Spirit in Management," *American Machinist,* April 18, 1912, Vol. 36, No. 16, pp. 612-615. See also his "The New Industrial Day."

They would bring to light the gaps in our knowledge and focus attention on the weakest links in our claim of practical applications.

The mapping out of related fields of activity would become possible so that every proposed improvement in method could be seen in its relation to the whole—a condition absent at the present time.

Consequently, he and Church insisted, "No apology is therefore necessary for an attempt to formulate some definite basis on which to build a truly scientific art of management."

As noted elsewhere in this study, the three regulative principles, (1) "systematic use of experience," (2) "economic control of effort," and (3) "promotion of personal effectiveness," were the result.

THE ALFORD-CHURCH PRINCIPLES

By "systematic use of experience" was meant a "careful analysis of what is about to be attempted, and its reference to existing standards of performance." New experience could be crystallized into new practice, and, even if present practice were not correct, it was an indication of the development of new standards. Finally new experience could be transmitted by detailed information to workers or by a connected body of new practice. The latter method was of course preferable.

Since "effort is experience in action," thought must precede action. But to get "organized action," effort must be controlled. This could be done by division, co-ordination, conservation, and, in industrial enterprises, remuneration. Division of effort was largely controlled by design, operative division, and administration. It must be followed by co-ordination, "prearrangement of a number of separate efforts" to produce the desired aim. This goal must be achieved "by proceeding along the line of least effort," conservation. And finally, since people demand wages in industrial work, it must be followed by remuneration.

In 1912, Alford and Church hailed the "comparatively modern discovery" concerning the close relationship between the welfare of the plant and that of its employees. For the promotion of personal effectiveness the individual must feel leadership, have adequate encouragement and reward, work under good conditions, and receive a definite allotment of responsibility. Of all of these, leadership, the authors maintained, was the most important. As a matter of fact, the trouble with some of the "management" consultants in practice at the time had been their substitution of mechanisms for leadership.

To show the validity of these three regulative principles, Alford and Church showed how the "principles" of Taylor and Emerson could be reduced to one of these three categories. Thus, Taylor's insistence on "planning" was merely a manifestation of "co-ordination of effort." His wage payment plan was an aspect of "remuneration of effort." Again, Emerson's "determination of standards" was merely an expression of "systematic use of experience."

In their treatment, Alford and Church were careful in setting forth limiting conditions, a matter that the enthusiasts of a particular type of management seemed to disregard resulting in an inevitable disrepute. As Alford and Church insisted, "It is not enough to know that a principle can be applied—it is even more important to know when not to apply it."

Both Kimball and Calder, writing in the *American Machinist* [5] on June 13, 1912, were in "hearty accord." Kimball felt that the statement of the "basic principles" was "not far from the truth." He was particularly pleased that a distinction had been made between "basic management principles" and "common sense" characteristics that were set forth as principles by partisans of certain management cliques. Of course, Calder informed the periodical that "your correspondents do well to emphasize the human element in the success, or otherwise, of the best laid schemes of industrial economy."

Church maintained that to these principles—which, of course, were incorporated and adopted in the ASME Report of 1912

[5] "Principles of Management." Separate articles by D. Kimball and J. Calder, *American Machinist, 36,* No. 24, 965-966 (1912).

—Alford had added a fourth principle,[6] "Transference of Skill." This is not completely correct for, as Alford pointed out in that report, skill transference was a fundamental that was set forth by means of the three regulative principles.

In the years that followed, Church wrote a series of articles for *The Engineering Magazine* (January-June, 1913), called "Practical Principles of Rational Management," in which he attempted to work out the application of the regulative principles. His book, *The Science and Practice of Management,* was an expansion of these articles. Lieutenant J. G. Meyers[7] of the United States Navy also set up some "laws" in *The Science of Management.* In 1912, Towne[8] presented a paper on "Axioms Concerning Manufacturing Cost," in which he set up twenty-three "axioms" on this subject. And there were others, of course.

By the time Alford wrote his 1922 Report on the status of management, a good part of the science-versus-art fracas had subsided. Consequently, when he turned his attention to the compilation of a handbook that engineers in the management field could use, it was not unnatural for him to attempt to bring together the fundamentals into a Code of Laws.

THE ALFORD CODIFICATION

The 1926 paper read before the ASME was the result. But this was just a beginning. As Alford wrote on September 12, 1928, so "animated, extensive, and on the whole favorable" was the comment and so "active ever since" has been the correspondence and so "continuing" has been the interest of "industrial managers, factory executives, engineers, and educators," that the suggestion that the laws be put in book form was followed. Alford's own Ronald Press Company published the book, *Laws of Management Applied to Manufacturing.*

6 Church, *Science and Practice of Management,* pp. 509 ff.
7 *Journal of the American Society of Naval Engineers, 23,* 94 ff. Reprinted in Thompson, *Scientific Management,* pp. 132-152.
8 *Trans. ASME, 34,* 1111-1123 (1912).

Here Alford expanded his discussion but adopted a "semi-popular" style. ("That is," he wrote, "technical terms and reasoning have been omitted as far as possible.") The changes from the early paper were not great. However, by the time he issued his *Cost and Production Handbook,* in 1933, he had made some changes, not only in some of the ideas but in the over-all concept: he now referred to "principles" and not to "laws."

Of course, he further expanded and revised his codification for the last book he wrote which, in the very title, reverted to his original term, *Principles of Industrial Management.* As for the *Production Handbook* in 1944, though it is based on the earlier Alford work, it must be remembered that Alford had died, and the treatment of his work, though authoritative, cannot be completely considered as his own.

In Part I of the Appendix an attempt has been made to trace in tabular fashion the growth and revision of Alford's concepts from its "law" phase in 1926 through its "principle" phase in 1940. However, some discussion of the matter is in order at the moment.

The cycle from *principles* to *laws* to *principles* can be partially explained by the fact that a curious mixture of idealism and practicability was involved here. On the one hand, Alford was attempting to give to management a set of logical laws as fundamental as those in the mathematical sciences. On the other, realizing full well the pragmatic nature of those who would use them, Alford had to assign, as he admitted, a "semi-popular" tone to these fundamental concepts. Furthermore, those who saw some practical use in them did not care what they were called as long as they were understandable and applicable. Then too, later when Alford himself began to apply the more rigid distinctions of Urwick, he felt some were "valid in all cases," while others were "sufficiently applicable."

Perhaps Alford himself was to blame. Perhaps when he began to consider the matter, he should have made clear the distinction between *laws* and *principles* and between *rules* and *axioms,* for all these terms were used somewhat interchangeably. But a reiteration of the strict definitions given by the logic texts would probably have frightened away the very "practical" persons who might use the concepts. Certainly it was difficult enough to introduce a "new" concept, without including theoretical embellishments horrifying to those who might use it. Hence, he adopted the popular conception in spite of all of its difficulties.

Unlike the "older engineering sciences" whose "body of fundamentals" had "always existed" and had been formulated by workers in these fields, management pioneers did not aim at such "completeness of survey" but contented themselves in "expressing such knowledge as was at hand in a number of statements."

These "statements" were known by various names: "principles" (Emerson), "underlying principles" (Taylor), "regulative principles" (Alford and Church), "axioms" (Towne), "law" (Gremple). As a matter of fact, Alford [9] himself in referring to Gremple's Law—"like conditions plus like causes necessitate like effects"—used the description of "the single axiom or aphorism of management." Hence it seems clear that little attempt was made to distinguish between them.

As late as 1928, Alford in his book insisted that "no one has spoken with more certainty" than had Henry Ford [10] when he maintained: "We have not found it necessary to alter the principles and I cannot imagine how it might ever be necessary to alter them because I hold that they are absolutely universal." Yet in that very book [11] Alford had assigned three characteristics to the *laws* of management: "They are resistant to change. They are universal in application. They are imperative to the highest success."

Although Alford asserted that the early statements "lacked the outstanding characteristics of natural law, that is the results of their operation could not be closely predicted nor precisely measured," he did not depreciate their importance. Fur-

[9] "Laws of Manufacturing Management," *Trans. ASME, 48,* 393-418 (1926).
[10] Quoted by Alford, *Laws of Management,* p. 30.
[11] *Ibid.,* p. 46.

thermore, he was convinced in 1928 that there was a growing evidence of the existence of many rather than a few fundamentals. He seemed then to negate the very thesis that he and Church set out to expound. For did they not attempt to show that all of the cited fundamentals could be reduced to their few regulative principles?

This was in fact seemingly contrary to the trend, in, say, physics, where a single all-encompassing concept was the goal. Usually a "special theory" was followed by a "general" one. Nevertheless, it must be admitted that Alford maintained that the very codification of the fundamentals would form the building blocks with which additional knowledge could be built.

Furthermore, Alford hoped that his codification would also serve in aiding engineering students to prepare for work in executive and management fields and in allowing all practitioners to apply these fundamentals to daily problems.

Envisaging some indication of what the future might hold, Alford pointed to the article on finding causes of quality variances that Shewhart had written for his *Manufacturing Industries:* [12]

Let us look upon the industrial development based upon applied scientific laws, making use of only a fraction of past experience, and think of the future based upon applied laws and laws of chance, thus making the best use of all of our data.

And he set himself to the task of examining the management fundamentals, theorizing on their origin, formulating many of them in "uniform language," and supporting their validity with citations from leaders in the field. All this was done with the high hope that investigation would be so stimulated that the "laws of management" would be fixed "as securely as the laws of mathematics, physics, and chemistry."

In his earlier works he admittedly felt that, because of the wide scope of management, he must restrict his discussion to "manufacturing management." This was justifiable. After all, he had defined "management" as the "science of getting work

[12] Shewhart, "Finding Causes of Quality Variances" in *Manufacturing Industries, 11,* 128, No. 2, February (1926).

done." Furthermore, this was the aspect in which the pioneers of the movement had worked, and it remained the main interest of the ASME members before whom he was presenting his paper.

But why, to come back to the fundamental question, did his work in the 1920's involve "laws" and those of the 1940's "principles"?

Certainly he began with the popular notion that characteristically made no distinction between them. Certainly he wanted a very close analogy to the "established engineering sciences." What could be more practical than concentrating on the term that these sciences had already established? Hence, his choice was for "laws."

By 1933, however, in his *Cost and Production Handbook*, he devoted a section (Section 25) to "Principles of Industrial Engineering." Here he refers to Fayol's *Principles*, Taylor's *Principles or Laws* (sic), and his own *Laws*. Even here he still was adamant on the interchangeability of the terms *fundamentals, principles, laws, axioms,* and *rules.*

He was aware, however, of two definitions formulated by Lyndall Urwick: [13]

PRINCIPLE. A general proposition sufficiently applicable to the series of phenomena under consideration to provide a guide to action. . . . A principle is a mechanism of thought.

LAW. A relationship between cause and effect which, so far as the total of existing experience goes, has been proved to be valid in all cases. . . . A law is a statement of fact.

Alford labeled Urwick's definition of a "principle" as a definition of "a principle of industrial operation" and added a definition of his own: [14]

LAW (MANAGEMENT). Uniformities, sequences, and results relative to given courses of action in management are designated as laws. They have a somewhat different significance than the laws of the physical sciences, for they deal with different phenomena.

[13] Urwick, "The Principles of Direction and Control," in the *Dictionary of Industrial Administration*, 17.
[14] *Cost and Production Handbook*, p. 1327.

From these three definitions it would seem that Alford had begun to recognize the distinction between these concepts. But this was not so, for in connection with them he said: "Two definitions of a law, and a third of a principle, of industrial operation, show that there is no essential difference in the meaning of these commonly used terms."

Yet only six years later, in his text, *Principles of Industrial Management,* he was emphatic in the distinction. On the basis of Urwick's original definitions, he set forth, "with considerable assurance," the following (pp. 63-64):

LAW OF MANAGEMENT. A relationship between cause and effect which, so far as the total existing experience goes, has proved to be valid in all cases.

A law is a statement of fact to govern decision.

PRINCIPLE OF MANAGEMENT. A general proposition sufficiently applicable to the series of phenomena under consideration to provide a guide to thought. A principle is a statement of probability to guide judgment.

What is more, so convinced had he become concerning the distinction that every one of the fifty or so "laws" were renamed as "principles." Of course, the title of the book itself was indicative, and in it only one *law* appeared.[15] This, a carry-over from his *Laws of Management* text,[16] was E. H. Thompson's Law of Ancient Work: "Given human power, practically unlimited and unpaid for, powerful machinery is needless."

Of course, the posthumously issued *Production Handbook* as well as the Beatty revision of the management text use *principles.*

Although there may be some question as to whether Alford's vacillation from *principles* to *laws* and back to *principles* was as much a manifestation of "weakness" in his thinking as an indication of his progressive thought, there can be little question that it served as a great force. Be that as it may, there was one factor that he, to his credit, did not fail to recognize throughout the development.

15 P. 5.
16 P. 248.

This unwavering concept was the belief that, whether it be a management *principle* or *law,* "it must connect cause and effect or, at least, indicate an established trend."

ORIGIN OF MANAGEMENT FUNDAMENTALS

From whence came the management fundamentals? Alford traced them as an outgrowth of customs. W. G. Sumner, in his *Folkways,* spoke of *mores* or *folkways* or "ways of doing things which are current in a society." Yet the mores, these ways of doing things, were not planned; they grew up and are practices "unquestioningly, unconsciously, and automatically." Analogous to an individual's habits, A. G. Keller's *Evolution of Man* insists that they make up society's behavior code.

Keller believed that division of labor was typical of these expedient ways. Alford included others (transfer of skill, incentive reward, exercise and response to leadership, fixing responsibility and authority, transfer of skill to machines and mechanisms, etc.) among the "accepted ways of getting work done."

All of these, their origins traceable to antiquity, were ready for use as the Industrial Revolution took over. These management fundamentals came from the "customs of mankind in doing work," and their *beginnings, growth,* and *continuing progress* were, are, and continue to be of a "societal or organic evolution."

Although this evolution still goes on, Alford insisted that the law of evolution itself is a law of irreversible transformations. Thus we cannot imagine that, having adopted division of labor, we will ever generally revert to "methods of the 'jack-of-all-trades,'" or wages having increased steadily that they will generally drop, or working hours having decreased that they will increase again.

Alford felt that his theory of the origin of fundamentals was independently justified by B. A. Franklin, vice-president of the Strathmore Paper Company. Franklin [17] maintained that man, whether he was aware of it or not, was ruled by laws—laws that

[17] *Open Shop Review,* May, 1926, p. 185.

he did not make (natural laws), laws that he did make (governmental laws), and laws that were neither nature-made nor man-made (laws of human relations and economics). An attempt to break any of these laws was either entirely impossible or possible for only a short while. In any event such disobedience courted disaster.

The codification of the laws applicable to management, therefore, was an important task. It was a difficult one as well. Not only did they have to be formulated into uniform language, but few of the experiential factors and the statistical quantities necessary for the relationship of cause and effect had, as yet, been determined.

Originally, Alford had forty or more laws grouped under about twenty-five headings. As the years passed, the number was increased, and the headings renamed. In the ensuing analysis of some of the more important fundamentals, the more comprehensive grouping adopted in later years has been used.

SPECIALIZATION

Of all the *laws* that Alford discussed in his early work and of all the *principles* that he treated in his later writings, perhaps those on "specialization" had been under his consideration for the longest time. Even the most casual reference to his 1912 Report is indicative of this fact.

In his treatment of specialization, he was very insistent that the matter be subdivided into specialization of "job," "individual," "tool," and "product." For he felt that particularly the first three had been frequently but incorrectly grouped under "Division of Labor." The first was of ancient origin, and Alford, citing Lardner's *Porcelain and Glass,* showed that an early manifestation was the Babylonians' division of the manufacture of porcelain into sixty operations. The "tool" subdivision, of course, came into prominence with the Industrial Revolution, but the breakdown concerning the "individual" was the direct result of the rise of "scientific management" and its attention to the "scientific selection of the worker." The fourth sub-division Alford based on Hudson's treatment, in his own *Management's Handbook,* of a concept extensively practiced in American industry.

Even Alford's citations from Smith and Babbage, in their contention as to why "division of labor" increases production, seemed to fortify Alford's subdivision. Nevertheless, Wallace Clark felt that the breakdown was confusing, and he suggested that perhaps Kimball's more concise statement, "As the worker restricts his field of endeavor, his product rises in quality and quantity," would not only be clearer but it would be closer to Roe's idea that "ideas must be verifiable by measurement."

Although Wallace Clark hailed Alford's attempt at codification, he made one more detailed criticism. It pertained to Alford's acceptance of "Functional Foremanship" as applied to managerial duties. Both Babbage and Kimball had claimed that division of labor need not be restricted to manual work, and Alford combined this concept with Taylor's idea of specialization of the individual. Certainly, if any of Taylor's ideas had become obsolete, "Functional Foremanship" is that one.

Unless the scattering of responsibilities was counterbalanced by greater organizational co-ordination, Wallace Clark felt that "functionalized management cannot equal non-functionalized management." He therefore suggested, as a substitute, the following: "As the scope of his responsibility is narrowed, the efficiency of an executive increases." Evidently Alford agreed, for his *Laws* book made the change.

STANDARDIZATION

Even if Alford did not have an early interest in standardization, he would not have had any other logical choice but to turn his attention to this subject. For specialization of the job calls for "standard methods, instructions, and times for doing work." Specialization of the individual calls for standard job specifications. Transfer of skill gives rise to standard tools and machines.

Specialization of product necessitates "rating, quality, and proportionality" standards.

Although he at first limited standardization to the physical aspects of a product, he soon felt the need to widen the concept to include results and procedures. His deep insight as well as his interest in standard costs and standard times made him aware of the "predetermined results," while safety codes and job specifications showed him the value of standardization procedures.

Of course his early emphasis, in his study of standardization, on the physical aspect of the product was unquestionably influenced by the admitted importance of "interchangeability," which Simeon North called the "principle of American manufacture." But Alford himself was certainly aware of the widening scope of standardization, for he was an early contributor to the movement in standardization of plant and equipment. When he served as a mechanical engineer for the United Shoe Machinery Company, at Beverly, Massachusetts, he, as his own writings reveal, "standardized the screw machine parts of that firm's line of shoe machines with an estimated saving in production costs of $150,000 per year."

J. Gaillard and F. J. Schlink, of the American Standards Committee (now Association), felt that the Alford statements on standardization ought to be expanded in its application to products. Asserting that standards were essentially "compromises" and subject to revision from time to time, they suggested that five laws be added to Alford's list. These Alford adopted as corollaries: they appeared in the *Laws* book and the *Principles* text, although Bangs omitted them from the *Handbook*. Admitting their correctness, the wording was unfortunately lengthy and intricate.

LEADERSHIP AND ORGANIZATION

Although Alford's later work laid great stress on organization, his earlier study of the subject did not emphasize the matter to any extent. In the beginning he was content merely to focus attention on the laws relating to leadership, exceptions, and authority and responsibility.

The reason seems simple. Beginning with a Napoleonic historian's "Wise direction is of more avail than overwhelming numbers, sound strategy than the most perfect armament," and Gantt's industrial paraphrase, "Wise policy is of more avail than a large plant, good management than perfect equipment," Alford himself gave the "observed relationship between creative power and concrete result" in terms of "Wise leadership is more essential to successful operation than extensive operation or perfect equipment."

And, if further evidence of Alford's early beliefs is necessary, consider his citations of the successes of North (who had no modern organization), Westinghouse (who died before modern organization reached any appreciable growth), and Ford (who condemned organization and felt that a man's title and duties were "limited by the circumference of his berry" on a chart that resembled a "family tree").

In later years, however, Alford quoted Carnegie, who felt that, even after losing his factories, trade, money, and transportation paths, he could, given four years and "our organization," find himself again. Furthermore, Alford soon came to the conclusion that, as important as leadership might be, to be effective it must be exercised over groups of people striving toward a common goal. These people, with their duties, authorities, responsibilities, and their relationships among themselves and their leaders, constituted the "organization for control."

In his contemplation of organization, Alford later began to recognize the functioning of a "healthy human body" [18] as the ideal toward which industrial organization itself might strive. Although in this connection he recognized the engineer Knoeppel's [19] description of the human body in engineering terms

[18] *Principles of Industrial Management,* p. 93.
[19] Knoeppel, *The Practical Application of the Principles of Industrial Engineering,* pp. 128-129.

and the physician Haggard's [20] treatment of the integrated action of the human body, Alford himself made the human body–industrial organization analogy, a matter that even today is not too widely recognized.

It is likely that Alford had been aware of the analogy as far back as at least 1913. For at that time Church in his book, *The Science and Practice of Management,* a follow-up of the inquiry he started with Alford, also used "the analogy of the human body" [21] and came to the conclusion: [22] "But it is from the fact that the human body is the most highly co-ordinated and efficient mechanism with which we are acquainted that we may expect to find helpful analogies and even practical hints."

It is surprising that "control," a matter with which Alford was concerned in his 1912 paper with Church, did not receive its full due in his 1926-28 works. By 1939, however, he had expanded his idea of what "control" meant and began to associate it with an objective. He was very close to today's concept of an association with a standard. However, he became interested in the distinction between "man control" and "fact control." And of course Gantt's comparison between "facts" and "opinions" played no little part in his later emphasis of fact control and its related fundaments: e.g., "co-ordination," which he treated as an element of control.

It is surprising that Alford, whose discussions frequently treated historical beginnings and applications,[23] did not show the Biblical reference (Exodus 18:12-26) to the "exception" fundamental as more recent writers have. However, Alford not only showed the relation between the "exception" concept and "standard cost systems" but called attention to its being "a principal control feature." [24]

[20] Haggard, "Physiology for the Engineer," in *Mechanical Engineering, 61,* No. 1, 8-12, January (1934).

[21] Pp. 3 ff.

[22] Pp. 5-6.

[23] For example, Alford gave the industrial organization of Solomon in building the Temple (*circa* 1000 B.C.) as an early application.

[24] *Laws of Management,* p. 77.

PRODUCTION PLANNING AND CONTROL

Although the posthumously issued *Production Handbook,* following the *Cost and Production Handbook,* uses the group heading "Production Planning and Control," Alford's term in 1928 was "Production Management." Of course the newer title is more expressive of modern trends, but the older one probably better explains why such fundamentals as Economic Production, Mass Production, Manufacturing Cost, and Indirect Expense are found in this grouping.

After the work is specialized and detailed, some agency—management—must direct and co-ordinate. And the fundaments in this grouping were those through whose application the physical factors were planned and directed.

Bangs and Hagemann put the Work Assignment aspect under this category, since it relates to a division of the work. Alford himself treated it, in his *Principles* text, under Employer-Employee Relations. It might even be appropriately considered under Individual Productivity. The point is, however, that Alford surprisingly did not consider it among the fundaments until later in his career.

As for the two concepts on Economic Production, a word of explanation is needed as to what Alford meant by a *production factor.* This was a term used by Church, first in a series of articles in *The Engineering Magazine* from October, 1909, to April, 1910, but which in the latter year were expanded into a book, *Production Factors.* For Church and for Alford the term referred to "any expense that has a *definite* relation to the cost of production."

The corollary, added in 1928, was the result of a mathematical study,[25] made by C. W. Cobb and P. H. Douglas in that very year, from a study of United States Census production records from 1899 to 1922. They ascribe 75 per cent of the product during that period to labor and 25 per cent to fixed capital. Even more important, as far as Alford was concerned, than the

[25] *The American Economic Review, 18,* No. 1, March (1928).

actual 3:1 ratio was the effect this mathematical measure had: for it was one of the forerunners of the Alford-Hannum kmh concept.

When Alford first stated these laws, G. Charter Harrison deplored the omission of the Law of Diminishing Returns. Thus, as production is increased and additional units of capital and labor are added, the unit cost of production will decrease up to a certain point. It was particularly significant at the time, because Ford had asserted that, as he reached 1,000 cars per day and jammed Detroit's freight facilities, he began to examine critically the size of his plant. Furthermore, a concentration of such a large working population in one locality was also objectionable. And Harrison quoted Ford as saying, in his *Today and Tomorrow,* "It is better to avoid difficulties than to overcome them, and not only do we find it easier to manage smaller plants but also—which is most important—*the costs of production in the smaller plants are lower."*

As a matter of fact, Kimball in his *Principles of Economics* restated the Alford laws in terms of the Law of Diminishing Returns.

Alford was well aware of the importance of these fundamentals in connection with the control of costs. Influenced greatly by Gantt,[26] who claimed that "only those expenses needed to produce" an article should enter into its cost, he introduced here his statements on Manufacturing Costs and Indirect Expenses. In his *Principles* text, he regrouped these particular concepts under "Cost Accounting."

Of course the mass production concept would be expected to have been included in Alford's early treatment. But it is of interest to note that he did not realize until two years later that, to obtain minimum production time or maximum output per unit of time, many operations had to be performed simultaneously. Hence he accepted E. P. Blanchard's Simultation (or Co-ordination) concept.

Of course, his ideas on Planning and Production Control were codified rather early. Since a fuller treatment of them is

[26] Alford, *Henry Laurence Gantt,* p. 181.

given below, in connection with his paper before the SPEE Summer School in 1929, there is no need to expand on his views here.

But one further aspect deserves attention, namely, his statement concerning the most effective means of controlling Operating Performance. This was a concept that came out of the kmh studies.

MATERIALS CONTROL AND HANDLING

Because of the close association between the expedient use of materials and the control of production, it was logical that the consideration of the materials problem begin early. Aside from the pioneers in the modern management movement, Alford traced materials control back to Nebuchadnezzar's Babylon where each year's harvest was systematically stored.

The first of the Alford fundaments on Material Control admittedly bears strong kinship to Gantt's emphasis on having material when, where, and in the condition needed. The second statement that Alford gave on this subject was merely another expression of the folk maxim relating to a place for everything and everything in its place: by 1939, he realized it was inherent in some of the other aspects and he omitted it. As for the third statement, which Alford adopted in 1928, it was strongly influenced by R. G. Tugwell.[27]

It was natural that Alford, as industry became more and more interested in the problem of inventory and obsolescence and varying price levels, treat these matters under Inventory Control. As a matter of fact, C. M. Bigelow suggested that Alford might add a corollary because of price changes. However, this matter was somewhat considered in the formulas on Economic Lot Sizes.

Again, because of the management movement's early emphasis on production proper, it was only in later years that Alford set forth some fundamentals on handling materials. In reality, though, these were an expansion of his original statement on

[27] *Industry Coming of Age*, p. 161.

the Flow of Work, which itself bears a substantial relationship to the entire problem of plant layout.

QUALITY CONTROL AND INSPECTION

In the early days, when the inspection process was practically synonymous with the quality control function, one would have expected to find in the listing of the fundaments an emphasis on inspection. This is clearly not so, for Alford's early insight into the relation of quality and costs was matched by his quick recognition of the importance of the statistical aspects that came in the 1920's. Furthermore, although he recognized Shewhart's contribution in the Statistical Quality Control Chart as one of the main contributions during the 1923-32 period [28] and although with Juran [29] he looked forward to the "more scientific way" these problems would be handled, and although he opened his *Manufacturing Industries* [30] for discussions on probability and on mathematical and measurement aspects of quality control, he did not lose sight of the management aspects of the quality problem.

His fourth statement, which he added later and which suggested the folly of obtaining conformance by inspection after fabrication, was typical of his fuller realization of the problem.

INDIVIDUAL PRODUCTIVITY

The Gilbreths' concern for the "one best way" was an adequate manifestation of the great part these pioneers played in the establishment of Alford's fundamentals dealing with the subject of improving and increasing the output of the individual worker.

Of course Alford's statement that, for highest individual productivity, a worker be assigned duties in keeping with the high-

28 Alford, "Ten Years' Progress in Management, 1923-1932," *Trans. ASME, 55,* No. 5, MAN-55-2, 1-16 (1933).

29 *Ibid.,* p. 11. Also Alford, *Principles of Industrial Management,* p. 315.

30 *Manufacturing Industries:* Shewhart, February, 1926, p. 128; Hall, "Quality Control," *16,* No. 1, 17-19, July (1928).

est type of work for which his natural abilities fit him, can be traced to Taylor. And on it is based achievement testing and its allied personnel fields, once described by the term that Alford used, "vocational guidance."

It is interesting to note that J. Younger suggested that, because of the tendency to add more unskilled workers, a converse be added: "It is advisable in a particular job to use the least skilled workmen capable of doing the job."

As for his three principles on the acquisition of skills, the first two are from the psychological laws of habit formation. The third was recognized by C. M. Bigelow,[31] who studied the manner in which workers reacted to unfamiliar tasks.

The Gilbreths' "Hand Motions" were given prominence, first as five *laws*, then as *rules* of *human* motions. However, according to authorities such as Lytle, the *law* (or *principle*) of Segur [32] on motion time is not on the same level. Even Alford [33] himself admitted that such an analysis might be "a modified technique of micromotion." Hence, the "law" has its basis in the Gilbreths' work. Possibly Alford thought it might be the answer to the "great schism" between motion and time study, a matter he greatly regretted. He was pleased with the proper balance that Roe and Lytle gave to these subjects in his *Handbook,* and in his *Principles* (page 322) he emphasized their combined power. Finally, for balance, Alford's 1926 paper gave, as the "Law of Delay Allowance," the empirical formula developed by Barth from Merrick's data. Even Barth maintained that it, too, was not deserving of "being elevated to the dignity of a law."

WAGE PAYMENT

Alford felt that his statements on "Relative Wages" and "Wage Level," supported by J. D. Cox of the Cleveland Twist Drill

[31] Roe and Lytle reported on this matter in connection with "Incentive Plan for Beginners" (pp. 962 ff.) of their section (Section 16: "Wage Payments and Timekeeping") in *Management's Handbook.*

[32] Alford, "Motion-Time Analysis: A New Step in Operation and Rate Study" in *Manufacturing Industries, 12,* No. 5, 341-344, November (1926).

[33] *Cost and Production Handbook,* p. 579 and p. 1341.

Company, and by F. W. Taussig in his *Principles of Economics* (vol. 2, p. 220), might better be classed as "economic" rather than purely "managerial," because they were indicative of "trends rather than relationships."

The fundamentals in this group dealt with the bases from which wages were set as well as the methods applicable to monetary incentives and the hours of work.

The first of the fundaments on Task and Wage Incentive is, of course, based on Taylor who, by a "most practical turn," insisted that "the more elementary the worker's mind and character" the shorter should be the period for which the work is assigned in advance. In 1928, Alford omitted from the second of these fundaments the "adequacy" of the wage incentive. The third was suggested by Barth who, on reviewing Alford's early statement on "Wage Rates," insisted that there was a misstatement. "It is not the wage rate that should not ever be changed as stated," he declared, "but the production time on which the wage rate is based." Alford agreed, and the "Base Time" statement was the result.

Alford raised to the level of a *law* in early works and a *principle* in later ones the "Hours of Work" that Cox had stressed. In 1923 President Harding, supported by the American Engineering Council's report of the previous year, *The Twelve Hour Shift in Industry*,[34] appealed to Judge Gary, who then headed the Iron and Steel Institute, to do away with such working periods in the industry.

Later, when the industry had acquiesced, Alford liked to refer to a letter he had received from Bradley Stoughton, who had written the AEC report: "Some employers truthfully say that they believe that labor costs have not risen much, if any, from the old 12-hour day."

This must have given Alford a good deal of satisfaction, for it was a matter with which he was concerned for many years—since Gary stated, "personally I am not certain that the 12 hour day is bad for employees. . . . I was brought up on a farm, and many, many days worked more than 12 hours. I am sure that

34 See below, pp. 206-8.

most of the busy officers of companies work more than 12 hours every day." [35]

OTHER "LAWS" AND "PRINCIPLES"

Alford's early experience in shops and with shopmen undoubtedly had its effect in his early inclusion of a statement in regard to maintenance of equipment. However, as his interest in "Safety" grew, particularly through the efforts of the American Engineering Council in this field, he began to treat maintenance as "accident protection applied to plant and equipment."

In his early work he included, as *laws,* various concepts relating to Labor Saving Equipment and Economic Lot Sizes. The former, consisting of formulas for the computation of resulting economies, were developed by J. A. Shepard and G. Hagemann for the Materials Handling Division of the ASME. These were repeated in his 1928 work. The formula for Economic Lot Size was that of R. C. Davis, and, in the *Laws* book, it was expanded into formulas relating to Economic Manufacturing Lot Sizes. These were the ASME formulas which, on behalf of the Management Division, F. E. Raymond undertook to examine and combine in his paper, "Economic Production Quantities." Included here were the work of G. D. Babcock, G. Pennington, and Raymond on the Economic Lot Formula and Davis' Economic Purchase Quantities. These, together with P. N. Lehoczky's approximation of the Raymond Formula, were included by Alford in his *Laws.*

Perhaps Alford was most deeply moved by the mathematical expressions that he felt were necessary for the quantitative approach. If so, Lytle's mathematical and graphical analysis was certainly worthy of similar treatment. In any event, for whatever the reason, Alford's later treatment excluded the economic formulas.

[35] Alford, *American Machinist,* editorially commented, on June 13, 1912, concerning the "supposed judicial mind" responsible for these remarks. And that was as long ago as 1912.

It is possible that Alford took heed of Barth's criticism of including the "preferred numbers" aspect of the Law of Discriminations. Barth maintained that even though such numbers follow a mathematical law, "the mere fact that such numbers are preferred implies a choice and not a law."

In later years, as the management field and research opened up even further, Alford understood and included some *principles* on Administration and Management Research. He also added the "Principle of the Objective," a fundamental requiring that "first things" be done "first" and the advance determination of "what to do and how to do it," even though the latter part of this fundament is close to his "Planning" concept. In many of these, the Urwick influence is again apparent.

One concept, surprisingly enough, he failed to include after his first treatment in 1926. This was the "Law of Profit," and it tied "profit" to "service." This came very close to the "spirit" that he attempted to breathe in the laws he codified.

"THE SPIRIT OF THE LAWS"

When Alford first presented his paper before the ASME, C. M. Bigelow suggested the serious need for a "preamble" to proclaim that there is "an underlying something," a soul or "spirit of scientific management," that transcends mere methods, principles, and laws.

Alford "heartily" agreed, and as he pursued the matter further, he felt that although the application of the fundamentals he expounded was so great a force in the development of America's industries, the spirit and motive behind these fundaments also had their effects "in terms of human life and happiness." Not only had they been instrumental in furthering the property, material wealth, leisure, comfort, and well-being of all the people, but they had also fostered a spirit of liberty, progress, and service.

The growth of liberty in industrial relationships, Alford found, was evident in the development of attitudes toward labor. The ancient world's "Make the wretches work" and the preindustrial revolution's "Keep the low orders poor and make them work" have given way to modern management's "Teach and lead your workers and so develop active co-operation between them and you."

The laws and principles expressed the existence of causal relationships. Therefore, it is quite fitting to examine the effect of their own causes. This has been continued improvement in management and engineering. As Alford noted,[36] "Progress becomes rapid only when facts are organized and principles are formulated."

There was also the doctrine preached by Gantt, which had greatly influenced Alford, the motive of "Service." Certainly here was a manifestation that a good doctrine could, at one and the same time, be good religion and good economics.

And what of Bigelow's "underlying something"? It was not in the laws or the applications but in "a real conscious belief that things can be improved." With such a spirit, success is assured.

ALFORD'S CODIFICATION ATTEMPT

Despite the unanimity of acclaim for Alford's statements of the fundamentals of management and his focusing of attention on causal relationships in the field of management, it cannot honestly be said that the true significance of the attempt, much less the potency of the result, has even yet been fully recognized.

Admittedly he was far in advance of his times. But a quarter of a century has since passed. Have we not as yet caught up?

Unfortunately the explanation, if at all possible, is not a simple one. There can be no explanation in terms of one factor, but rather in a combination of many. There is the nature of the presentation. There is the nature of the audience. There is the nature of the subject. And there are the times. All these

[36] *Laws of Management*, p. 251.

are factors, but it is not easy to discuss any one of these without the others.

Perhaps as good a starting place as any is Alford's own presentation. By the very nature of the subject, plus the pioneering aspect of the attempt, it was natural that his ideas on the subject should have initiated further development. However, to the beginner and to the practitioner who attempts to use the Alford statements in a manner that has become known as "handbook fashion," this very development, so essential to progressive thinking, appears confusing.

For the vast majority, the Alford statements are to be found in the handbooks. An examination of the posthumously issued *Production Handbook* (which, according to the Preface, "follows the lines laid out by Dr. L. P. Alford"), under a section titled "Principles of Management," yields some definitions of a *law* and a *principle* and a listing of *principles,* but no *laws.* The earlier *Cost and Production Handbook* has a section, "Principles of Industrial Engineering," which contains a list of Alford's Laws (sic).

Is this the Law or the Principle of Exceptions? In the face of such a contradiction, a novice's rereading of the definitions is assuredly confusing. An examination of the *Principles* text does not help matters. Here, if anywhere, an explanatory statement by Alford himself, because of his rich historical references and background, would have been exceedingly helpful.

Aside from the reference to *laws* and *principles,* the use of such terms as *corollary* and *axiom* seems to imply a listing with the logical order and rigor of a geometry. Whether this should or should not be so is not the point. Psychologically, it is true, and a "letdown" is the result.

Back in 1926, Barth maintained that some of the statements were not "lofty" enough to qualify as *laws,* a fact that took Alford several years to realize. Barth, at that early ASME session, suggested that "A Code of Axioms, Laws, and Principles for the Guidance of Industrial Managers" might be a more appropriate title. Perhaps that would have had at least one point in its favor: it would have avoided a suggestion of an air of finality, a concept that Alford did not want to convey (but actually did).

As might be expected from any pioneering work, some of the detailed statements could have been clearer, and some of the titles could have been more distinct. For example, the *Production Handbook* lists, under "Organization and Leadership," the Principle of the Undertaking and the Principle of the Objective. The *Principles* text, on the other hand, omits the Undertaking Principle but includes one Principle of the Objective under "Ownership of Industry" and another Principle of the Objective under "Organization for Control." [37] And then still another Principle of the Objective is given, this time in connection with "Administration and Management Research."

Of course, it may be said that a good part of this would be "confusing" only to those—and there are many—who do not understand the real significance of the fundaments and who are completely unaware of the progressive nature of the entire subject. It must be understood that this is a dynamic and not a static affair.

Unfortunately, Alford was concerned not only with the theoretical aspects of the problem but also with the practical ones. He was well aware of the great practical advantage of such a codification.

Certainly, a good part of his audience must have been "practitioners by choice." Unfortunately too many, bent on the accomplishment of their daily tasks, do not or cannot take time to stop, consider, and reflect. Too many are involved in the necessary "practicalities" and too few realize the great practicability of the theoretical. And, for too many, the importance lay in the classification for easy reference rather than in the

[37] Note the Urwick influence: "Principle of the Objective. It is a necessary preliminary to all activity to have a complete and clear statement of the object of such activity in the form of a policy or of instructions. Action must be so arranged as to subordinate all secondary consideration to that object." (Urwick, "The Principles of Direction and Control," in the *Dictionary of Industrial Administration*, pp. 17 ff.) Alford quoted this statement, with proper credit to its author, in the *Cost and Production Handbook*, p. 1344.

underlying causal relationship necessary for true understanding.

There are undoubtedly some true practitioners whose abilities transcend the usual run. Unhappily, they are few in number and have little time to devote to such a program. There are also those who have the time but not the experience—and only by a combination of all factors can the problem be further studied.

Specialization also has come to the management field. Codification and interpretation of management fundamentals require continuous analysis, and very few people exist with Alford's over-all outlook.

Today each of the management practitioners has his own particular remedy that is applied with all too automatic precision in all situations, no matter how diverse. Too few can size up a general situation. Too many carry their own particular pills. Too many come with just a statistical control chart and a set of sampling tables. Too few come with even a knowledge of the management of quality control, much less an acquaintance with the broader field of management. Too many come with only a stop watch, too few with an all-round knowledge of the management picture.

And this dynamic field of management fundamentals needs the general outlook. Otherwise, it will display an overemphasis in one field and an underemphasis in another.

Many years ago Coes called attention to the many pseudo management laws, "deftly borrowed from some other science and dressed up for the occasion," which have had results that have "not redounded to the credit of the scientific management movement." He had hoped that eventually perhaps a science might be developed that could be "visualized as a pyramid, with all other basic sciences forming the base and body of the pyramid, and management forming the pinnacle or apex."

Again comes the call for the broad and over-all viewpoint.

It must be remembered that Alford only devoted a small part of his life to the problem. Unfortunately only fifteen years remained when he started to give the matter serious thought. For many of these significant years, his physical health was not of the best.

But he had made a beginning. It remains for the management field to renew and continue a genuine interest in this problem. Unquestionably further progress will come, for a very firm basis has already been established.

This much we owe to Alford—and ourselves.

Chapter VI

KMH

THE QUANTITATIVE APPROACH

As pointed out above, only a very few were unconcerned with Taylor and his work. Generally speaking, one was either keenly in favor of or profoundly against "Taylorism." Hence, when Church first raised the question as to whether "scientific management" was truly "scientific," his article was viewed with favor by one camp and with contempt by the other.

Even Church would hardly have expected Taylor and his followers to realign their principles and writings to suit his own criticism. Consequently, there could not have been any spontaneous and universal movement to follow the suggestion that, if "scientific management" were not now "scientific," it be made so. Of course, occasionally there were individual attempts to make the "correction."

By the 1920's a good deal of the fervor of this controversy, along with that of the accompanying "science-versus-art" question, had subsided. Yet this did not mean that no further thought was given to the matter.

By now the change of emphasis, from mere "classification" to quantitative measure, was becoming more and more apparent in all the sciences. To express it briefly but succinctly, Huxley's "Science is nothing but trained and organized common sense" had been replaced by Lord Kelvin's "When you cannot measure what you are speaking about, when you cannot express it in numbers, your knowledge is of a meager and unsatisfactory kind; it may be the beginning of knowledge, but you have scarcely in your thoughts advanced to the stage of a *science,* whatever the matter may be."

This quantitative approach soon became the *sine qua non* of scientific method. Certainly those who had been trained in engineering were keenly interested in this procedure in connection with industrial problems in general, and management problems in particular.

In his discussion of Alford's "Laws of Manufacturing Management" before the ASME in 1926, Roe pointed out that laws—interrelations of observed data—do not make for a science unless they are "verifiable by measurement." Hence, in addition to the ideas on the use of measurement in management operations that he had previously expressed,[1] he suggested that Alford add to his list the following: "Since exact observation underlies all science, measurement, i.e., comparison with uniform standards, can be applied to such phases of management as have a scientific basis and in so far as this is done it will aid in predicting results and in the execution of work."

Although there is no evidence that Alford ever included it in his codifications, there can be no doubt that it expressed a spirit that led Alford on to his search for some measurable concepts that could be used and generally accepted in management.

Furthermore, Alford felt that if planning was to be a factor in industry, it could only be achieved by means of, and along with, the basic concept of the measurement and evaluation of operating performance. He therefore decided that a unit was required for this purpose that could serve as a standard in terms of which such measurement could be made and that would be capable of supplying facts that could be interpreted for control purposes.

Although a further discussion of this matter is not required at present, it might be noted here that what Alford was suggesting was the inseparability of planning and control. Although a quarter of a century has passed, there are yet too

[1] Roe, "Measurement of Management," *Trans. ASME, 45,* 825 ff. (1923).

few printed records (like Rathe's [2]) emphasizing specifically the very close affinity of the two concepts.

Admittedly a great number of units were, from time to time, developed, used, and frequently either entirely discarded or assigned to a role of lesser importance. Thus operating, cost, and financial ratios—turnovers, percentages, rates, ratings, empirical factors, comparisons, and efficiencies—were developed. But the rise and decline of more than one hundred of such items seemed ample evidence to Alford that there was, conservatively, a lack of universal acceptance.

THE DEVELOPMENT OF THE ALFORD-HANNUM CONCEPT

Of course, it would have been typical of Alford to see the existence of a problem, set himself to its solution, and come up with the "kilo man-hour" (kmh) as the answer. But this would not be historically correct. In this connection, Alford's private papers are of immeasurable value:

Joshua E. Hannum was director of the Safety in Production Study of 1928. I was vice-chairman of the committee that conducted this investigation and produced the report. We recognized that in the data that had reached our hands at that time were many facts not directly applicable to the safety problem. We, therefore, at a convenient time explored these facts and developed the kilo man-hour method of analysis for business and industrial operation.

This, then, is how Alford, with Hannum, eventually set out "to undertake a search for a basis of evaluating operating performance."

They started their kmh study in February, 1928, and their first paper, which Alford's files call a "by-product of the principle study," was presented to the ASME in December. This was "A Basis for Evaluating Manufacturing Operation" [3] for which, as Alford noted in his private papers, Hannum had done a great deal of the detailed work, "for he carried through

[2] "Management Control," in *Advanced Management, 45,* No. 3, 8-11, March (1950).

[3] *Trans. ASME, 51,* MAN-51-2, 9-15 (1929).

all of the statistical computation that yielded nearly a hundred tables of data."

For the next four years, Alford and Hannum continued their study, expanding it and making new applications, which they presented at the December, 1932, meeting of the ASME: "Applications of the Kmh Method of Analyzing Manufacturing Operation." [4] At that time, *Mechanical Engineering*, according to Alford's personal records, "asked for an article on the kmh method and the findings which had come from its use." The "short paper," [5] written in response, gave "particulars regarding the kmh system and findings bearing upon the present industrial system."

The *Mechanical Engineering* article was too much of a "review" to give full significance to the analysis and the implications that had been developed. It may, however, serve to give the "general" reader a hurried but inadequate recapitulation:

Briefly stated, the kmh system for evaluating industrial operating performance is based on the theory of control of rates, that is, if the rates of expenditures for labor, material, and expense factors are controlled, the total expenditure is controlled. The base of the rates, or denominator of the principal ratio fractions, is the man-hour, a factor common in all industry, and permitting a maximum degree of comparison of results. For convenience only, the base is taken as 1000 man-hours, or a kilo man-hour (kmh). This unit has given its name to the system.

The possibilities of the method for revealing pertinent facts are indicated by a few . . . (of the) . . . findings . . . rates of production, expenditures for supervision, annual working times for most favorable operating performance, optimum size of plant, selling value of product, and percentage of profit.

SOME EARLY ADOPTIONS

The authors of the kmh system were indeed hopeful when at least two governmental bodies adopted the system: (1) the Com-

---

[4] *Trans. ASME, 55*, MAN-55-7, 59-66 (1933).
[5] *54*, 821-824, December (1932).

mittee on Technological Employment and (2) the Census of Manufactures.

On May 11, 1931, W. N. Doak, President Hoover's Secretary of Labor, appointed a Committee on Technological Unemployment. This committee in turn established a Subcommittee of Technological Studies, according to its report, "realizing that it did not have within itself all the necessary information, thought, and experience to deal adequately with the task assigned to it," and asked about thirty individuals and about the same number of technical, labor, and research groups for help.

Under the direction of B. M. Montgomery and M. W. LaFever of the Bureau of Labor Statistics, the subcommittee was aided by the Man-Hour Committee of the American Engineering Council as well as the Committee on Technological Employment from the American Institute of Architects, AIChE, AIEE, AIMME, ASCE, ASME, American Iron and Steel Institute, Bureau of Railway Economics, Institute of Economics, National Industrial Conference Board, and Silk Association of America.

Alford and Hannum, members of the Man-Hour Committee of the AEC along with G. E. Hagemann and R. A. Wentworth, made up the ASME's Committee on Technological Employment.

Basically the recommendations of Alford and Hannum were accepted by the Committee and made part of the report submitted by the Secretary of Labor on November 14, 1931. Later the report and its recommendations were made part of Report 964 of the U.S. Senate under Senate Resolution 483 (71st Congress). This document was again referred to by a Select Committee on Unemployment Insurance that held hearings in April, October, November, and December, 1931. The report was ordered printed on June 30, 1932.

The Report of the Committee on Technological Employment carried the following

RECOMMENDATION. The Department of Labor adopt and put into use at the earliest practicable date the Alford-

Hannum method for determining the influence of technological change upon employment and unemployment.

But in 1934 Alford noted in his personal files that "these
recommendations have not been followed fully up to the present time, but numerous studies involving man-hour data have
been made and published by the Bureau of Labor Statistics
since our report was made."

Again, the Bureau of the Census briefly took up the system.
In a supplemental return in the Census of Manufactures for
1929, it secured information from four industries—Blast Furnace Operation, Machine Tool Building, Petroleum Refining,
and Lumber Manufacturing—and analyzed the data by the
kmh method.

This recognition, however, was brief. In all likelihood, these
bureaus could not have been expected to continue its use. For
American industry had failed to show any overwhelming move
toward its adoption. It was not yet ready for this manifestation
of Alford's farsightedness.

SOME MEASURES OF PERFORMANCE

Although Alford noted in his personal files that "the concept
of the kilo man-hour was new, so far as we could determine,"
he surely did not mean that it was the first attempt at measuring
operating or administrative or managerial performance. Many
methods and measures had appeared before this time.

In addition to the widely applied (and sometimes questionable) ratios such as the current ratio (current assets to current
liabilities), turnover (production requirements to average inventory), etc., there are the ratings made by means of rating
scales and evaluation sheets. The unemployment scores of
Cooke [6] and the evaluation sheet of the Committee on the
Elimination of Waste in Industry [7] are good examples. Then,
too, there was the familiar index number.

[6] Cooke, *Bulletin of the Taylor Society, 6,* No. 4, 163-170.
[7] *Waste in Industry,* pp. 34, 117.

A. L. DeLeeuw [8] attempted to measure over-all operating effectiveness in order to compare a plant's operation under actual and under ideal (where the maximum amount of product is obtained through a minimum of outlay) conditions. He defined the plant's efficiency (E_i) as

$$E_i = E_t/E_p$$

where E_t is the total efficiency and E_p is the efficiency of purpose (i.e., the greatest possible efficiency). Waste (W), that part of the expended material or effort not utilized, becomes

$$W = 1 - E_i$$

It should be noted that some of the "measures" actually set up a "rate." Thus the Gantt Chart, where for the same interval of time requirements are plotted against actual performance, really sets up a rate for the selected period. Again, a rate of expenditure is established for each subdivision of time in connection with a budget, which essentially estimates expenditures for a longer period of time and divides these estimates into the smaller subdivisions noted. Even standard costs imply rates of input of labor and material costs and burden charges in producing an article.

The importance of setting up a rate, it will be shown, can best be appreciated when there is a realization of the fact that a dual-purpose tool is set up. On the one hand, it sets up a plan, and on the other it controls its operations.

Despite this property of some of these measures, none had, as will be seen, all the characteristics that Alford believed necessary. Hence he felt they were, for the most part, unsatisfactory. Furthermore, there was no wholehearted attempt on the part of either industrial or governmental agencies to come to even the remotest agreement on any measuring device.

[8] *Management Engineering, 1*, No. 3, 141-146. See also C. H. McKnight, "Reducing Material Waste," in *Mechanical Engineering, 54*, No. 2, pp. 109-112, February (1932).

KMH AND PLANNING AND CONTROL

Although Alford and Hannum first presented their system as "a basis for evaluating manufacturing operation," during the years that followed they began to realize the fuller significance of their creation. Consequently, they felt that what they had not only could measure operation but was fundamental to the national planning and control of productive work.

Fundamentally, they maintained:

One hour of human work is the objective equivalent of any other hour of human work, when

Each hour is averaged from the total number of productive hours worked by the group to which the worker belongs, and when the

Measure of equivalency is the result of the effort expounded.

Here was the principle of economic or exchange equality on whose enforcement depended the stabilization of the interchange of goods and services between members of different producing groups.

An individual's reward for an hour of productive work, they felt, must be directly proportional to the results of that hour's work. This man-hour and individual reward ("payment for results") [9] was a demonstrated fundamental in industrial planning.

The process by which each of these fundamentals was put into effect implied a control of *rates* and *quantities*. Thus Alford saw, in the plowing under of crops, the reduction of acreage of tilled land, the reduction of weekly hours of manufacturing machinery operation, and the prohibitions on the increase of productive equipment, attempts to control (in these cases, to lower) farm and factory output. Crude and unscientific as they were, he felt that they were a beginning of planning in terms of national rates.

The rate advocated by Alford and Hannum for control in industrial planning was—and the reasons will be made apparent

[9] This was added as a "principle" by Alford in 1940.

—the time rate based on 1,000 productive man-hours (kmh).[10] Thus, the productive rate for men's shoes production may be, say, 750 pairs per kmh. The rate for wheat production may be, say, 4,000 bushels per kmh.

The return to a group for the work done by its members should be based on the output per average hour of work. The individual's reward should be based on his personal output, and hence can be the same, less, or more than his group's average. Thus, using the above figures, 4,000 bushels of wheat are the exchange equivalent of 750 pairs of men's shoes. But an individual farmer's reward may be at an equivalent rate. If he produced only 3,000 bushels of wheat, his reward in pairs of men's shoes is 562; if he produced 5,000 bushels per kmh he is entitled, under normal conditions, to 937 pairs.

Planning is not an easy matter—particularly planning with rates. Dependable facts are essential to any planning that attempts to control events by controlling the rates of movement of contributing factors. And the kmh system was Alford's method for analyzing rates for planning applicable to the nation, to an industry, or to an individual concern.

The advantages he claimed for the method were that (1) it presented all facts in the same mental focus, (2) it revealed obscured and unrecognized relations, and (3) it showed up cause and effect more readily since it put the information and the interpretation in the same time relation.

The Alford-Hannum studies attempted more than mere analysis applicable to any kind of productive work. They gave and analyzed hundreds of actual rates for all principal factors in American business, industry, and agriculture. They presented major findings of great importance in man-hour planning. Some were in sharp contrast to accepted belief, but all showed points of agreement between good management and good economics.

For convenience, the findings may be grouped under six headings: Production and Productivity, Costs and Values, Wages

---

10 Rautenstrauch, *Economics of Business Enterprise,* p. 378, giving credit to Alford, used a rate based, not on 1,000 hours but on the number of productive hours per year (2,000) or per month (175).

and Salaries, Employment and Work Hours, Plant and Organization Capacities, and Financial Results and Profits. However, their disclosures can be postponed until after a closer examination of the kmh method, the kmh rate, and (naturally) the law of operating rates.

THE KMH METHOD

After the first collection of man-hour data for the AEC had been made in 1926 and after the resulting report on Safety and Production had been issued in 1927, there lay before Alford and Hannum, to use Alford's unpublished words, "a mass of material . . . [which] . . . like a promising mine . . . had been partially opened by shafts and tunnels, but where some of the richest ore-bodies had not been exposed, much less assayed."

Three one and a half billion man-hours worked in American industry by two and a half million men and women formed the basis for the analysis by the kmh method. From almost one hundred tables of manufacturing rates came the kmh method of measuring, evaluating, and controlling operation and performance in industry, business, and agriculture. The original tables had been computed and studied, hitherto obscured relations had been recognized and investigated, and facts had been formulated into statements and checked—and, Alford's private writings reveal, "not until all these steps were taken, did the kmh method begin to emerge as an idea."

BASIS OF THE KMH METHOD

The kmh method of industrial analysis, planning, and control is, of course, based on the man-hour—a derivative of *time,* one of the most universal of all measures used in industrial operation. *Time* is a factor used in determining standard times, computing payrolls, and finding labor costs.

However, the kmh method reverses the usual relationship. In ordinary industrial use, time is the variable and the factor under discussion is the constant: 4.5 minutes per piece, 72 hours per 1,000 pieces, etc. The kmh method allows the factor to be the variable that is expressed in terms of the man-hour: 750 pairs of shoes per kmh.

An example may better demonstrate Alford's argument for the greater concreteness offered by the kmh method of expression. Consider the following sets of figures of production rates at three hosiery mills:

Mill Number	Time in Hours Per Pair	Dozen Pairs Per kmh
1	0.508	164
2	0.208	400
3	0.150	555

In short, the kmh method allows concentration on the factor under study, while the usual method diverts the mind to focus attention on a none too familiar division of time.

Kmh rates for simultaneous events often allow the determination of additional rates by inspection. Thus if for an industrial process there is a productivity of 309 tons of output per kmh, a wage rate of $355 per kmh, and a supervision cost of $70 per kmh, etc., an easy comparison can be made between labor and supervision costs.

CHARACTERISTICS OF THE KMH BASE

The main reasons for the lack of acceptance of many of the previous attempts at formulation of a base measurement or rate can be found in one or all of the four characteristics which, Alford insisted, such base factors must possess:

1. It must be measurable by a common established unit.
2. It must have universal use in industry.
3. It must be easy to handle in computation.
4. It must be influential in its effect on industrial operation.

A good example of such a compound factor, although limited to the safety question, is the expression of accident frequency in terms of lost-time accidents per 1,000 man-hours worked.

The time factor seems to satisfy the first three characteristics, but what of the fourth? To satisfy it, there must be a relationship between time and human effort. The requirements set forth the demand that, as changes take place in operation, they must exercise major influences on the results. Clearly, then, a production factor is indicated.

Few production factors are similar, none is the same. Plant sites and layouts, processes and methods, materials and products —all vary one from the other. Definitely, management and operating methods, as well as financial and administrative policies, are far from the same.

Is there, then, any production factor that *is* the same?

Alford implied that there was, and it was *human effort.* Workers are much the same wherever they are found in industry. They are, for the most part, little skilled. Labor turnover records indicate their mobility and their movement not only from one plant to another but from one industry to another. As for training, generally speaking, only a few days—sometimes only a few hours—comprise an effective period in which a worker may be brought up to a satisfactory rate of production on the most specialized manufacturing operations. Finally, according to the Segur "Law," any expert worker on standard operations has the same capacity for doing work as any other.

Thus, the production factor—human effort as applied in manufacturing—has many of the characteristics of the desired constant, were it only possible to express it by a measured unit. Unfortunately, it is not possible, at least not at the present development of industry, to evaluate it satisfactorily by any acceptable unit of measurement. All that can be done at present is to apply a time measurement to the interval during which the effort is applied and thereby measure the rate of output in terms of time worked. In all this, of course, there is an underlying assumption: on the average, an hour's work in one industry or plant is the substantial equivalent in human effort (mental, manual, or combined) of an hour's work in another industry or plant.

The use of time measurement of the duration of human effort in doing work has the support of other investigators. Probably one of the most important of these is W. N. Polakov,[11] who maintained:

The practical task of controlling production must begin with measurement, and, to be correct, measurement must be in the proper dimension. We cannot use for measuring work the units of mechanical power, such as the foot-pound or the horsepower, which embraces only the muscular work of man, even though these expressions contain the time rate, for it would be a comparison of the part with the whole. The time rate of man's work (that is, the man-hour) is the only measure of production which is of the same dimensionality as the energy causing it.

Thus the fourth requirement of the kmh base—relating to its influence on industrial operation—is satisfied by the selected time factor. It is to be noted that what is actually being taken is "human effort or labor expressed on a time basis."

For evidence that labor, of all the production factors, has the greatest effect on output, "for equal percentage changes," Alford went back to a matter that had concerned him during his codification of the management fundamentals.[12] This was the production formula that Cobb and Douglas had deduced mathematically from a study of the manufacturing production of the United States during the 1899-1922 period.

$$P = bL^{3/4}C^{1/4}$$

where P = production
  b = 1.01
  L = production factor *labor*
  C = production factor *fixed capital*.

In brief, this implied that a certain change in the labor factor alone had "three times" the effect on production of the identical production change from the single factor, fixed capital.

Another manifestation of the importance of the labor-effect factor is the emphasis that is placed on it in "cost reduction"—a

[11] "The Measurement of Human Work," in *Management Engineering*, 2, No. 2, 911-913, February (1922).

[12] See above, pp. 153-54. See also 1928 Corollary to the second law of Economic Production under Production Planning and Control in the Appendix, Part I.

matter that has been given a prominent place in every manufacturing program since the decline of handicraft production and the rise of modern management.

MAN-HOUR SPECIFICATIONS

It was typical of Alford not to leave matters to chance. Since there often is an opportunity for a choice of man-hours for which computation may be made, it was not enough merely to maintain that there must be an operating relation between the hours worked and their associated factor and that care must be exercised. Although the details need not be given here, he actually set down three detailed specifications adopted by the AEC and the Committee on Safety and Production, the U.S. Bureau of the Census, and the Committee on Technological Employment of the U.S. Department of Labor.

KMH COMPARISONS

On the basis of the kmh, many factors of operation may be expressed. Some of these are:

Productivity: Physical Volume of product per kmh
Employment: Number of workers per kmh
Fixed Capital Investment:
 Buildings: Dollar investment per kmh
        Floor area per kmh
 Machinery: Dollar investment per kmh
        Horsepower utilized per kmh
Primary Power: Horsepower utilized per kmh
Industrial Accidents:
 Fatality: Number of deaths resulting from accidents per kmh
 Severity: Number of working hours lost per kmh
 Frequency: Number of working hours lost per kmh
Costs:
 Wages, Material Costs
 Prime Cost, Overhead
 Charges, Manufacturing
 Cost, etc.: Dollars per kmh

Profit:
  Manufacturing
  Net, etc.: Dollars per kmh
Selling Price: Dollars per kmh

Some examples may be culled from the numerous applications made by Alford and Hannum. Thus, accident severity in telephone service may be indicated by 3.93 days lost per kmh; productivity in sheep-killing by 1,450 dressed hundred weight per kmh and in laying of water mains by 6,650 linear feet per kmh; seed cost in potato-raising by $360 per kmh; administrative cost in a plywood concern by $53 per kmh.

Of course other combinations are also expressible, such as optimum capacity range of blast furnace operation (270 to 640 kmh per year), maintenance cost of steam railway equipment ($941 per maintenance of equipment kmh), and so on.

Then, too, comparisons can be made: "kind with kind of product" (260 tons per kmh for anthracite and 655 tons per kmh for bituminous coal), "year with year" (36.8 tons per kmh for zinc products in one year compared with 45.4 tons per kmh in another), "area with area" (75 acres per kmh for oat production in the Piedmont Plateau compared with 78 acres per kmh in the coastal plains), "store with store" ($7,170 per kmh for one grain store compared to $12,300 per kmh for another), etc.

Without even going into details, the power of such comparisons is immediately apparent.

THE KMH RATE

It must be remembered that, under the kmh method, emphasis is on the fact that it is concerned with *rates*. Just as our striking mechanical progress came from a clearer understanding of the laws of motion, so too is the control of our agricultural and industrial production dependent on an understanding of the fundamentals of motion.

For the control of any productive performance—be it that in a plant, an industry, or a nation—must be "the control of rates, rates of change, and energies, rather than the control of the quantities of the factors of input and output."

Without going into the details of the numerous tables that fill the Alford-Hannum discussions of kmh, perhaps a suggestion of the attack may be of interest. Take, for example, the very familiar data given for a particular industry by the Census of Manufactures. Here are the unclassified data of "number of establishments," "number of employees," "value of product," etc. Suppose the analysis is to be done in terms of wages. The data will be regrouped, and the same items mentioned will be given for groups or classes of "average amount paid as wages (dollars)": under 100,000, from 100,000 to 199,999, from 200,000 to 299,999, etc. Next these classes will be treated not in terms of dollars but in terms of "wage rates" (dollars per kmh), and the corresponding items will be determined (still in regular units: value of product in dollars, quantity of product in tons, etc.). Finally, the corresponding items for each of the classes will be calculated (now as value of product dollars per kmh, etc.).

Now the comparisons may be made. The firms, being classified in accordance with the average wages they pay, can now be seen to have a certain value of product (dollars per kmh): those in one wage category may be seen to have a definite value of product, those in the next higher wage category have another value of product, and so on.

The kmh method does not stop at comparisons, for it is also possible to consider the kmh change of rate. To use an analogy from mechanics, it is possible to study accelerations as well as differences in velocities. Once again the significance should be apparent.

THE LAW OF OPERATING RATES

Are there any laws or principles applicable in this study? The one that Alford formulated here is the Law of Operating Rates. Since his original formulation came before he was completely influenced by Urwick's distinction between *law* and *principle*, he called it *law*. Of course, in his *Principles* text, he later changed it to *principle*.

Be that as it may, he formulated this fundament under consideration as follows:

> Operating performance is controlled most directly through control of the rates of expenditure of labor, material, and expense.

Alford liked to explain this fundamental by an analogy: "We wish to drive our automobile from our home to a certain city that is precisely 350 miles away, and we wish to cover this route in 10 hours driving precisely." With three measuring devices at our disposal—an odometer, a chronometer, and a speedometer—our objective can be accomplished in any of three ways. First, make time the major factor, and, at definite intervals of time, note the distance traveled to see if the mileage at each is too little, too great, or just right. Second, do the reverse and make the distance the major factor, noting the time at definite intervals of distance.

These two methods require (1) two simultaneous observations for each check and (2) a comparison, after the figures have been obtained, with a prepared schedule to determine how the actual is comparing with the planned.

The third method is more direct and fits in better with the relation between cause and effect. All that is necessary is to watch the speedometer and keep the car at 35 miles per hour. If the speed is more, use the brake; if less, use the accelerator.

The kmh rate is of equal value in connection with the control of operating performance that the mph rate is in regard to the car's journey. Each rate has a time basis, and each connects a major operating factor with time. Each may be checked at any place or time or situation during the operating performance. Each, if correctly determined and properly maintained, can give advance assurance of realizing the ultimate objective.

PRODUCTION AND PRODUCTIVITY

Alford and Hannum used the kmh system to probe *production* ("goods, articles, and services which are the physical work-result of effort expended in agriculture, construction, extraction, manufacturing, public service, and transportation") and *productivity* ("kmh rate at which physical volume of goods, articles, and services is produced"). Their analysis showed proof of a fact that is even today being demonstrated: "American industry can produce an abundance of all the good things in life for all the people, much more in volume than has ever before been turned out, even in the years of greatest business activity."

COSTS AND VALUES

Cost relations and relative values are important but not easily studied. There is essentially no universal agreement among businessmen, accountants, engineers, and economists as to their application, treatment, and philosophy.

Alford and Hannum presented their kmh method as a means of solving many cost problems and overcoming difficulties in value determination. Basically these authors insisted that there are two (and only two) components in costs and values for pricing: labor and materials; every other item, analyzed back to its source, is either one or the other of these two elements of cost. And the most practical instrument for their measurement is labor—human energy expressed in time (i.e., the interval during which it is expended).

Thus, the kmh is applicable both to the budget and to standard costs, and in these time rates rather than quantities are considered.

WAGES AND SALARIES

Among the relations revealed by the kmh method were the accompaniment of high wage rates with high salary rates, high wage rates with high production rates, and high salary rates with high production rates. Even these few revelations are significant. They imply in the higher range unit factory cost and high selling value per unit of labor and supervision cost. The kmh findings challenged the often used practice of wage, piece-rate, and salary cutting to achieve cost reduction.

EMPLOYMENT AND WORK HOURS

The difficulties involved in understanding problems relating to employment and hours of work, Alford and Hannum insisted, were aggravated by the lack of organized facts and data, in turn due to inadequate statistics, analysis, and interpretation. They wanted an enormous amount of information concerning inanimate goods and deplored the dearth of data on the potentialities and utilization of human energy at work: "It appears that in our economic thinking we have put corn and cattle ahead of men and women."

Polakov, in *The Power Age: Its Quest and Challenge,* in 1928, suggested the adoption of the kmh method for these studies. Some governmental agencies did adopt the method in connection with employment studies:

If A = Average number of workers employed

B = Total number of man-hours worked

C = Total quantity of product output

D = Total number of workers employed

then $B/1000$ = Employment rate (Number of kmh worked per year)

$C/(\text{kmh worked})$ = Productivity rate (Quantity of product output per kmh)

$D/(\text{kmh worked})$ = Working force requirement or labor stability rate (Total number of workers per kmh)

A/C = Labor utilization rate (Average number of workers per unit of product output)

C/A = Labor performance rate (Quantity of product output per worker)

B/A = Labor time rate (Number of kmh worked per worker)

B/C = Time utilization rate (Number of man-hours worked per unit of product output)

Here, for example, the authors maintained that the number of kmh worked and not the average number of workers employed was the correct measure of the employment trend. Thus the trend is indicated by a *rate*.

PLANT AND ORGANIZATION CAPACITIES

Alford illustrated "American exuberance" by referring to the usual answer given by too many to the questions as to how much a plant could produce and how much business an organization can do: "The sky is the limit." He was emphatic in showing that the "controlling factors are quite different from the atmosphere."

The kmh method showed factually the effectiveness of small plants in the matters of rates and costs of production as well as in earnings on capital investment—a matter amply demonstrated in the trend toward dissolution of large industrial units.

The method again advocates the use of man-hours worked as a measure for capacity of plant or organization, because of the universality of time. Money value of product was not a proper measure of capacity because of value variations, and physical volume had only limited application to simple products and continuous processes.

The kmh system was concerned in the main with the measurement of five types of capacities: Maximum (or Potential), Break-Even, Optimum, Operating, and Excess.

FINANCIAL RESULTS AND PROFITS

One of the great shortcomings of accounting methods is that they show only end results, in dollars and cents, and are based on the idea that the sole purpose of business and industry is to earn a profit on the capital invested. In the face of Alford's serious infection by Gantt's service doctrine, it would not be difficult to surmise that the kmh plan would have nobler motives.

The kmh method attempts to connect the items of both the

balance sheet and profit-and-loss statement by means of the man-hours worked. It thus shows how invested capital provides employment for workers and how changes in capital assets and surplus relate to kmh—matters which are not shown by the commonly used financial ratios.

SOME FINDINGS BY THE KMH METHOD

A summary of some of the more important findings, authenticated by numerous tables, graphs, and analyses, serve to give not only some indication of the method but the reasons for Alford's staunch advocacy:

1. Industries that are recognizable as prosperous have high selling rates. (These products are largely in the luxury class.)

2. Low selling-value products (largely staples and necessities) are connected with industries "notorious because of business troubles."

3. The selling-value rates of agricultural products are in the same range as manufactured necessities.

4. Low prime-cost rates accompany high production rates.

5. High prime-cost rates accompany low production rates.

6. High wage rates accompany high salary rates.

7. Low wage rates accompany low salary rates.

8. High wage rates accompany high production rates.

9. Low wage rates accompany low production rates.

10. High salary rates accompany high production rates.

11. Low salary rates accompany low production rates.

12. The number of hours worked is a more accurate measure of the trend of employment than the average number of workers or a census of the unemployed.

13. Man-hour employment in well-managed companies can be reduced about 4 per cent annually as a result of increasing productivity without reducing the quantity of product output.

14. An analysis of operating factors (in four major industries: Blast Furnace Operation, Machine Tool Building, Petroleum Refining, and Lumber Manufacturing) shows that, if the productivity of the less efficient plants could be raised to the average efficiency for the industry, as much as 25 per cent reduction in man-hour employment would result, and, if the productivity of all plants were

at that of the highest in the industry, more than 55 per cent reduction in man-hour employment would result. (Hence, fewer and fewer man-hours per unit of product will be needed by American industry, and "man-hour employment can be increased only by increasing the volume of business.")

15. High production rates accompany short work periods.
16. Low production rates accompany long work periods.
17. High wage rates accompany short work periods.
18. Low wage rates accompany long work periods.
19. High salary rates accompany short work periods.
20. Low salary rates accompany long work periods.
    (Hence, these findings indicate the advocacy of a shorter work week.)
21. For the most effective operating performance, the optimum capacity of an industrial plant should be small.
22. In general, the small-capacity plant is more efficient than the large-capacity plant.
    (Question: Is effective operation closely associated with intimate, personal, managerial supervision?)
23. In agricultural operation, as opposed to industrial operation, the optimum size should be large.
    (Hence, an increase in size of such operations in the U.S. would be a sound policy.)

THE MODUS OPERANDI

Coming as it did during a time—the late 1920's and the early 1930's—when business stability was a paramount question, many of the "popularizers" seized the kmh method and its planning aspects as being a panacea for the current economic ills. Although the authors might have admitted its applicability to the times, they never claimed or attempted to peddle any patent remedy. Alford and Hannum, however, did offer kmh as an aid to the major problem of the ever-increasing distribution of the necessities, comforts, and luxuries of life. To attain the goal, the authors advocated an increase in production—which can be achieved by increasing the application of human energy (of which there is an abundance), improving the effectiveness of below-average plants (for which there is a great opportunity), and increasing the productive capacity of the average worker (which is a continuous process).

Even then both Alford and Hannum recognized America's possession of great productive powers and capacities which, they felt, were sufficient for any foreseeable demand. Consequently, they maintained that real national planning must set forth a doctrine of "abundant plenty for everyone as an inalienable right."

Alford claimed that the two basic steps in such a planning program were the formulation of the goal in clear statements and the continued use of this goal as a gauge for planning and performance decisions and details.

For the achievement of these steps, the answers to six questions must be found. The first three questions:

1. What services and goods *will* be needed?
2. How much of each of these *will* be needed?
3. When *will* they be needed?

The next three questions that need answering are merely the restatement of the first three questions with *must* substituted for *will*.

The answers to these questions give the rate of demand for goods and services by consumers during a definite period as well as the rate of production that must be maintained to satisfy that need. In short, what is *needed* is the knowledge of a demand rate followed by a control of a production rate-making for proper correspondence.

Additional planning steps may now be added. Alford advocated such additional requirements as "getting the facts," determining the content as well as the form of the information, deciding which agency shall be responsible for gathering, compiling, and publicizing the facts, and, finally, how the facts shall be organized and interpreted.

Kmh was, of course, Alford's suggestion as to how the last step should be taken. To repeat, he felt that the rates were needed and that these rates should be time rates. He allowed any factor to be used as the numerator providing the event took place in the identical time used for the denominator. But, "because men are more important and of more value than things, materials, and machines, we advocate the use of man-hours for the denominator."

The last step in planning concerned the responsibility for and the enforcement of the schedules. Here the mechanism of control is implied, a matter which, Alford insisted, would be greatly facilitated by the latent power of the kmh system.

Again and again, in his treatment of kmh, Alford stresses on the one hand the planning aspects, and on the other the control aspects. He passes from one to the other with remarkable ease. This ability, although he does not express it in so many words, is an indication of his proximity to the elements of what is now known as "Management Control."

Alford had come so close to this "new" concept that it deserves closer attention. It is one of the paradoxes of the present management development that so little has been published on so important a subject. Conceived and nurtured in semisecrecy, few of its present proponents have given it any of the publicity it deserves and management needs.

One reason for the lack of widespread publication is the fact that it is more easily practiced than preached: it lends itself more to action than to the printed word. Furthermore, too few have given proper attention to the fundamental concepts on which it is built.

Curiously, the very term "management control" is inappropriate because *both* planning and control are involved. In addition, Rathe, for example, feels that the very word "control" seems to imply, to many, some kind of restraint out of tune with the popular notion of "freedom." He has entertained the possibility of describing this planning-control notion by the term "management service." However, because of Gantt's use of "service" in another connection, he, for one, is more inclined toward "management guidance," a term derived from the function of the "executive's instrument panel."

Whatever the term, there must be, in the concept itself, an "interplay of planning and control." Not only do these two have an affinity for each other but, if either is to be meaning-ful, they must be inseparable. Thus, the budget is an exam-ple of this planning-control combination. So, too, is Alford's kmh.

Aside from the concomitance of planning and control through all Alford's treatment, his favorite analogy also shows his an-ticipation of the "new" concept. What more tangible evidence is needed than his description in terms of the speedometer? Of course, "the Executive's Instrument Panel" may include many more dials than a mere speedometer, but Alford had the basic one—and the fundamental idea for his "rate" was not only a "planning" device but a "control" as well.

RECAPITULATION

As the fundamental principles of kmh have already been set forth, some of its aspects should be emphasized. It must be remembered that these are not obvious concepts. As a matter of fact, the fact that kmh was not accorded complete accept-ance is evidence of its not having been completely understood.

Three concepts that merit emphasis are:

1. Operating performance is not "capable" of direct meas-urement.
2. Time is the basic unit in the kmh scheme.
3. Kmh involves rates and not quantities.

Mention has been made of Polakov's assertion—inserted by Wallace Clark in the Appendix of the first edition of *The Gantt Chart*—that the mechanical measurement of work in terms of foot-pounds is inadequate, for it concerns only the muscular aspects of man's work. This is in line with the views of Knoeppel who insisted that the basic item in production was not the material object, but rather the "thinking." (Emer-son himself had expressed the notion that a single idea may have more importance than all the physical labor of men, ani-mals, and machines.) Thus, the objects that roll off the as-sembly lines—radios, automobiles, fountain pens—are not the real products but only manifestations of the true product, namely, thinking. According to this concept of Knoeppel, "a successful industry is successful because time measures an efficient thinking, or productive human energy." Obviously, an unsuccessful industry is just the opposite.

Alford looked on these views of Polakov and Knoeppel as supports of his "contention that the time factor is basic." His next step, however, was a logical necessity.

Since many persons contribute their work, it was necessary to recognize the parts played by all. Hence, he introduced the concept of combining the time all spent, man-hours. For simplification, he divided by 1,000 and obtained kilo man-hours.

An analogy might be appropriate here. Every engineer has had the opportunity of studying—if not in practice then during his training in a calculus class—the rates of flow of liquids into and out of tanks of various shapes. The fact that shapes differed—here was a spherical tank, here was a conical one, here a cylindrical one, and so on—did not deter his study. All he did was calculate the volume and express the rate in terms of dV/dt.

Instead of differently shaped tanks, here are different items —industrial accidents or physical volume of product or dollars of invested machinery. The problem now is to determine the respective rates in terms of performance, or rather in terms of the substitute measure that is being used, namely, time. Thus, for example, although Alford talks of the rate expressed as the number of deaths resulting from accidents per kmh, it would have been more appropriate had he talked of the rate d(number of deaths resulting from accidents)$/d$(kmh).

To express it graphically, the quantity under consideration (e.g., capital investment, industrial accidents, etc.) is measured along the Y axis, while time (or rather kmh) is measured along the X axis. Thus the familiar dY/dX now can be translated in terms of Alford's kmh rates.

Just as it is easy for the engineer to compare rates of flow among different-sized cylindrical tanks, so is it easy for him to compare dollar investment per kmh in different-sized plants.

If the engineer could express all these different concepts—capital investment, wages, etc.—in some relationship just as he can bring all the different-shaped tanks down to a volume formula, then he could have universal measures of performance. Even Alford admitted that "not all the compound factors that may be built up from the kilo man-hour base are applicable" in instances where the products are different.

However, one point must be realized: as industry becomes more and more mechanized, the more and more similar do the performances in all industries become. That is to say, as industry goes to servomechanisms, push-button mechanization, and automation, the less will be the distinctions between labor in a bakery, for example, and that in an aircraft plant.

Juran has often remarked about the high degree of interchangeability at both the top and the bottom of the organization ladder. The president of an automobile company does equally well as president of a food concern. So, too, the sweeper in a plant manufacturing radio tubes works as efficiently in a candy factory. It is only in the middle that there is what Thorstein Veblen called "trained incapacity," that is, the inability that restrains persons from working with any product other than that with which they were trained. Increased mechanization should reduce the number so affected.

THREE PERSONAL COMMENTS BY ALFORD ON KMH

Among Alford's private papers there are three references that he personally made and that are particularly descriptive of the high hopes he had held and the resulting disappointment he had encountered in his kmh investigations.

The first of these was written in 1931. He was reminiscing about the reception afforded the first paper that he and Hannum presented to ASME at the December, 1928, meeting:

. . . The discussion was most animated, and in the main friendly. We had to meet only one vicious attack from an economist. About 70 individual professional papers were presented at this meeting of the Society, and distributed in reprint form. One quarter of all the copies of all the papers distributed were of this paper of ours. During 1930 this same paper was the "best seller" of all of the Society's publications.

Possibly the most gratifying response, however, was the letters we received, in the main asking for more information. About 250 came during the first few months of 1930, and they are still coming (in 1931) at the rate of about one a week. Newspapers and magazines gave the paper and its idea space in both news columns and editorial comment. Clippings have come to us from Canada, England, France, and Sweden. Assuming that any collection of clippings does not represent more than one tenth of the publicity obtained, the amount accorded us for the Kilo-man-hour idea and method was most gratifying.

In addition, Alford referred to a "particularly happy appreciation" by E. E. Free, "in 'New York' for February 2, 1930." It commented that "all the best ideas are simple," that Alford and Hannum had given enterprises a method comparable to that used by electrical engineers in rating electric motors and locomotives, and that, with the justified popularization and publicity afforded by the *New York Evening Post,* the authors "promise to be credited with nothing less than a revolution in business assaying."

The second comment was one made by Alford, in his personal files, in 1934. It was not as lengthy as the first but was essentially hopeful. It referred to the second paper that he presented to the ASME meeting in 1932: "The discussion was extensive and complimentary, particularly in regard to the significance of the major findings. The general publicity on this paper was not so extensive as its predecessor of 1928."

The third reference was made in 1937, and it referred to the fact that in 1934 "Mr. Joshua E. Hannum and I wrote a book based on our KMH studies." Alford's comment, though very much shorter than the other two, was more meaningful: "We failed to find a publisher." It is on this unpublished manuscript, *Man-Hour Planning*—which remained in the Alford files at Montclair for more than twelve years after his death and which was included in the papers given by his son, Ralph, to the department Alford once headed at NYU's University Heights—that much of the analysis presented here is based.

CRITICAL ANALYSIS OF KMH

What had happened between the heralded rise of kmh and its eventual resignation to limbo, all in a matter of little more than five years?

Was its decline due to its own basic fallacy of fundamentals? Was it due to any fault in its presentation? Was it caused by any unjustified overextension of its own? Or was it the victim of an unappreciative audience, an unsympathetic environment, and perhaps the spirit of the times?

With the exception of the first question—its basic dependence on the time measurement *is* fundamentally correct—the answers to the other questions have a bit of the affirmative in all of them. A closer examination of some of the details may help to bring out these facts.

Perhaps the best place to begin this examination is with a consideration of the soundness of the basic fundamentals, namely, is time a sound basis for measurement of performance?

Even during the discussion that followed the presentation of the paper at the ASME meeting in 1928, Polakov, Knoeppel, and others agreed that this was proper.

At that time, too, G. D. Bearce, who showed the application of the kmh analysis to a study of two paper mills, called the kmh "a logical standard." W. C. Wright based his agreement on the correctness of the unit by showing that it afforded the baking industry a method of studying even obsolescence of plant and equipment.

This does not imply that there was no criticism of the studies, for there naturally was to a certain extent. However, with only one possible exception, none challenged the fundamentals. Most of the criticisms asserted the need for further study of limitations and the impropriety of using the method

for interindustrial (rather than for only intraindustrial) analysis. There were also the criticisms implying that the method
was too constrained. Before considering any of these, an examination of the one which, in his private papers, Alford called
"vicious" is in order.

The "economist" was Hudson B. Hastings, Professor of Industrial Engineering at Yale, whose criticism was essentially
based on "productive efficiency of labor and capital," which,
he insisted, when increased reduces selling prices and consequently cannot make for any permanent increase in selling
value per kmh. Alford attempted to underestimate this criticism because of an unfortunate statement that revealed Hastings' lack of appreciation of the concept.

Much of the Alford argument was based on the greater importance attached to *rates* than to *quantities*. Yet in his criticism Hastings questioned the findings on the basis of underemphasis of *quantities*. Unfortunately, he gave no concrete
proof of the supposedly fallacious consideration. Hence, by a
single stroke, Alford nullified Hastings' criticisms, completely
incorrect or not, by asserting that "he seems to have reasoned
from opinions."

Alford must have felt deeply about the matter, for nowhere
else in his writings did he refer so pointedly to unfavorable
opinions.

Among other of Hastings' criticisms was the question as to
whether, in making interindustry comparisons, consideration
need not be given to labor and depreciation costs accumulated
before the product reached the plant in question. The point
in question, of course, does disregard the question of rates!
However, before Hastings can be accused of any lack of appreciation of "our purpose" or a failure to "sense the possibilities of our analytic method," it must be remembered that
communication does not imply that mere words be transmitted.
Only meaningful words can be effective.

However, in many of the criticisms by others, the same
theme is constantly repeated: should not the method be limited to the same industry and product? As a matter of fact,

even Bearce, who used the method effectively in regard to two paper mills, asked this very question in regard to a wider application in comparing dissimilar industries. Alford hinted that "without doubt" perhaps not all of the compound factors resulting from the kmh base were helpful here, "but we believe that many can be used to great advantage."

Let us consider Coes's ideas on kmh. Realizing that there was a lack of any unit capable of being directly able to correlate human effort as applied in industry with production, he felt that the limitations imposed must never be lost sight of in building up a method of application. E. M. Herr, Westinghouse president, also regretted the inability to establish limitations on the method. Alford agreed that these must come only after much experimentation and trial—and it did require a great deal of additional operating information.

Coes felt that, "if there were a uniform basis of comparison," the method could develop a great many additional compound factors, such as raw materials per kmh, work in process per kmh, etc.

It may be of interest to note Coes's views of almost twenty-five years later when interviewed, without the benefit of any notes or references to his previous remarks, by the author of this study.

Among the main difficulties, he felt, was the collection of basic data. Without going into the problem of diverse skills among workers, various capacities among machines, and such matters, how can one easily account for the production and correction of "bad" parts? Of course, it might be possible with the growth of quality control that such a problem may eventually be reduced to a minimum, but the time is not yet here. Coes admitted that he was always "intrigued" by the idea, but that he had never used it. He questioned whether or not it might cost more to set up than it could save. Nevertheless, in numerous conversations with Alford, he always said that, once the method was begun and reached wider application, these difficulties would be overcome.

But the method never—at least, not yet—reached any wide application.

From the foregoing it can be seen that, although the method was *basically* sound, it needed more extensive study. But it could not be kept alive unless it was given wider application, and, of course, it could not be given wider application unless it was kept alive. Why?

For the most part, the method was not simple, and the studies were not completely understood. The lack of simplicity was to a large extent due to the fact that the basic measure was not a direct one, and therefore not easy to comprehend. The lack of understanding by the audience can also be explained by the fact that the presentation was often lost in detailed tables.

It is evident from the Hastings criticism, at least, that the first presentation was not too clear. It was not until the unpublished manuscript was written that there was any explanation for the emphasis placed on the "rate" aspect. Certainly, the "kmh rate" was mentioned frequently in the earlier presentation, but it lost its pointedness because it was used almost interchangeably with "kmh factor" and "kmh unit." This, no doubt, prevented the general reader from fixing in his mind the rate idea, which in itself is not an easy concept to the layman who already had a fixed concept in terms of quantities.

This concept might not have been lost sight of if the methods and terminology of the calculus had been used. However, any such attempt would have made the applicability even more limited.

Some of the "elementary" mathematical relations were not easy for many who were interested to grasp. In many cases, even after the reader was convinced that it was more concrete to think in terms of a rate having kmh in the denominator (e.g., 400 dozen pairs of shoes per kmh, rather than 0.208 hours per pair of shoes), the Alford-Hannum treatment would refer to a ratio with the kmh in the numerator (e.g., employment per month, 9,649 kmh per month). Certainly such a concept was both logical and necessary, but it was confusing to many.

And, if the difficult concept and treatment were not enough, the times must also be considered. One might think that, during those troublesome days when the faith in "rugged individualism" of many of our citizens was somewhat shaken and interest in "planning" began to rise, some attention might have been paid to this method which, as its authors showed, was capable of being applied in planning.

Unfortunately, many incorrectly connected it with "technocracy," which had a meteoric rise and fall. Again, as far as the government was concerned, there was some question as to the type of "planning" governmental authorities advocated: for the most part, they were influenced by pressure groups rather than by true scientific thinking.

Thus, throttled on the one side by difficult basic concepts and on the other by a difficult presentation, kmh remained undeveloped.

Evidently Alford considered it his unfinished business. As Juran told the writer of this book, when someone interested in management visited Alford at Montclair, it was not unusual for Alford to spend a good part of this visit in attempting to propagate a justified faith in kmh.

It must be admitted that kmh was and is a great accomplishment. And in its authorship Alford was far ahead of his time. Basically, Alford was on the right track, and there can be little doubt that, as Alford insisted, *time* can be helpful as a measuring stick.

But although the concept of "time" may be in the right direction, it must be handled with care. Despite Alford's insistence on the support afforded by Knoeppel's beliefs in the importance of "human effort in time—or thinking in time," and in its being "the truest gage we can use in measuring and evaluating productive processes," this viewpoint is not completely free from difficulties.

Knoeppel's belief that "the less the relative cost of a thing, the greater the proof of laborsaving or saving in time, and the higher the output in the way of effort or thinking in time" is not entirely accurate. To say that an automobile has a value

of $6,410 per kmh while a certain quantity of bituminous coal
has but $1,140 per kmh is no testimony to the efficiency of one
compared to the other. Even if, for argument's sake, the com-
parability of x automobiles and y tons of coal, the economic
aspects of pricing, and other such matters were to be neglected,
this would assume to a certain degree that wages—admitting
their fundamental importance in the setting of prices—are com-
mensurate with productivity. Certainly this is a matter that is
not entirely in accord with the labor-management picture today.

It is one thing today that 750 pairs of shoes are equivalent
to 4,000 bushels of wheat on the basis of the man-hours of
work involved. As mechanization increases and as labor becomes even more similar, this statement may have some meaning. However, it is something entirely different to introduce
here that rubber yardstick called "dollars." Even Alford was
aware of this.

Of course, the kmh concept attempts to give proper recognition to the nonmanual aspects of production by the very rejection of such manual measures as foot-pounds. Nevertheless,
any universal application of measures to creative skills—assuming that they are capable of being measured—is not without
pitfalls.

Even if the difficulties of setting standards for creative work
are for the time at least forgotten, certainly Alford's premise
that, generally speaking, all labor is alike does not hold here.
If similarity is the mark of manual labor, dissimilarity is the
distinctive feature of creative work. Just as there is a distinction between the work of a da Vinci and that of even the finest
copyist, so too is there a difference in the work of engine de-
signers. The celebrated mathematician, Poincaré, worked on a
theorem for many years, but its solutions "suddenly" came to
him while boarding a train. How is the time to be set for such
"work"?

In short, we know too little about man's mental processes,
at least as yet.

Certainly kmh has its merits. Not the least of these is the

fact that it can help management by making factual many matters that were formerly accepted as opinion. For example, it took a long time for many to realize the truth of the emphasis by both Taylor and Gantt upon the fallacy of indiscriminate wage cuts as the basis for cost reduction—because it was "opinion." Today, so generally has this doctrine been accepted that many may not realize that it still is opinion, substantiated in practice, but still opinion. On the other hand, here is a device that demonstrates mathematically that what was formerly opinion is really fact, or as nearly fact as mathematics can show.

In brief, though, the kmh system contains too many latent possibilities for it to be either discarded or treated with disdain. It must be restudied, particularly in the light of the additional experience that has now become history.

This may mean a forthright examination of its basic axioms. This may entail a more mathematical analysis. This may suggest a re-examination in the light of modern statistics, a matter that has certainly reached new heights since the Alford days.

Then and then only will kmh be able to make its just claim as a potent instrument for the guidance of management.

Chapter VII

THE AMERICAN ENGINEERING COUNCIL

AMERICAN ENGINEERING COUNCIL

Among Alford's proudest recollections was that of the work that he did in the organization and maintenance of the American Engineering Council. It is indeed a paradox that despite the recognition given the work of the AEC so little is generally known of the Council itself. In fact, one of the few sources of information concerning this "most ambitious attempt at engineering unity" is an unpublished paper in the ASME files, the "story" of the AEC, by A. F. Bohenik.

Even if Alford had not played so active a part, it would have been necessary to include here an account of the AEC's work in order to understand the engineering profession during the 1920's and 1930's. Because of Alford's work on the committees and his tenure of office as vice-president of the Council, it is imperative to include some information on this body.

In June, 1920, delegates from seventy-one national, regional, state, and local engineering clubs and societies decided "to achieve unity through an agency of an over-all organization." The AEC was the result. This was not the first attempt at unifying the engineering profession. The Founder Societies (ASCE, AIMME, ASME, and AIEE) had as early as 1917 established an agency, known as the Engineering Council of the National Technical Societies of America, in order to work with the government on engineering problems rising from the war.

As a matter of fact, in April, 1919, that organization, in an attempt at mobilizing the profession for "peacetime services of a public nature," sponsored a conference of the engineering societies in order to establish a "department of public works on a cabinet level." Out of this the AEC was developed, and it eventually, in January, 1921, took over the older Council.

The AEC, it must be remembered, was a federation of societies and not of individuals. Although Bohenik refers to the organization as the AEC and explains that it operated by means of a council (later known as an "administrative board"), the reports—e.g., *Waste in Industry*—refer to the AEC as the Executive Board of the Federated American Engineering Societies.

In any event, membership in the AEC was accorded to representatives of participating societies on the basis of one representative per 1,000 members. Financial aid was supposed to come from the member societies in the beginning on the basis of membership, but in later years in terms of a flat fee.

Although the AEC had a distinguished membership which, during its existence, included a president of the United States as well as presidents and officials of numerous engineering societies, corporations, and colleges, L. W. Wallace, who became the AEC secretary, wrote to Roe on May 11, 1942:

It may be said that throughout the life of the American Engineering Council, no man served it in more capacities, or with greater courage, loyalty, ability and devotion, than did L. P. Alford. To the interest and work of Council he gave unstintingly of his time, energy, experience, and balanced judgment. He made this contribution because of his conviction that Council was an instrument of public service. He made this contribution on the high plane of unselfish motives and as a mark of his devotion to the eternal principles of unselfish motives and as a mark of his devotion to the eternal principles of right and justice.

Even before the formation of the AEC, Alford was the ASME representative on the older Engineering Council and he continued on after the AEC was formed. His work in the organization of the AEC may be judged by the fact that he, aided by

Kimball and Wallace, was successful in including in the statement of purpose of the AEC the lesson he had learned so well from Gantt, namely, "service." Consequently the aim of the organization was clearly defined:

Engineering is the science of controlling the forces and utilizing the materials of nature for the benefit of man, and the art of organizing and directing human activities in connection therewith.

As service to others is the expression of the highest motive to which men respond and as duty to contribute to the public welfare demands the best efforts men can put forth, NOW, THEREFORE, the engineering and technical societies of the United States of America, through the formation of The Federated American Engineering Societies, realize a long cherished ideal,—a comprehensive organization dedicated to the service of the community, state, and nation.

To cite briefly some of Alford's other posts on the AEC, he held continuous membership as ASME's representative until January, 1925, and he had served as vice-chairman in 1924. In 1928, he was again reappointed and again served as vice-chairman. He continued his duties as representative until 1940, although in 1938 he was an alternate. Thus he was, except for a few years, a member of the Council throughout its life and, for a good part of this term, he was chairman of the ASME delegation.

Alford was originally appointed temporary executive secretary of the Council, and he continued in this post until Wallace took over. In addition to other duties he was for many years chairman of the original Committee on Publicity and Publications. On more than one occasion he served on the Public Affairs Committee. Several times he served as a member of the Executive Committee of the Council, as well as on its subcommittees.

However, despite his many posts and duties, Alford's great contributions, like those of the AEC itself, lay in the reports that were issued. As will be apparent, he played a large part in the preparation of the most important of these—*Waste in Industry, The Twelve Hour Shift, Safety and Production,* and

The Balancing of Economic Forces. Also, as AEC representative, he contributed to the renowned *Recent Economic Changes.*

Before discussing these reports more closely a review of the proud history of the AEC, plagued almost continually by financial matters from its beginning (during the recession of the early 1920's) to its end (during the depression of the 1930's), should be continued.

In addition to the reports cited, the AEC produced numerous others. These included such matters as a survey of Commercial Aviation (which led to the establishment of a Bureau of Aviation in the Commerce Department), a standard code on Street Traffic Signs, Signals, and Markings, to mention but a few. The AEC fulfilled its objective of public service by making available for the public interest the abilities, training, and experience of the best engineering personnel in the country. Thus it aided congressional committees on such matters as Forestry, Topographic Surveys, National Hydraulic Laboratory, Patents, and Public Health. For the profession it maintained a roster of names and records of 115,000 engineers.

Yet despite its brilliant record the AEC was eventually terminated: although there may have been other matters, no small part was due to finances. Despite the fact that seventy-one clubs and societies took part in the original organization meeting, the AEC was eventually supported mainly by the ASME, the AIEE, and (after its entrance in 1929) the ASCE. These three organizations contributed from 75 to 95 per cent of the total AEC income.

In 1939, unrest and dissatisfaction led to the appointment of a Joint Committee, made up of representatives of ASCE, ASME, AIEE, and AEC, for the re-examination of the basic aims. The report (July 22, 1939) still stressed the need of a strong engineering organization in Washington. Nevertheless, in 1940 both ASCE and AIEE decided to withdraw. Consequently, the Executive Council of ASME on November 8 suggested that AEC terminate its affairs. This took place officially on December 31, 1940.

In October, 1941, the five societies—ASCE, AIMME, ASME,

AIEE, and AIChE—established the Engineers Joint Council, which took over the AEC funds.

The AEC records were partially stored at George Washington University, although an incomplete file is in The Library of Congress. Just one year before his death, Alford was concerned lest the "valuable historical record of one of the great attempts of American engineering" remain confined to storage and out of reach of students of the engineering profession. Not only was he hopeful that these records would be placed in the Engineering Societies Library, but that their message would be recorded for the benefit of the profession.

WASTE IN INDUSTRY

Among the first of the reports in whose preparation Alford played a large part, was the now celebrated study, *Waste in Industry*, issued under the auspices of the AEC.[1] This report was the result of a suggestion by the Council's first president, Herbert Hoover, who favored a study of the "restrictions and wastes in industry." Exactly one day after the suggestion was made, the Executive Board approved the appointment of a committee to conduct the investigation. On January 12, 1921, Hoover named fifteen engineers—he later added two more—to the Committee on Elimination of Waste in Industry. These, in addition to Hoover and Alford, included J. P. Channing (chairman), G. D. Babcock, W. Bassett, F. G. Coburn, M. L. Cooke, H. Emerson, I. N. Hollis, E. E. Hunt, C. E. Knoeppel, R. Linton, F. J. Miller, H. V. R. Scheel, S. Thompson, L. W. Wallace (vice-chairman), J. H. Williams, and R. B. Wolf.

In accordance with its proposal, the idea was to conduct, as Hoover had expressed it, "an extensive study, carefully planned and rapidly executed" so that it could be helpful along "definite lines for further action." In less than five months, the Committee reported on an analysis of waste in six typical branches of industry—building, men's clothing, shoes, printing, metal trades,

[1] Federated American Engineering Societies' Committee on Elimination of Waste in Industry, *Waste in Industry*, McGraw-Hill Book Co., 1921.

and textiles—and presented an advanced version of its findings to the AEC meeting in St. Louis on January 3, 1921. On July 6 the complete report was edited, and publication took place on July 15.

Because it is not possible to single out Alford's contribution, any detailed discussion here would add little to this study of Alford's work. However, his influence is readily apparent to anyone who may care to examine the report, for here can be discovered the same message that runs through many of the Alford works. For example, there is the insistence that "management has the greatest opportunity and, hence, responsibility for eliminating waste in industry." (Compare, in this connection, the Alford contention concerning safety in industry.) [2] Again, waste is caused by (1) low production (faulty management), (2) interrupted production (idleness in men and equipment), (3) restricted production (by both owners and workers), and (4) lost production (accidents). The parallel with Alford's works needs no further elucidation.

Among the conclusions themselves, reiterated time and time again in the writings of Alford, is this: since the causes are known they can be pursued intelligently, providing mental and moral forces are added to the physical resources.

THE TWELVE HOUR SHIFT IN INDUSTRY

The very next year (1922) after the study on *Waste in Industry* appeared the AEC presented another report, *The Twelve Hour Shift in Industry*.[3] Like the report that preceded it, this one, the work of the committee on Work-Periods in Continuous Industry—which included, in addition to Alford, H. E. Howe (chairman), J. P. Channing, M. L. Cooke, D. T. Farnham, F. J. Miller, L. W. Wallace—also reached the status of a *classic*.

The beginnings of this study go back to about 1920 when

2 See below, pp. 225-26.

3 Federated American Engineering Societies, Committee on Work-Periods in Continuous Industry, *The Twelve Hour Shift in Industry*, E. P. Dutton & Co., 1922 (the data of the general survey were worked up by H. B. Drury; the data on the Iron and Steel Industry were worked up by B. Stoughton).

the engineering profession started a systematic study of the so-called "long day" (twelve-hour shift) in continuous process industries. The earliest recorded meeting took place at the Engineers Club in Philadelphia, in 1920, where the discussion involved the changing from the two-shift to the three-shift system in three particular industries.

Also, it was about this time that Cooke [4] made his well-known study of the progress resulting from the changeover of the steel industry to the three-shift system. Aided by a grant from the Cabot Fund, the field work was done by H. B. Drury, who reported his findings to a joint meeting of the engineering societies in New York, in December, 1920. (See *Bulletin of the Taylor Society*, Vol. 6, No. 1.) However, most of the companies included in the Drury report were rather small.

Consequently, in 1921, the Taylor Society requested the International Labor Office in Geneva to study the two-shift day in other countries. That study showed that "the shorter day is now more completely established in the fifteen foreign countries answering the questionnaire" than in the United States.

Again in 1921, Drury, aided once again by the Cabot Fund, which issued the report in 1922, studied the twelve-hour shift among the larger steel companies.

However, in 1921, the Cabot Fund made a grant to the Federated Engineering Societies to carry on two studies:

1. Extent of the two-shift day in continuous process industries (other than iron and steel).

2. Experience of manufacturers who changed from two-shift to three-shift operation.

The Committee of the Societies assigned these tasks to Drury and Stoughton, respectively.

Here, too, Alford's role is not too clear, even though his own writings emphasize the value of the shorter working day. How-

4 On August 28, 1920, Cooke wrote to Alford "informally and personally on a matter which impresses me as unusually important." It concerned the "twelve-hour shift," and Cooke asked for "counsel," "reactions," and "considered judgment," for "you are one of that type of engineer who believes that our profession has public responsibilities."

ever, it is unquestionable that he concurred in the report's conclusions:

1. The change away from the twelve-hour shift has been, for the most part, accidental, i.e., few, if any, have made any detailed "judgment as to its merits."

2. Departure from the two-shift system should be considered not so much on the basis of the extent of its usage but rather on the basis of its being too long in relation to the direction of industry "when measured by twentieth century ideas."

3. Current decisions must be made with due regard to "humanitarian considerations" and cannot be influenced *only* by purely economic questions of maximum production.

Alford, in his *Laws of Management,* pointed out that the economic loss sustained by both industry and worker in changing from the two- to the three-shift system was not great. The report came to a similar conclusion. But it did warn that a sudden change can be the cause of lowered production, and that it can be avoided if there is preplanning and co-operation with worker, management, and public.

SAFETY AND PRODUCTION

By 1928, the country was aware of the problem of industrial accidents to such an extent that forty-three states had already enacted workmen's compensation laws and the safety program was being enriched by the efforts of thousands of people and the efficacy of millions of dollars. The general trend of the accident mortality curve was downward, a phenomenon that had been in progress probably since the opening of the century. Nevertheless, despite this general tendency the laws of probability indicate that such a trend would not manifest itself as an ever-decreasing curve, but rather as a curve made up of cyclical "ups and downs" with each successive "up" not going as high as the previous one and with each successive "low" dropping lower.

Paradoxically, however, a study of the *relative* rates seemed to indicate an increase in the number and severity of accidents. Obviously the casualty insurance companies were the first to observe this occurrence which, in view of the safety campaigns, was unaccountable. Early in 1925, the National Bureau of Casualty and Surety Underwriters, desirous of a "careful and dispassionate" nationwide study,[5] proposed that the AEC study the relationship between industrial accidents and production efficiency, a matter which, it believed, would uncover the reasons for the existing situation and lay the basis for future development of the safety movement.

The AEC, acting in its customary manner, appointed an advisory committee (consisting of prominent authorities) that met in Washington on May 14, 1925, and decided that such an investigation was "timely, practicable, and valuable," that data of the "character required could be obtained," and that the investigation was one that could be "properly" conducted by the AEC. Its recommendations were accepted at the AEC's annual meeting in January, 1926, and a committee—"Committee on Safety and Production"—was appointed: L. W. Chaney, L. A. DeBlois, L. W. Hatch, J. P. Jackson, C. F. Loweth, W. W. Nichols, B. Stoughton, L. W. Wallace, A. W. Berresford (chairman), and L. P. Alford (vice-chairman). In February this committee selected J. E. Hannum, who was then research engineer for the Eye Sight Conservation Council, to direct the work and P. E. Holden of Stanford University to help him.

In less then two months, the committee approved its general program and organization, and by June it had set up its detailed field work plan. It is of more than passing interest to note that the type of person entrusted with this investigation— e.g., C. W. Lytle, who was then Director of Industrial Co-operation at NYU, headed the Investigation Center in New York— was indicative of the caliber of the work. The field work was accomplished within four months, for by October the preliminary

[5] American Engineering Council, *Safety and Production: an Engineering and Statistical Study of the Relationship Between Industrial Safety and Production.* Harper & Brothers, 1928, p. 3.

analysis of the data was started and, before the end of 1926, the preliminary outline of the final report was approved by the committee. In April, 1927, the draft of the final report was in the hands of the committee, which sent it on to the publisher in June, twenty-five months having elapsed from the original meeting of the preliminary advisory committee of the AEC.

The findings of the committee were full of meaning concerning both particular and general problems. The rise in severity and number of accidents was clearly shown to be the result of the increased intensity of the industrial process, and the increase in production per man-hour had gone up so impressively that the accident rate in terms of production had really decreased. However, these phenomena—less accidents per unit of product, but more units of product, more accidents—are not entirely happy ones. Although the matter is not too disturbing when considering production, it is alarming when considering working conditions, for men's lives and well-being are matters of great concern. And the suggestions for the "new" viewpoint in a safety campaign must consider more than safety per unit of product: it must be aware of the difficulties brought about by an industry that was becoming more intense.

In more detail, the study found that (1) industrial accidents can be "controlled," (2) accident rates can be reduced while production rates go up, (3) industrial executives have as much responsibility in accident prevention as in productivity improvement, (4) accidents have incidental costs that cannot be neglected, (5) maximum production can only be achieved at minimum accident-performance, and (6) too few plants keep or analyze accident records, and too many do no real organized safety work.

As a result, the committee recommended that industrial agencies, trade associations, and engineering societies co-operate to secure accident data, publicize analyses, and further the safety movement. Furthermore, it asserted that the same executive attention be given to accident prevention as was given to increasing productivity.

RECENT ECONOMIC CHANGES

Although Alford's contributions to the survey, *Recent Economic Changes,* are more clearly marked than those he made for either *Waste in Industry* or for *The Twelve Hour Shift,* the analysis as a whole was not made entirely under the auspices of the AEC, as will be evident after further discussion.

For too many the efficacy of this survey on *Recent Economic Changes* is measured, as far as present-day observers are concerned, in terms of how correctly or incorrectly it called the turn on the impending recession which, for want of a more startling beginning, was heralded by the reaction on the New York Stock Exchange in October, 1929. Since the report was issued in that year, many may turn back to look at the study for some sign of prophetic vision.

Such expectations would be doomed to disappointment: not because the predictions were either true or false, but rather because it attempted to make no clear-cut prognostication. Perhaps an excerpt from W. C. Mitchell's contribution [6] may be taken as indicative of the general tenor:

. . . For the country as a whole, both current opinions and statistical indexes indicate that production, transportation, and distribution have been maintained for the last few years on a high, but not exceedingly high level, with brief periods of contraction, to which the term "depression" seems scarcely applicable.

The relative stability has encouraged optimists to say that "the business cycle" has been "ironed out" in the United States, that our last cycle ended in 1921, and that we need not fear a serious reaction in the future. The forecast in this statement we may leave for the future to test, reserving our attention to what has already happened.

This, then, is what each of the scholars, scientists, and observers who contributed to the report [7] was asked to do: unearth facts as "to what had already happened." Prognosis was

[6] Mitchell, "A Review," in *Recent Economic Changes,* Vol. 2, p. 890.
[7] *Recent Economic Changes,* Vols. 1 and 2, McGraw-Hill Book Co., 1929.

not asked for, and, even had it been, it would probably have been rejected as having no place in an opinion-free diagnostic report.

E. F. Gay,[8] in his "Introduction," in presenting the report to the National Bureau of Economic Research Investigation, said:

But with such prognostications as to the possibilities of the future or with recommendations as to control of tendencies of which the symptoms seem now discernible, the National Board of Economic Research is not concerned. As a penetrating fact-finding organization, it has been employed, with the enlistment of a staff of specialists, in bringing together in summary form the best information it could find as to the recent economic experiences of the United States.

The postwar depression of the early 1920's had led to the establishment of the President's Conference on Unemployment in 1921. This conference resulted in three surveys that had been set up to investigate the general aspects of the nation's economic system and to further the reduction of unemployment: (1) *Business Cycles and Unemployment* (prepared in 1922-23); *Seasonal Operation in the Construction Industries* (prepared in 1923-24); and *Recent Economic Changes* (prepared in 1928-29).

The third of these three surveys, modeled after David A. Wells' *Recent Economic Changes* (for the period 1864-89), was intended as an analysis of American economic life with particular reference to the developments that had taken place after the 1920-21 recession. It was made on behalf of the Committee on Recent Economic Changes of the President's Conference on Unemployment, chaired by Hoover who, in the midst of its preparation, was elected to the presidency of the United States and who, in the later discussions, absented himself in favor of A. W. Shaw, the acting chairman. The members of the committee included W. T. Brown, R. W. Dunlap, W. Green, J. Klein, J. S. Lawrence, M. Mason, G. McFadden, A. C. Miller, L. E. Pierson, J. J. Raskob, L. J. Taber, D. Willard, C. M. Wooley, O. D. Young, and E. E. Hunt (secretary).

8 Vol. 1, p. 12.

The basic investigation of the committee, like those of the Committee on Business Cycles and Unemployment, was made under the auspices of the National Bureau of Economic Research, Inc., with the aid of a great number of governmental and private agencies, among which was the AEC. Financed by Carnegie and Rockefeller funds, more than two dozen organizations, numerous colleges and universities, scores of federal, state, and municipal bureaus, divisions and departments, and over one hundred persons co-operated to perform the field work and obtain the necessary data for the survey.

However, the underlying survey that resulted was made up of reports on such matters as "Construction" (J. M. Gries, U.S. Department of Commerce), "Transportation" (M. T. Copeland, Harvard, W. J. Cunningham, Harvard, and E. C. Gregg, U.S. Department of Commerce), "Marketing" (M. T. Copeland, Harvard), "Labor" (L. Wolman, National Bureau of Economic Research), "Management" (H. S. Dennison, Dennison Manufacturing Company), "Agriculture" (E. C. Nourse, Institute of Economics), "Price Movements" (F. C. Mills, National Bureau of Economic Research), "Money and Credit" (O. M. W. Sprague, Harvard, and W. R. Burgess, Federal Reserve Bank of New York), "Foreign Markets" (J. H. Rogers, University of Missouri), and "National Income" (M. A. Copeland, Cornell). Although these matters were reviewed by W. C. Mitchell (National Bureau of Economic Research) in a concluding chapter, the entire study was prefaced by analyses of three aspects of industry: the "Changing Structure of Industry" by W. L. Thorp (National Bureau of Economic Research), "Changes in New and Old Industries" by D. S. Kimball (AEC), and "Technical Changes in Manufacturing Industries" by L. P. Alford (AEC).

Before treating Alford's contribution,[9] it may be best to touch briefly on the highlights of the entire report:

1. "Acceleration rather than structural change is the key to an understanding of our recent economic development" (1922-29).[10]

[9] Vol. 1, pp. 96-166.
[10] Vol. 1, p. ix.

2. Despite variability in activity among groups, areas, and industries, the rise in standard of living generally throughout the country, although not new, has taken on some importance because of its scope and degree.

3. The increased availability and utilization of power have speeded production, reduced the unit cost of production, eliminated drudgery, and maintained or increased wages.

4. "Business has thus developed a new degree of economy in the use of credit, which may be set down as another characteristic of the period." [11]

5. Because the period under consideration "is perhaps too brief for a definite judgment," the report recommended a close study in the relationships between prices, wages, and the cost of living.

6. Industrial leaders have begun "consciously to propound the principle of high wages and low costs as a policy of enlightened industrial practice." [12]

7. Increased productivity has been fortified by a concomitant increase in the consuming power of the American consumer.

8. The American has become less concerned about primary needs (food, clothing, shelter) and has a greater portion of his earnings available for "optional consumption" (i.e., it may be spent or saved according to his tastes).

9. The utilization of increased leisure has gone hand in hand with the increased production-consumption rate.

10. There has been phenomenal growth in American service industries—travel, entertainment, education, insurance, laundries, hotels, etc.

11. The natural advantages of the United States—abundant raw materials, numerous sources of power, wide markets—coupled with an almost insatiable demand seem to indicate remote saturation points and the fact that this country has only touched the fringe of its potentialities.

12. "Until recently we have not diverted savings from productive business to speculation. There has been balance be-

[11] Vol. 1, p. xiii.
[12] Vol. 1, p. xiv.

tween economic forces—not perfect balance, but a degree of balance which has enabled the intricate machine to produce and serve our people." [13] However, it was felt that the country must learn to "develop a technique of balance." Information is vital to such an equilibrium—information of the type supplied by the "economists, engineers, and statisticians who prepared the survey."

It was this last recommendation with which Alford eventually concerned himself.

The Alford study treats the "technical changes in manufacturing industries" from a quantitative point of view. Consequently, any criticism must for the most part be limited to the source of the data rather than Alford's interpretation of it. On the whole, the figures are as reliable as could have been obtained: they come from a variety of publications such as the *U.S. Census of Manufactures*, the *American Economic Review* (particularly compilations by W. Thomas, C. W. Cobb, and P. H. Douglas, in the *Supplement*, March, 1928), and the National Industrial Conference Board, and from, as in previous Alford reports, correspondence and personal contact.

Using the increase in productivity (i.e., output per worker) as a key to "recent" technical changes in manufacture, he studied this phenomenon in relation to other factors "capable of quantitative study on a national basis." His treatment was broken down into three parts.

First, he analyzed and uncovered, among the national changes in technical production factors, *increases* in (1) physical value of product, (2) productivity of the industrial worker (or man-hours worked), (3) primary power utilized (both as to total volume and as to amount per employee), (4) fixed capital costs (i.e., manufacturing, buildings, equipment, and machinery), (5) wages and weekly wage rates, (6) cost of materials for manufacture, and (7) prime costs. He also discovered *decreasing trends* for (1) number of wage earners and (2) average hours worked per week. From these he derived quantitative measures of the in-

[13] Vol. 1, p. xxi.

crease in productivity per wage earner and of the decrease in unit prime cost over the period under consideration.

In the second part of his study, Alford was concerned with specific changes in certain technical production factors. Thus, he explored the figures he had gathered concerning the development of industrial research and found a marked increase in the attention given, resources available, and funds spent in this highly important field. He painstakingly classified, as a result of a survey which he conducted, "fifty typical developments" in products and materials and a similar number in connection with industrial processes. Even though his selections were made a quarter of a century ago, it is of more than passing interest to note that his choices were particularly appropriate in view of the fact that their full potentialities have only lately been realized. He included, among others, cellophane, dry milk, panchromatic motion picture film, various alloys in metal production, paper products, glass and glass substitutes (quartz, ultraviolet, etc.), leather substitutes, silk substitutes, lacquers, carbon dioxide ice, etc. His process selections vary from the refining of edible oils to the elimination of crazing (in pottery drying). Alford would naturally be expected to include an analysis of the widespread effort at cost reduction together with the increased attempt to improve operating effectiveness, particularly because of his work on *Waste in Industry*. He found three principal lines of endeavor here: (1) simplification of product, (2) standardization of product, and (3) concentrated effort, particularly by reclamation and reuse of materials plus development of byproducts, to reduce waste. His interest in the over-all effects is evident from his analysis of the increase in the utilization of industrial power and power machinery, for he carefully noted the "shift" in the "machine civilization" from one "created by steam power" to one "created by electric power." Consequently, he took cognizance of Glenn Frank's observation, at the Midwest Power Conference, February, 1928, of the effect resulting from the fact that, under the "steam" civilization, the "worker must go to the power," and under the "electric" era, the "power can be taken to the worker."

Continuing his treatment of these specific changes, Alford pointed out that the increase in industrial buildings was more marked before rather than after 1922. Graphically he showed that, although the curve indicating the increase in value of manufacturing machinery was higher than that of industrial building, it was not nearly as indicative of marked increase as the one for primary power. However, Alford showed that there was a tendency toward not only improving the capacity of manufacturing equipment but also in increasing its economy. In this connection, too, the increase in material-handling equipment had a dual purpose: (1) reduction of the costs of transporting materials and products and (2) use as a pacemaker for the increase of production speed. Alford did not find it inappropriate to insert here the findings of his AEC Committee on Safety and the correlation it made between productivity and accident prevention. Finally, he treated the effects of the improvement in artificial illumination and other technical considerations capable of modifying work surroundings.

In the third and last part of his analysis, Alford considered the "changes in technical production factors for twelve industries." Because it would have been misleading to have allowed the over-all average figures to convey a general impression of universal success, Alford attempted to show that there were variations among industries: some exhibited trends far in excess of what the averages showed, while others had not progressed that far. Hence, he treated two groups—six industries in each —"the first commonly looked upon as prosperous, and many of the second as notoriously in trouble and beset with economic and business difficulties." [14]

The first class of industries included automobiles, rubber tires, petroleum refining, cement manufacture, blast furnaces, and steel works and rolling mills; the second category, flour milling, slaughtering and meat packing, leather tanning, cane sugar refining, paper and wood pulp, and boots and shoes. Thus, to point to a single example, in a comparison of derived figures for the automobile and shoe industries the former showed, on

[14] Vol. 1, p. 166.

the basis of 1919 and 1925 figures, percentage *increases* in 139 in productivity per man-hour and 41 in primary power per man-hour and a *decrease* of 56.5 in unit prime cost; the shoe industry, on the other hand, showed, for these same items, percentage *increases* of 1 and 38 and a *decrease* of 22, respectively. In general, Alford felt that on a further examination of these items for all the industries considered here, the second group had not made increases in the utilization of production factors comparable with the first. Hence, it seemed apparent that this fact indicated "the place where improvements may be initiated."

There is little doubt as to the importance of Alford's contributions to the report, for they furnished much of the fundamental and quantitative basis on which the entire report was based.

However, the value of his work here cannot be limited to the report. For it was here that he was able to probe industry for facts and figures and trends. Certainly it was here that he reinforced his thinking as to both industrial practices and measurement of performance. The first was to be expected, for his thinking at the time was still vibrant with his search for "laws" of manufacturing management. The second aspect eventually gave rise to his ideas on kmh, even though he insisted that it was directly from his studies on safety that the kmh concept grew. However, it seems apparent that such a concept could not have come full grown like Minerva from the brain of Jupiter. Certainly, an occasional seed was planted from time to time, and indeed this report contained several of them.

Chapter VIII

MORE REPORTS AND A TRIBUTE

THE CLOSE OF THE *1920's*

Although the year 1912 was of considerable importance in Alford's professional life—a year in which he made his mark in the management aspects of the engineering profession—other years indicate the development of newer interests. The close of the 1920's is a period that deserves further analysis.

In this chapter, a sincere attempt has been made to present and analyze what is believed to be his most powerful writings and addresses of this period. His ideas on production control have been chosen primarily because he himself thought the subject important enough to bring to the attention of the engineering educators of the times. Again, the invitation extended to him to address the World Engineering Congress in Tokyo was more than an indication of the respect that he had earned. It was also a manifestation of his expert evaluation of the status of management in that all-important year 1929. His concepts of the importance of safety in industry were significant not only because they displayed his humanity but because he was convinced that here was a sound objective, as well as a definite management responsibility. His 1932 survey of management, as he rightly maintained, came at a time when the country was entering a new and important phase in its history. His talk before the Industrial Conference at Pennsylvania State College was an early public admission of his acceptance of Gantt's Service Motive. But even more important, it served as formal notification of an endeavor in which all could join, with resulting success and benefits to all concerned. And it was his address at the Stevens Institute of Technology that formed the basis of his more widely known book on the author of the managerial philosophy of "Service."

ALFORD AND PRODUCTION CONTROL

It is not easy in the wide field within which Alford worked to pinpoint his main interest. For, once he entered the field of industrial and management engineering, his "current" interest was his "main" interest. And the "current" interest was the one that he felt was of most importance to the profession.

When he felt that there was a need for a clarification of the fundamentals of scientific management, that was his interest. When he thought that the interest of the worker needed more attention, that was his concern. When he thought that some mathematical measuring device might be of value, that was his problem.

Nevertheless, on July 31, 1941, less than six months before his death, when in his customary anxiety to serve his country and profession he supplied answers to a questionnaire submitted by the National Roster of Scientific and Specialized Personnel, he checked, as the fields of his greatest interest, (1) Administration and Management, (2) Production Control, and (3) Plant Layout.

He had a deep interest in production control, for he felt that "modern production control started in the machine shop." And it was there that he too began his professional career. Again, after the Hoover Report on *Recent Economic Changes* and its picture of the progress of American industry since 1922, Alford, with due regard for "the increased productivity of the American worker," felt that much of the credit was due

> to the development of management; to industrial engineering in general; to production control in particular; to the gain in knowledge of "how to get work past the point of the tool."

Hence, in 1929, when the Society for the Promotion of Engineering Education (now known as the American Society for

Engineering Education), conducting its "Summer School for Engineering Teachers" at Purdue University, invited Alford to speak, he chose as his topic "Organizing for Production Control." He presented this paper on July 5, 1929, and it was later [1] included among the papers of the Production Division of the Mechanical Engineering Sessions.

The situation was custom-made for Alford's distinctive abilities. Here was a group of engineers to whom he was to introduce and emphasize this very useful tool of modern management. Here was an audience to whom he could talk meaningfully of principles and fundamentals. In about six pages, he briefly but completely presented the main concepts of the subject: for, he contended, despite the complexities that the details might assume, the topic was "fairly simple in principle."

ORGANIZING FOR PRODUCTION CONTROL

A good part of the matters he discussed were based on the previous works of others as well as his own. Thus, his definition of *production control*—"that system which, existing over a long period of time, controls the order of movements of the elements of a productive program in relation to each other and to the whole"—can partially, at least, be traced to G. D. Babcock, who treated the subject in Alford's *Management's Handbook* (Section 12). Alford's statement of the "Principle of Production Control,"

> The highest efficiency in production is obtained by producing the required quantity of product, of the required quality, at the required time, by the best and cheapest method

he culled from his own *Laws of Management Applied to Manufacturing* (p. 135). In this connection, it is of interest to note that he did not, as do some writers today, restrict the subject to merely a "control of quantity," but like Kimball he was aware of the quality and economic aspects.

[1] Paper No. 12, SPEE, February (1930).

Aside from bringing this important subject to the attention of American engineering educators, the value of the paper lay in its conciseness. Alford's proficiency at systematization is clearly evident in the almost military precision and logical order of his treatment of the topics of Material Control (investigating the demand for, requisitioning, purchasing, receiving, inspecting, storing, and delivery of material), Production Planning (analyzing orders, determining tool and machinery equipment, estimating process times, fixing beginning and ending times, determining operations and job sequence, fixing material requisites, checking estimated costs, and originating necessary paper work), and the Principal Procedures in Production Control (production planning, material procurement, routing, scheduling, dispatching, inspecting, storing, and handling work-in-process). One immediate effect of his line of attack was the establishment of a pattern that management textbook writers seem to have followed ever since.

He showed the roles that could be played by an analysis of past performance records, operating reports, budget estimates, and statistical studies in the establishment of a production schedule. Although few writers included cost analysis as part of production control, Alford was emphatic in stressing its relation to the subject. Furthermore, he was mindful of the mechanical aids, particularly the Gantt Charts.

Above all, Alford was not content as were many to measure the proficiency of a production control system by a mere compilation of the increased quantity of product. Anticipating today's vanguard of "management control" leaders, he suggested a more realistic "measure of success," namely, "the percentage of orders shipped on the dates promised." Citing instances, he felt that meeting delivery dates from 85 to 95 per cent of the time was an indication of "good practice." Whether this range is considered high or low is not important. What is important is this early manifestation, so frequent in his writings, of attempting to find some mathematical measure that could effectively replace biased judgment.

THE WORLD CONGRESS IN TOKYO

The year 1929 was an eventful one in the American economy. A good opportunity to consider management's progress at that time was afforded by a paper that Alford wrote for the World Engineering Congress, meeting in Tokyo during the fall of the year.

On this occasion, the Japanese Embassy in Washington extended individual invitations to about three hundred engineers in this country to attend and participate. As Alford's private files reveal, "I was one of those invited, and a little later was asked to prepare the paper on 'Scientific Industrial Management.' " The paper was read on October 30, 1929, at the Management Session, "by Joseph W. Roe, who kindly acted for me in my absence."

Alford was moved by the letter of appreciation that he received from Baron Koi Furuichi, President of the Congress, in December, for he mentions it at length in his personal papers. Alford was commended for "the kind support given by your good self in presenting such a valuable paper," and the Congress felt "highly honored" that it "could include your good name in the official list of its paper contributors" and was deeply grateful "for the great sympathy that you have shown the Congress in that way."

The paper, No. 341 of the Congress, was printed in English in Tokyo. It depicted compactly the development of "modern American industrial management, most frequently referred to abroad as 'scientific management' " during the quarter of a century that intervened between Taylor's paper on "Shop Management" (1903) and the meeting in Japan. There is no need to comment here on its details, but a careful selection of its outstanding concepts will give an additional appraisal of Alford's insight in charting management's progress.

TWENTY-FIVE YEARS OF "SCIENTIFIC INDUSTRIAL MANAGEMENT"

To begin with, Alford felt that although it was not easy to give a satisfactory definition of management, "in simple words it is 'The art of getting work done.' " He found the celebrated ASME definition of the word "unsatisfactory and incomplete in certain respects, for it does not convey an idea of the mental attitude, the scientific approach, the application of enlivened intelligence."

He insisted that there were "three principal initiatory steps," which "in chronological order are: the development of production control, personnel management, cost control and budgeting." He fixed these "milestone dates" as "respectively, 1903, 1908, and 1917."

He stressed again and again the importance of "the new viewpoint and way of thinking," and he was adamant in a belief in the importance of the worker and in "the purpose of industry as service to the public." Alford also heralded the "doctrine" that he and Hannum expressed in "A Basis for Evaluating Manufacturing Operation," which "imposes the obligation, on the one hand, to conserve human effort and prevent its waste, and, on the other, to use the greatest of managerial skill and effectiveness in doing the work of industry."

Aside from the principles of Taylor, the rules of Person, and the mechanisms of Hathaway, Alford set down what he considered to be "the more important management methods in use in progressive American industrial concerns": (1) Organization for Operation, (2) Production Planning and Control (which he illustrated with diagrams by Bangs), (3) Quality Control, (4) Stores Control, (5) Process and Operation Analysis, (6) Wage Incentive (referring particularly to Lytle's analyses), (7) Labor Maintenance, (8) Plant, Equipment, and Machinery Maintenance, (9) Standard Costs, (10) Budgeting Control, and (11) Market Analysis.

He modestly but rightfully considered his own codification

of the "Laws of Manufacturing Management." And he insisted that there was a growing acceptance of two principles: (1) "High wages accompany high production and low costs." (2) "The worker is entitled to leisure in which to enjoy the reward of his labor."

His ideas on the trends of management were along three lines: (1) simplification, (2) expression of "management fundamentals including codifications and the use of formulas and experiential constants," and (3) an expansion of management principles and methods to additional fields of human effort.

He took issue with those who felt that advances in industry and manufacturing were of the nature of "a second industrial revolution." He took his cue from the report, *Recent Economic Changes,* to which he had made an important contribution, and he maintained that "industrial evolution" was a much more appropriate description.

SAFETY

At the ASME's annual meeting in New York in December, 1930, a symposium was conducted by the Safety Committee. Here Alford reiterated and expanded the findings his committee made two years previously in the AEC's Safety and Production Report—the same report so largely responsible for the formulation of the kmh concept. His paper, indicative of the "newer" point of view, was entitled "Management's Responsibility for Industrial Accidents." It called attention to the fact that, as a result of expanded studies of both accidents and industrial organizations, there was a gradual shift away from the idea that a worker was responsible for all events that befell him, especially when he had slight control over his environment in a plant.

In short, it was Alford's contention that an industrial accident was "evidence of some fault of the control of the operating conditions and forces," and that physical injury was a horrifying and spectacular signal of some basic maladjustment.

On the basis of a thorough examination of accident and production experience of about two and a half million workers in about fifty-five billion man-hours of operation, the AEC's Committee on Safety and Production asserted: [2] "In other words, the key to the new safety movement, which will substantially reduce the number and cost of accidents now being experienced, is the industrial executive."

Alford gave another finding of the AEC Report, which had been conceived with the objective of exploring the idea that "the safe factory is an efficient factory," namely, that the coefficient of correlation between industrial safety and industrial production was 0.835.

Alford's message was, therefore, obvious: if management could achieve a high production record, it could also achieve a high safety record. As a matter of fact Alford two years before had added this production–safety correlation to his *Laws of Management*.[3]

To avoid criticism of this humanitarian appeal for improved safety, Alford also discussed the truth of the converse: to achieve a high production record, it was necessary to achieve a low accident rate.

As one method of attack, he suggested a reduction in labor turnover, mindful that there is a relationship between this factor and accident experience. Here, too, he showed that humanitarian considerations made for good economics, for a conscientious effort to improve safety conditions would, in turn, reduce labor turnover. Another vindication of the Gantt idea with which Alford was so thoroughly imbued!

ALFORD'S REPORT ON THE PROGRESS OF MANAGEMENT, 1923-1932

By a strange coincidence, the year 1932, a year to which many political, social, and economic historians attach great importance, marked the second decade after Alford's 1912 Report. Consequently, the Executive Committee of the ASME's Man-

2 *Safety and Production*, Report of the American Engineering Council, p. 33.
3 P. 206.

agement Division, Alford's private files show, "asked me early in 1932 to write a report on the progress of management for the decade closing with that year."

Alford was particularly pleased by the "peculiarly fortunate" nature of its "timing," for, as he noted in his personal papers, "Immediately thereafter, in 1933, came the major efforts to change the social and industrial efforts of the United States of America. The report presents one comprehensive study of the conditions, situations, and trends as they existed before the efforts to change had been made."

The paper, "Ten Years' Progress in Management, 1923-1932," was presented at the ASME's annual meeting in New York, in December, 1932, and it appeared in print in the same copy of the *Transactions* [4] that carried the second kmh paper by Alford and Hannum.

THE REPORT'S BACKGROUND

The ten years under discussion were marked by "violent fluctuations in industrial activity and sharp contrasts in the results of operating performance." The business cycle was marked by an expansion to 1923, a contraction to 1924, an expansion to 1926, a contraction to 1927, an expansion to 1929, and a contraction to the time at which the report was being written.

Throughout it all, management's progress was steady. And, at the midpoint of the 1923-1932 period, H. S. Dennison [5] noted the prevailing high rates of production per man, wages per man, horsepower per man, and management per man.

In the preparation of the report, difficult as the times made it, Alford leaned heavily on the ASME's *Bibliography of Management Literature* (published in 1927 and revised in 1931) and files, as well as the *Report of the Committee on Recent Economic Changes*, to which Alford himself had been a contributor. All these indicated, as Alford pointed out, that man-

---

[4] *Trans. ASME*, 55, No. 3, MAN-55-2, pp. 7-16, April (1933).
[5] "Management," in *Recent Economic Changes*, Vol. 2, chap. 7, pp. 495-546.

agement itself had become specialized.[6] The works on the broad subject of scientific management had been replaced by treatments of specific phases, such as safety, material handling, etc.

THE FINDINGS OF THE REPORT

Alford selected some twenty-five items that he thought were indicative of the management picture during the decade. All these, though capable of individual discussion, were not entirely independent:

1. National Planning

Although Person, in presenting his paper on "Principles and Practices of Scientific Management" at the World Social Economic Congress in 1931, asserted that a step-by-step stabilization—material factors and human relations, production and distribution, individual enterprise, and industry, national and international—was necessary, Alford felt international planning was as yet at least "a stimulating speculation." However, national planning was another matter, and the AEC's Committee on the Relation of Consumption, Production, and Distribution was [7] one of the bodies studying the matter.

2. Service Motive in Industry

Alford, though fearful that "profit management" might negate Taylor's sincere efforts to establish mutually agreeable employer–employee relations and Gantt's insistence on the "service" motive, found comfort in the fact that there was some evidence of employer responsibility toward employees. He pointed to statements by G. Swope and B. A. Franklin and the unemployment plan of General Electric in 1930. He believed that eventually unemployment insurance would become a matter for the legislators.

---

6 This was a "fate" that awaited even the writing of the 1942 "Management's Progress Report" for ASME.

7 See below, pp. 247-48.

3. Changes in Mental Attitude

The search for exact facts and the shaping of action on them rather than on opinion were still in progress. Forecasting, budget planning, and standard costs were indicative of this trend. The important management reports of this decade included those of *Safety and Production* and *Recent Economic Changes* for the AEC, *Economic Life of Equipment* for ASME's Management Division, *Cost Reports for Executives* and *How to Set Standards* for NACA, *Industrial Standardization* and *Budgetary Control* for NICB, as well as Anderson's *Industrial Fatigue* and Lytle's *Collegiate Courses for Management.*

4. Economics in Industry

In this category are numerous mathematical formulations, formerly expressed linguistically. Many of these are listed below. However, many required simpler expression before they could be afforded wider industrial application.

5. Management Principles

Here Alford referred to his own "two codifications of laws and principles." In this period, however, he maintained that three laws had been formulated: Motion-Time (Segur), Simultation (Blanchard), and Operating Rates (Alford and Hannum). He particularly singled out the work of Kimball on Minimum Cost Points; Davis, Lehoczky, Pennington, and Raymond on Economic Manufacturing Lot Sizes; Coes, Hagemann, Kurtz, Norton, Raymond, Shepard, and Vorlander on Economic Life of Equipment; Roe on Economics of Small Tools; Davis on Economic Purchase Quantities; Shewhart on Economic Control of Quality of Manufactured Product; and Knoeppel and Rautenstrauch on the Break-Even Point.

6. Advance in Doing Work (Transfer of Skill)

The increase in the productivity of the individual worker was a remarkable manifestation of the period. It should be noted that Alford implied that this productivity was, to a great extent, the result of the expanding use of mechanization and the extension of the principle of skill. In this connection, notice was taken of the Alford-Hannum studies, which maintain that increase of productivity is a continuous affair in well-managed concerns and goes on during good times and bad.

7. The Human Factor in Industry ("Employment Management")

Alford called attention to the fact that, during the 1920-21 depression, many concerns curtailed personnel activities. However, the unemployment rate for personnel managers during the recession following 1929 was no greater than that for any other supervisory and staff employees. Furthermore, the industrial relations programs of most companies had been maintained. (It must be remembered that the Alford report was written before the passage of the Wagner and similar acts.)

8. Management Method (Organization)

In addition to a renewed study of the operating structure itself, there came during this decade an increased emphasis on the functionalization of duties and specialization of personnel. But in this connection there was one field where progress, up to now at least, has been slight, but which is a necessary part of a system of control, namely, measurement of operating performance. Shewhart, in his *Economic Control of Manufactured Product,* maintained that standards of performance for every management function can be established "in accordance with the normal distribution of each characteristic of the function when influenced solely by a constant system of chance causes." In addition to the three most widely used mechanisms, Gantt Chart, budgets, and standard costs, the kmh system of Alford and Hannum was introduced.

9. Management Methods (Cost Accounting)

Cost accounting was one of the most significant of all management procedures that came during the 1923-32 period. For this the NACA founded in 1919 played a great part. This association not only raised the status of cost accounting but furthered budgetary applications (after J. O. McKinsey's publication of *Budgetary Control* in 1922) and extended the use of standard costs (after G. C. Harrison's first presentation of its methods in 1918).

10. Management Methods (Waste Elimination)

Although the AEC's *Waste in Industry* report was typical of this movement, the decade also saw savings effected by the simplification of practice recommendations of the Bureau of Simplified Practice, a co-ordinating agency, as well as the economic and engineering advantages resulting from the movement to create "American Standards," which was initiated by a group of technical societies that formed the American Engineering Standards Committee (reorganized in 1928 as the American Standards Association).

11. Management Methods (Wage Payment and Profit-Sharing Plans)

Financial incentive wage plans made steady progress during the period, although profit-sharing plans did not. The complete story of this aspect of management has been told by Lytle in several reports.

12. Management Methods (Job Standardization)

Reduction of labor costs was a stimulating factor in the study of jobs and operations during the 1923-32 decade. The early motion versus time study controversy of the early 1920's subsided. As noted, the harmonizing of these methods of job standardization by Roe and Lytle (in Alford's *Management's Handbook*) did much to bring about the change in attitude.

13. Management Methods (Inventory Control)

The shortages of World War I and the excessive stocks of the 1921 recession acted as stimuli for better inventory control.

14. Management Methods (Materials Handling)

The extension of assembly equipment to allow "straight-line production" was one of the developments. Then, too, there were numerous applications of better handling in many diverse industries.

15. Management Methods (Accident Prevention)

The AEC's "Report on Safety and Production" in 1928 summarizes this aspect of management. There was a fuller appreciation of the facts that industrial accidents can be controlled, that "safe" plants are more "productive" than "unsafe" ones, and that industrial executives have a responsibility in accident prevention.

16. Management Methods (Work Councils)

Alford recorded the growth during the early 1920's of the work councils (employee representation plans) and their resulting effect on the retardation of the growth of organized labor. However, he was unable to determine any future trend at the time he wrote his report.

17. Wage Levels

Alford hailed the spectacular rise and acceptance of the theory that high wages accompany high production. He was, however, concerned by the fact that wage cuts during 1931 and 1932 became common. Nevertheless, he was steadfast in the hope that the high wage–high production theory would return to favor and widespread acceptance.

18. Working Hours

Ford's announcement of the five-day week came in 1926, as a result of attaining a high productivity per machine and per man-hour. Alford felt that the trend toward shorter working hours was definite in all industrial management.

19. Working Conditions

Alford recorded the increased attention that was being paid to work environment and conditions in general, and air conditioning, lighting, fire prevention, noise elimination, and fatigue in particular. As a manifestation of the enlightened view, he pointed to Anderson's studies, which showed that, alongside good management, fatigue is of minor importance.

20. Industrial Plants

Two trends were becoming apparent. First, there was a tendency toward locating industries in small centers. Second, the small unit was beginning to be favored because of its economy in operating performance.

21. Obsolescence of Equipment

Equipment studies showed the relation between equipment obsolescence and production costs. They also ushered in an intensified search for better obsolescence evaluations and provisions in cost accounting.

22. Industrial Research

A great impetus here was the (First) World War. So fully had industrial research shown its value by reducing costs, improving and developing products, and fostering good will that there was an increase in this activity despite the adverse business conditions of the times.

23. Industrial Engineering Courses

The number of institutions of engineering giving industrial engineering courses increased from 10 (in 1922) to 35 (in 1931). The enrollment increased as well. Lytle's well-known survey seemed to indicate a promising future for this program.

24. Marketing

The growing importance of this phase was indicated by the fact that about one fourth of the *Recent Economic Changes* was devoted to marketing. Although the Taylor Society began the application of scientific management methods to marketing and the American Management Association had a division devoted solely to distribution problems, progress had been slight. Some trends, however, were beginning to be indicated: sales quotas, sales budgets, market analysis, scientific pricing.

25. Association and Society Activities

The decade saw an increase in the number and scope of trade organizations and management societies. Management Weeks here and Management Congresses abroad made their appearances. The American Committee, representing jointly ASME, SIE, AMA, Taylor Society, and NACA, had participated in five International Management Congresses from 1924 to 1932: Prague, Brussels, Rome, Paris, and Amsterdam. There was a Management Session at the World Engineering Congress in Tokyo in 1929, and American support had been given to the International Management Institute (Geneva).

ANALYSIS OF THE ALFORD REPORT

The Alford report was favorably received. What discussion it evoked at the ASME meeting was for the most part not so much an expression of fundamental differences as it was an indication of items that some believed should not have been omitted and developments that others believed did not have the proper emphasis.

Clark, Kimball, and Polakov enlarged on national planning. Kimball also stressed the need of emphasizing distribution rather than production, a matter in which Alford concurred. Kent felt that stronger statements should have been inserted in the report to show that mechanization of industry was not, in the long run, a cause of unemployment, with which Alford agreed but maintained he was unable to offer complete and satisfying quantitative evidence. Lillian Gilbreth pleaded for a greater interest by management engineers in psychology, with which Alford agreed.

However, the effectiveness of Alford's role as historian of the management movement may in this instance be ascertained. Just four years earlier, H. S. Dennison of the Dennison Manufacturing Company was chosen to report on Management during the years 1922 to 1929 for the Report of the Committee on Recent Economic Changes. A comparison of the methods of Dennison and Alford in this regard are indeed of interest.

The Dennison report [8] was based on a Field Interview Schedule that was given with a set of "standard instructions" to field investigators. After completing the survey, the investigator was supposed to check, in accordance with the opinion of the ranking person of the plant visited, the particular practice and relative importance of certain management methods. Thus an attempt was made to record the importance of organization, planning, budgeting, etc., in industry. From a list of several thousand companies selected by trade associations, "100 were chosen as nearly as possible to be fair samples." The sampling omitted "failures and the large Babbittry of business" as well as others. No treatment of management principles and little analysis of management applications were evident.

However, it is only by a reading of the complete reports that the reader can properly judge for himself the effectiveness of both Alford and Dennison in this field.

FURTHER HISTORICAL REPORTS

Unquestionably the ASME had in Alford a man who was not only anxious to serve and devoted to his task, but one whose abilities, particularly in recording the ten years' progress of management, could hardly be matched and never be surpassed.

Alford took his task of writing these decadal reports seriously. His associates still tell how he would, during the intervening years, begin to assemble data that he felt might be needed. Lytle and others tell how, during the years following the 1932 report, he continued in his task of collecting data for the 1942 report.

Alford's health began to fail in the 1930's. He must have had a premonition that the 1932 report was to be his last for, according to George Stetson, ASME's editor emeritus, Alford hinted that perhaps some search ought to be made for a potential author for the report of the next ten years. This was typical of Alford's concern for planning. Unfortunately, Alford's death

[8] Dennison, "Management," in *Recent Economic Changes,* Vol. 2, pp. 495-546.

came at the beginning of the year in which the new report was due.

Under the editorship of G. E. Hagemann, who had been associated with Alford for many years, the 1942 report was written and expanded. It was a fitting tribute to Alford that his writing task was accomplished by almost a score of persons of such import and caliber as L. S. Fish, J. M. Juran, A. S. Knowles, H. B. Maynard, and W. A. Shewhart.

INDUSTRIAL CONFERENCE OF 1932

Ever since 1907, when Beaver, a former governor of Pennsylvania and president of Pennsylvania State College's Board of Trustees, spoke with Taylor at the Union League Club, in Philadelphia, that college has had a proud history in the field of industrial engineering. At that time, Taylor was asked to recommend a man who could teach "mechanical engineering" from the standpoint of production rather than machine performance. Taylor recommended Hugo Diemer, who had taught what Lytle [9] believed to be our earliest individual course in shop management at the University of Kansas as far back as 1902. Taylor had also been familiar with Diemer's articles for the *Engineering Magazine* of C. B. Going. Consequently Pennsylvania State College had in 1908 the first Industrial Engineering Department in the country.

Another achievement of this college was the annual industrial conference, which has since become so popular. It was such a conference in June 1932 that Alford's private reminiscences show he was asked to attend: "Dean R. L. Sackett urged me to attend . . . and talk on some economic topic. I accepted and endeavored to express my belief that the 'service motive' must dominate the 'profit motive' in industry, and that some

[9] Lytle, "Collegiate Course for Management: A Comparative Study of Business and Engineering Colleges," *Proceedings of the S.P.E.E., 39,* 806-839 (1931). (According to Lytle, the Wharton School of Finance, established at the University of Pennsylvania on the recommendation of James Wharton, in 1881, was the first to recognize that "management should be separated from ownership and be developed as a profession.")

form of national planning must come. Within a year both were being experimented with in America." The Alford talk was titled "Some Economic Factors in an Industrial Program."

ALFORD ON PROBLEMS FACING THE ENGINEERING PROFESSION

Alford at that time felt concerned about the fact that engineers and industrialists alike were being accused of being the creators of the physical means that led to the 1929 recession. Technological unemployment and an alleged responsibility that was greater toward capital than it was toward labor were the core of many of the criticisms.

Alford, on the other hand, mindful that conditions must not only be immediately alleviated but must, in the long run, be prevented from recurring, was convinced that the engineer and the engineering school must take the lead in this more comprehensive move "toward a better economic balance."

He therefore suggested to the conference ten factors, four related to American industry in general, two concerned with the individual plant, and four connected with operating performance, to which the engineering profession ought to pay some attention.

Although these points were set down in a period when returns to both the plant and the worker were low, their true worth can be better appreciated today, approximately a quarter of a century later, after having gone through tighter national governmental controls and violent international wars and unrest.

1.Profit Motive

The attacks on both the profit motive and free enterprise by various groups were met by progressive industrial leaders who had themselves, before this time, gone on record maintaining that "ownership is no longer, if it ever were, a warrant for profit, for profit must come from the public." Furthermore, profit can come only to that industry yielding the "best service."

Thus the doctrine that "industry is a service," already established, needed wider expansion. As for doing away with free competition, its penalty is the imprisonment of the individual within the confines of a bureaucratic state.

2. Interchange of Industrial Information

The growth of trade organizations, the dissemination of technical information, and the adoption of standards have proved to be very worthy. However, care must be taken lest under the pretext of spreading industrial information for the purpose of allocating production and stabilizing prices, the Anti-Trust Laws are relaxed.

3. National Planning

There seemed to be an apparent trend toward national planning. Although many contend that a government agency should be set up to tell industry what it can make and the price at which it must sell, Swope and the U.S. Chamber of Commerce have suggested either voluntary co-operation or a national planning organization with affiliations in all industries. The exact form planning was to take was questionable, but not its eventual existence.

4. Unemployment Insurance

Alford expected a dual attack here, General Electric and Procter and Gamble taking the lead in private initiative, while Wisconsin and other states were proceeding from the legislative point of view.

5. Optimum Size of Plants

On the basis of his kmh studies, Alford suggested that attention be paid to the fact that the small plant's high productive rate was promising.

6. Decentralization

Alford believed that the argument set forth by the AEC's Committee on the Relation of Consumption, Production, and

Distribution was worthy of notice: decentralization afforded a "useful method of striking a balance between agriculture and manufacturing." Thus he felt that this tendency should be encouraged, for "human" as well as "business" reasons.

7. Lower Costs

The trend toward lower costs, reinforced by the depression, will demand more attention.

8. Increased Productivity of Labor

This trend is evident in good times and bad. Its existence in good times is obvious. In bad times, it manifests itself by the fact that only the more productive workers are retained. Although Alford suggested that the entire matter was worthy of additional consideration, is it possible that he did not anticipate the union's growing role here?

9. High Wage Rates

Alford accurately forecast this trend. His proposal that the matter was deserving of a closer study was justified.

10. Shorter Hours of Labor

Alford correctly focused attention on this trend as well.

In short, Alford expected industry in general and engineers in particular to take cognizance of the growing philosophy of social responsibility. It was only through a departure from the old idea expressed by Arthur Young in 1771—"the lower classes must be kept poor or they will never be industrious"—that Alford felt that business recessions could be minimized and industrial operations stabilized.

ALFORD AND GANTT

"As I look back over my own history," wrote Gantt, "I can pick out five or six men who have influenced my life more than all others combined." [10] However, perhaps none of the educators

---

[10] *Industrial Leadership*, p. 24.

and industrial associates whom Gantt could name could have been said to have exerted the influence that he himself exerted over Alford.

Throughout this volume, frequent detailed instances of Gantt's influence on Alford's thinking have been cited. Lillian Gilbreth, as a worker in the same field of engineering and as a resident of the same town, also bears witness to Alford's devotion and admiration for Gantt. As a matter of fact, it was more than a happy coincidence that the Gilbreths left Providence for Montclair, where both Gantt and Alford lived. Alford's son, Ralph, also relates that his father and Gantt spent much time together. As a matter of fact, Margaret Gantt Taber recalls "Mr. Alford from his visits at our home in Montclair."

Alford's monumental biography, *Henry Laurence Gantt,* is free from any detailed reference to himself, although he does refer on occasion to the "editors of *Industrial Management*" (p. 294), the library of L. P. Alford (p. 300), the assistance given by Mrs. Alford in the book's writing (p. xi), and the Alford-Hannum Law of Operating Performance (p. 294), which was a crystallization of Gantt's comment to Roe that "the essential element in any performance is time, not quantity." There is also (facing p. 242) a reproduction of the "certificate accompanying the medal awarded posthumously to Gantt" that bears Alford's name and signature as chairman of the Gantt Medal Board of ASME and the Institute of Management.

Even Gantt's frequent trips along Alps Road (then known as Ridge Road) to watch pensively the majesty of the setting sun are referred to in the book as being accompanied by "some friend" (p. 55). As a matter of fact, Alford's private files reveal much the same theme, except there he is more explicit: "Time after time, just before the coming of evening, Gantt would stop at my home and ask me to join him for a ride."

As a matter of fact, in addition to his published writing, Alford's own private papers bear *concrete* evidence of his devotion to Gantt. In fact, they may even be looked upon as the basis on which his book on Gantt was written.

THE BEGINNINGS OF ALFORD'S STORY OF GANTT

Two years before the book was written, Alford's private papers reveal:

The 1932 summer school for Professors of Engineers sponsored by the Society for the Promotion of Engineering Education was held at the Stevens Institute of Technology, Hoboken, N.J., in July. One evening was devoted to the contributions to modern industry of two eminent graduates of the Institute, Frederick W. Taylor and Henry Laurence Gantt. Conrad Lauer spoke on Taylor's achievements; I talked of Gantt's accomplishment.

Although for some time Alford had studied and expanded the ideas of Gantt, his talk at Stevens on July 12, 1932, which is in manuscript form in his files, shows a much more personal relationship with Gantt than he allowed himself in his book.

Thus, Alford asserted in his talk on "The Contributions of Henry Laurence Gantt to Modern Industry,"

On the one hand, I was eager to pay a tribute to one of the best friends I ever had. On the other, I was reluctant to speak because anything that I might say would be an all too inadequate summation of his great accomplishments. In one respect I was glad of an opportunity to try and lift his torch for a few minutes amid the gloom of today's industrial recession; and in another respect I was fearful that whatever interpretation I might give would lack even the reflection of his prophetic fire. At one moment I was urged to accept your invitation in the belief in the soundness of his teachings and practice; at another moment I felt like drawing back lest I becloud the issues he so clearly saw, or weaken the vigor of his presentation.

But the urges to accept have won over their negative rivals and for a few minutes I shall talk to you about my friend; the one who influenced the thinking of my mature years more than any other; an engineer whose contribution to modern industry is positive, constructive, creative; a gentleman possessing the charm of a warm personality, a heritage possibly from the warm south from whence he came.

Nowhere except for a very brief meaningful statement did Alford make any pointed comparison between Taylor and Gantt. His talk, like his book, indicated that not only was Gantt an associate of Taylor but "to a great extent his follower." Alford recalled that both had worked, planned, and faced pioneering hardships and difficulties together. Again, despite the fact that "the warmth of their friendship cooled somewhat during the last decade of Taylor's life," Gantt had paid generous tribute to "his former chief."

Alford's significant differentiation came in his reference to the fact that Taylor's *Shop Management* and Gantt's *Organizing for Work* were, "in my mature judgment," worthy of consideration as "the two greatest books in the field of industrial management." In describing them, Alford said, "The first is concerned with principles and practice, the second with principles and philosophy."

As far as Alford's personal files reveal, he considered Gantt's "three outstanding characteristics" to be "his engineering mind, his firm decision and quick action, and his leadership." Certainly the proximity of their homes, Gantt's "Oakleigh" at 18 Hoburg Place and Alford's at 9 North Mountain Avenue in Montclair, gave Alford additional opportunities to observe his mentor. Thus he could testify to Gantt's aesthetic nature and the "inspiration and strength for his daily work" that he could draw from even the beauty of a sunset.

Alford named as the "three dominant qualities of Gantt's nature" loyalty, courage, and vision. Not only did Alford maintain that Gantt's "parting of the ways" was applicable to the then current economic conditions, but

. . . it seems that during the past three years we should have paid more attention to Gantt's teaching. He saw clearly that a nation's wealth and well-being depended upon its powers of production. These powers we have lost during this period of depression. On one side stand our factories and their equipment, capable of producing but inactive; on the other rises an increasing mountain-like accumulation of human need for the necessities, comforts and luxuries of life. The one is not operating to satisfy the other. There seems to be no power to do a comparatively simple act, to start production.

Although Alford paid tribute to Gantt's insistence on facts as well as to his chart (whose application to ammunition shops was begun by David B. Porter and whose universal application was stressed by Wallace Clark's book), he felt that Gantt's "teaching, his vision, his spirit are still an active influence toward better things in American industry"—"this life after death" —can be traced to "the simple slate marker of his grave." The Biblical quotation, Alford felt, was Gantt's motive, source of action, and measure of accomplishment: "I am among you as he who serveth."

Consciously or otherwise, Alford evidently made that his guide as well.

THE GANTT BIOGRAPHY

It was natural that Alford would open his magazines to Gantt's great work. As a matter of fact, the first Gantt Chart to be *published* appeared in the February, 1918, issue of *Industrial Management*. (It showed the orders and output of five items of war material. Of course, Porter had plotted his chart even earlier—June, 1917.)

However, it was to be expected from Alford's devotion to Gantt's doctrine that he would eventually try to tell the story of the man's accomplishments. But even in his Stevens talk, Alford seemed to imply that there was a need to bring out matters that have "never been adequately presented in literature and many of our younger engineers do not realize" ever took place. He was referring to the "period which required men of courage, vigor, and determination"—the period when Gantt began his active practice and "when the newer ideas were making their way."

The biography was "written at the initiative and under the auspices of the Biography Committee of the American Society of Mechanical Engineers." Alford's writing was guided by the Committee's specification that the work should show, by the subject's "growth," the "manner of man he was," by his "tastes and attainment," his "place in this workaday world," by his "activities with their failure or successes," what he added "to the art and practice of his profession"—and, throughout it all, his contributions as a citizen and his influence as an engineer.

Alford's private papers reveal that, as far as Gantt was concerned, "It is easy to select out concise statements full of meaning. The reason for this highly desirable quality probably existed in the clearness of Gantt's thinking and the power of his expression."

Yet despite the clearness and accessibility of Gantt's writings, the hordes of Gantt's friends and admirers, and the editorial assistance and library research of Agnes M. McTiernan, the Alford task was not easy. Ralph Alford recalls the long and sustained work that his father put into this biography of a "Leader in Industry."

This book, which Alford's private papers of September, 1938, call "probably the best writing that I have done, judged from a literary standpoint," must have been a labor of love and a tribute to the man whom he recognized as a friend and counselor.

The book might also be considered as a climax to "a most pleasing honor" that came to him three years before the Gantt biography. His personal recollections noted in February, 1934, just about six months before the biography was issued, reveal:

It came to me on the evening of October 29, 1931. At a dinner at the Hotel Pennsylvania, the Henry Laurence Gantt Medal was presented to me, jointly by the American Society of Mechanical Engineers and the American Management Association. This medal is the highest honor in its field and is awarded for "distinguished achievements in management."

Harold V. Coes in presenting me as the recipient of the award said, "He has given generously of his time and thought to the formulation of the science of management and to its advancement, and has been an ardent proponent of the scientific approach and the scientific method to the solution of management problems."

Although many distinguished persons, including a famous engineer and President of the United States, have since received that award, none came closer than Alford to the man for whom the award was named and the man whose life and ideals he made his guide.

FURTHERING THE GANTT INFLUENCE

In order to honor one's friend and counselor, one may write, preach, and practice his philosophy. Even more, one can get others to do the same.

A brief quotation from a letter by one of management's leaders is indicative of Alford's success in this venture. In a letter to the writer of this book, Pearl F. Clark wrote:

Dr. Alford's suggestion to Wallace Clark, after Gantt's death, that he write a series of articles on The Gantt Chart, as Gantt himself would have done if he had lived, made him a real influence in Wallace's life. Not only did he suggest the articles, he added his guidance and advice as editor of *Management Engineering,* in which the articles appeared.

In the Preface to the book which came out of these articles, you will see the acknowledgment to Mr. Alford. As the book was published here, and then translated and published in other countries, Mr. Alford continued his interest and pride in it.

No further proof or more authoritative evidence of Alford's very own accomplishments is necessary.

THE DEPRESSION YEARS

The engineering profession was not unlike the rest of the country: it, too, felt the effects of the troublesome depression years. Alford was, of course, conscious of this, but he was also well aware of the more general and basic problem. While he felt that something must be done for his engineering brethren, he was convinced that here was a matter whose solution could not be even remotely considered without due regard to the entire problem. The problem, if it could be restated, was a paradox. Here were members of a profession crying for the relief of its misfortune when the clear logic of the methods and thinking of this very group was itself capable of helping others.

It is, therefore, important to analyze his engineering interpretation of the country's economic mishaps in general and the "balancing of economic forces" in particular. For, as he saw it, here was not only an engineering problem but an engineering obligation as well.

Despite the many writings and interpretations of the NRA Codes, there is a decided dearth of analysis of the managerial aspects of these techniques. In other words, the country was entering a "planning" stage, yet few management experts treated the problem from the broad point of view. Most were content to limit their endeavors to the question of how a code affected a particular industry in which they were interested.

Alford's interests here also carried him further, for he was led to his study of work assignment, particularly as applied to an aspect of the textile industry. These interests also led him to other considerations which, at the outset, may seem highly theoretical but which, on further consideration, were among the most practical observations that he ever made and among the most potent predictions he had ever postulated. These involved his formal recognition of the growing importance of the cost aspect of industry.

He was emphatic in his belief that just as the stress had up to these times been laid on the production side of industry, so now there was a transition to a greater realization of the role of costs. However, because he felt the importance of the cost point of view, it might be tempting—but it would not be true—to attempt to credit him with the development of today's concepts of management controls. Certainly cost control is an integral part of management control but, as important as this cost aspect may be, it is only a small portion of a much greater subject. In his appreciation of the information that costs may give, however, he might be looked upon as an early forerunner of the more general views being promulgated today.

Chapter IX

THE DEPRESSION

COMMITTEE ON THE BALANCING OF ECONOMIC FORCES

Alford's concern for economic stability, like his concern for any matter to which he felt a sense of responsibility and duty, manifested itself in his devotion to a study of the "balancing of economic forces." How he specifically started to study the problem is recorded in his private papers.

During the winter of 1930-31, President Hoover suggested to L. W. Wallace, who was then the AEC secretary, that the Council undertake the examination of the reasons for business recessions and then suggest how future depressions be either avoided or their effects mitigated. Alford painstakingly recorded the following details:

Wallace discussed the proposal with a few engineers and telephoned to me asking to join him in Washington the day before the meeting of the Executive Council which was to plan for the 1931 Annual Meeting of the American Engineering Council.

I reached Washington on Wednesday morning and spent the day on the proposal. Toward midday I dictated a presentation for the Council, revised the first draft, and then revised and improved a second draft. On Thursday morning the proposal was submitted to the Executive Committee. It was adopted with only a few changes and ordered to be presented to the Assembly at its session the next day which was Friday. The Assembly listened to the proposal and adopted it by unanimous vote and without discussion or debate.

The president of the Council appointed soon after a special committee on the Relation of Consumption, Production, and Dis-

tribution. I was made a member. The committee set for itself the
task of exploring the causes of the business depression that began
in the autumn of 1929. Its report was completed toward the end
of 1931, and was submitted to the Assembly of the American Engineering Council at its Annual Meeting in January 1932.

It was favorably received and ordered to be released for publication. Some two or three weeks after the Assembly meeting I went
to Washington and spent a day with Wallace editing the report,
and preparing it for publication.

THE FIRST PROGRESS REPORT

Although Alford was only a member of the committee—which
also included R. E. Flanders (chairman), F. J. Chesterman, D. S.
Kimball, and L. W. Wallace—he, by virtue of his editorial experience, did much of the editing on this first progress report,
"Balancing of Economic Forces: Suggested Lines of Attack on
the Interrelated Problems of Consumption, Production and
Distribution.[1]

The committee studied many of the popularly accepted interpretations of the economic situation of the early 1930's, including examinations of such prevalent explanations as technological unemployment, wasteful manufacture and distribution, general overproduction, speculation, installment buying, and the
breakdown of international trade and credit. The committee's
conclusion was that the effects of these matters on the economic
recession, though disturbing, were either questionable or inadequate.

The committee found that the typical business cycle was a
complex affair and contained elements of all the above explanations. Thus, any interpretation from the single viewpoint of
money, psychology, industry, etc., could give only an incomplete diagnosis. In its search for a working hypothesis, the committee found that the "most satisfactory" interpretation might
come from an analysis of the "lack of balance between production and purchasing power," a matter suggested in the report,
Recent Economic Changes.

[1] *Mechanical Engineering, 54*, No. 6, 415-423, June (1932).

The problem of the interrelation of these factors was complex and required unselfish, intelligent, far-sighted study, because social experimentation, since it involved human beings, was a serious matter. Here the notion that any indiscriminate rejection of current methods be rashly advocated was not implied. Thus the profit motive and free competition could continue to exert their effective influence in continuing to give society improved methods and lowered costs, even though they might have to be "restrained in their destructive and unsocial manifestations."

The report maintained that the problem was not only inevitable but involved "nothing less than the purposeful changing of the course of history."

THE SECOND PROGRESS REPORT

The importance of these matters on the "balancing of economic forces" is clearly indicated by the detailed notations recorded by Alford in his private files. Because of his usual conscientious nature, he undoubtedly felt that the others of the committee—which now took on two additional members, F. J. Chesterman and F. H. McDonald—should be kept informed.

On January 13, 1933, the second progress report was submitted by the committee to the AEC Assembly. The Alford private papers reveal that:

The discussion was extended and favorable. The vote was to return the report to the committee for final editing and publication. The representatives of the Assembly were asked to submit their views, comments and suggestions by February 1.

I was planning to go to Miami, Florida, for a six weeks' vacation. L. W. Wallace, Executive Secretary of the committee, agreed to join me with all the data and information appertaining to the report and we were to edit it amid flowers and sunshine.

Pressure of business in Washington prevented Wallace from joining me. So he sent me all the material and I spent the greater part of ten days editing the report to bring it so far as possible into agreement with the majority opinion of the representatives on the Assembly and the members of the committee.

The document was printed with substantially no change from my edited draft.

The second report, still maintaining the over-all title, "The Balancing of Economic Forces," was published in two parts: I, "An Analysis of Forty Causes of Business Instability," [2] and II, "An Analysis of Twenty-three Plans for Business Stabilization." [3]

The first report, submitted by the committee on January 16, 1932, and approved by letter ballot from members of the Assembly in February, had received such wide distribution by publications throughout the country that two comprehensive files were set up; one contained more than two hundred reviews with detailed discussions by eminent and competent persons in business and the professions while the other contained more than fifty remedial plans offered as suggestions. The committee's dependence on these files as a major source for the second report was to be expected.

As the subtitle suggests, forty alleged reasons for the depression were analyzed. To accomplish this more effectively, they were grouped into seven general classes: (1) psychological, (2) technological, (3) business performance, (4) savings and investment, (5) financial, (6) agricultural, and (7) governmental, and were studied particularly with reference to their effect on business stability, scale of living, and distribution of goods.

From this entire study there was only a "single finding" that the "Committee is willing to support at this time," namely "no one all-inclusive cause can be designated as the forerunner of business depression."

Twenty-three remedial plans and programs were selected from the more than fifty in the file that the committee had built up. This selection aimed at obtaining a proper cross section, and it therefore avoided an inclusion of similar plans. Listed alphabetically by author, these included the views of

[2] *Mechanical Engineering*, *55*, No. 4, 211-224, April (1933).
[3] *Mechanical Engineering*, *55*, No. 5, 295-304, May (1933).

historians (e.g., C. A. Beard), economists (e.g., F. D. Graham, J. R. Smith, J. M. Clark), labor leaders (e.g., W. Green), industrialists (e.g., W. B. Dickson, G. Swope), engineers (e.g., C. R. Stevenson, J. S. Lennox, E. Lissner, H. C. Dickson), lawyers (e.g., C. A. Roberts), organizations (e.g., U.S. Chamber of Commerce), and others. Each was analyzed as to Classification (e.g., "Unemployment Cure"), Author and Origin, Objective, Theory or Principle, Methods Advocated, Author's Evaluation, and Status.

Although the committee in its objective treatment neither approved nor condemned any of these, its conclusions in this part of the report could be anticipated on the basis of those in the previous part. There being "no one all-inclusive cause," there could not be "any one all-inclusive remedy" that could serve as either a "preventive or cure."

Finally, the committee felt that this conclusion ought not to lead to discouragement, for the problem "is of such magnitude that its solution will be a major event in the history of civilization."

ALFORD'S OWN "APPRAISAL"

From even the most casual examination of the two reports, it is not difficult to imagine that they would be considered by a general but impatient audience as being "inconclusive" and lacking any definitely recommended "remedial measures" for the cure of economic ills. And many, full of anxiety but unmindful or unappreciative of the complexity of the problem, expressed their disappointment.

In response to a request, Alford felt that "it may not be inappropriate for a member of the committee to express his personal views by way of interpretation on some of the issues raised by the report." His paper, "An Appraisal of Economic Forces," [4] in which he specifically maintained that he was "speaking solely for myself," is consequently of greater signifi-

[4] *Mechanical Engineering,* 55, No. 6, 345-346, June (1933).

cance for this study than the reports themselves that provide proper background material.

As for the reports, Alford maintained that even though the views of the "general reader" might be considered "reasonable," so too were the actions of the committee. To realize the enormity of the job one must consider the fact that what was involved was the "assembling of 40 economic variables into one expression and then solving that expression." As for alleviating the depression, that was a matter that was most effective before and not during a depression.

Alford's personal views are of interest not only because they display his good engineering sense but because they are also indicative of his stalwart moral character. Thus, even though many asserted the inevitability of business movements, Alford with righteous indignation maintained that "a natural cycle of economic events can hardly be blamed for acts of betrayal of trust, or criminal speculation, or credit and price manipulations." And even if business cycles were "natural phenomena, we can change and improve the man-made regulations of business, the rules of the game of living."

Again typical of his character was the fact that he saw some hope in the fact that a good part of our prosperity was due to "intelligent work," and this would again redeem us.

These, then, were his over-all views. However, his detailed opinions are of great interest, as well.

There must not be restrictions on the development and improvement of machines, tools, processes, in either engineering or management. That is to say, scientific and technological progress must go on, but compensation must be made for the resulting disturbances of human relations.

Unemployment is not a temporary problem: it is one that must be considered even in the future. It can be attacked from at least three angles: (1) expanding the production of "constructive" services and luxuries so that they will be within the means of all, (2) shortening working hours with "high penalties" for overtime work, and (3) unemployment insurance.

Wage cuts reduce purchasing power, and the doctrine of high wages must prevail. Decentralization of industry and relocation of many industrial units to smaller urban and rural communities—matters of vital concern today, almost a quarter of a century later—must be seriously considered.

Other matters that he accurately forecast as of major concern in the future included: "providing of wages and income is not enough to stimulate and maintain buying: pricing must also be fair"; as to the money situation, "if taking the working-man's glass of beer was a noble experiment, increasing the price of his loaf of bread is a bold experiment"; instead of being "a political football," the tariff must be considered as "a tool of conscious social control"; the agricultural situation, a "particularly complex" matter, must be given increased attention; public construction must be accompanied by long-time planning, a procedure engineers have long advocated; and, under the business economy of the "present" and "the immediate future," the profit motive must be maintained, even though the profits should be "reasonable" and speculation must be curbed.

If these matters are not sufficient indicators of his foresight, his forecast of the power of America's production will give additional proof of his farsightedness. It must not be forgotten that Alford's appraisal came at a time when many believed, with relief, that the peak production of 1929 was an exception rather than the rule. Alford looked at the matter much more hopefully, considered that want was no longer a problem, and forecast our ability to "produce a tidal wave of goods and services."

He reiterated his contention that our main problem was a problem in control, "of matching production and consumption." Hence, he re-emphasized the need of paying more attention to rates and rates of change than to quantities. He felt that "both the new planning and new control are distinctly engineering problems, capable of solution only by the engineering method."

THE THIRD REPORT

The committee, in its second report, and Alford, in his "Appraisal," held promise for the third report. The committee ended its second progress report with the expectation that its next effort "may well be to select and present those elements of remedial programs which seem feasible and practicable." Alford reiterated this expectation and wrote that the next report was "scheduled for about a year hence."

The third report did not come in 1934, as suggested, nor did it receive any widespread public notice. It was, however, written, and a manuscript copy is in Alford's private files, which also contain the notation that it "has never been published." As far as its contents are concerned, the manuscript also contains Alford's accompanying remark that "It reviews, in question and answer form, the field of the two earlier reports and is called 'A Catechism of Fundamental Factors.' "

The Alford manuscript bears the notation that it was written during 1935-36, presented to the AEC on January 10, 1936, and revised on April 18, 1936. Although Alford maintained that "I have been a continuing active member" of the committee since its "formation" five years before, nowhere does he lay any personal claim to this third report. He did, however, note that at the suggestion of L. J. Fletcher, who had become a member of the committee, the earlier findings reinforced by the additional "knowledge and experience gained during the last two years," were reworded "in terms of 108 questions." Furthermore, these were the "experience and observations of the members of the Committee and are presented herewith, as a Third Report of the Progress of the Committee."

The mere fact that Alford failed to take credit for a report emanating from a committee on which he served was no indication that his role in its formulation was a minor one. As a matter of fact, even in instances where he might not have even done the actual writing and editing—matters for which he was widely recognized in the engineering profession—he certainly was a very dominating force. And this report was no exception.

This report, whether it represented individual or combined thinking—combined in dealing with economic and social objectives, industrial balance, business competition, labor, agriculture, foreign trade, banking and credit, taxation, public works, and social security—expressed restrained, studied, and, for the most part, justified opinions. Since it cannot be unequivocally identified as Alford's individual work, a closer examination is not in order here. However, in view of its message, it was deserving of much wider circulation.

Its conclusions testify to the complexity but not the impossibility of the solution. They imply that there are many causes of depressions, and there are many remedial measures possible. These should include the raising of the standard of living, the wider distribution of goods and services, a lessening of the violent fluctuations in living standards, a greater possibility for the equality of opportunity for all, as well as the ending of the "justifiable fear" of an individual that he and his dependents will lack the essentials of food and shelter.

DECLARATION OF ABUNDANCE

One cannot say that it was solely because of his work with AEC that Alford was concerned with problems relating to the nation's well-being. Even if there never had been such a body, his keen feeling of responsibility as an engineer and as a citizen would have compelled his consideration of such matters. Perhaps just as significant as the AEC's influence on Alford is the question of Alford's influence on AEC. Wallace on more than one occasion has testified to this influence. So, too, have many leaders at ASME and elsewhere, for Alford's concerted effort to vitalize the spirit of engineers was not limited to the meetings of AEC, ASME, or any other engineering body.

His general industrial and economic philosophy, particularly as it related to the welfare of the people, is of particular interest here. A re-examination of the high points of even the AEC reports with which he was concerned would surely yield such information. Nevertheless, in his file at ASME, as well as in his own personal files, there is a paper that Stetson believes to have been based on some of the AEC work. Entitled a "Declaration of Abundance" and dated October 13, 1933, an analysis of this paper results in an expression of his beliefs, a representation of his thoughts, and an indication of his hopes for America, which, at the time, was plunged in the depths of a seemingly bottomless economic abyss.

Fearful because many had—temporarily, he hoped—forgotten the simple relation between wealth and work, between plenty and effort, between abundance in living and expenditure of human effort, or between the good things in life and the ability to produce them, he attacked the defeatist attitude—"to take what can be had without a thought, or a struggle, for what is better"—that was then so prevalent.

Pledged to the ever-continuing task of raising the American living standard, he favored constructive efforts to (1) shorten the work week (because of the increased leisure this would entail) and (2) increase wage earnings and reduce prices (in order to afford a satisfactory spread between wages and prices). He considered as particularly harmful all movements to curb productivity, to destroy the relation between wage earnings and performance, and to prevent the expansion of productive equipment. He pleaded for a re-emphasis and a practical manifestation of certain fundamental truths which, for about fifty years, engineers nurtured, developed, measured, and codified:

1. High wages (as well as high salary rates) accompany high productivity.

2. Low wages (as well as low salary rates) accompany low productivity.

3. High productivity (as well as high wage rates and high salary rates) accompany short work periods.

4. Low productivity (as well as low wage rates and low salary rates) accompany long work periods.

Alford was determined that some effort be made to demonstrate the untruth of the idea that the machine had been harmful to the worker and to the country. In the final analysis a machine is merely an accessory to man—an addition to his energies, an apparatus to conserve time and human effort in the production of goods, a means of relieving drudgery and increasing the volume of goods. To it man has transferred his skill and power; consequently, it is inferior and not superior to man.

Clearly, he was disturbed by the unintelligent attack on the machine and the fallacious assumption that industry was primarily responsible for America's economic mishap. Probably much of this indignation was the result of the fact that these false assertions implied a condemnation—by innuendo, if not directly—of the engineer who played so great a part in the creation of these devices. This was especially disturbing, for Alford had always considered the engineer as a source of man's material salvation and not as a creator of Frankenstein monsters.

Alford asserted that the time was ripe for (1) the elimination of the unfair privileges of *both* the employer and the employee so that both could fulfill their responsibilities to the community and (2) the recognition that all industries producing commodities and services that were socially necessary must be free from all selfish and autocratic control. The "way out" for America, he felt, lay in the rehabilitation and extension of its physical equipment in order to ready it for the satisfaction of the ever-increasing living standard that had always asserted itself in goods, articles, and service.

Although the AEC afforded Alford a place to reaffirm the Gantt philosophy, the times were, he felt, seasonably appropriate for making a choice along the "parting of the ways." And the road to take was that posted by the engineer and guided by the service motive.

ENGINEERING EMPLOYMENT AND THE CAPITAL GOODS INDUSTRIES

"In September, 1933," Alford's private files reveal, "the Council of the American Society of Mechanical Engineers appointed a committee to study the relation of the situation in the Durable Goods Industries and engineering employment." And, he added, "I was made Chairman."

Serving with Alford on this Special Committee on the Capital Goods Industry were R. E. Flanders, W. W. Macon, and L. C. Morrow. An attempt was made to study the prospects of a revival in this section of the economy that concerned itself with such matters as making and installing mechanical equipment, involving about thirty billions of America's eighty billion dollars of business, and accounting for the employment of eight million workers "normally." These industries, it was felt, were particularly deserving of attention by virtue of the fact that "mechanical engineers by inclination, education, and experience" ordinarily found employment in these industries which, at the time, were involved in less than one third of their normal activity.

The committee began its survey in five selected cities (Worcester, Philadelphia, Atlanta, St. Louis, and Milwaukee) and investigated the capital goods industries, giving due regard to production, prices, and general prospects.[5] However, the course of the committee took a more definite turn as the result of the ASME's Semi-Annual Meeting, held in Denver. Here the Local Section Delegates adopted and sent on to the Council a resolution which, in turn, was transmitted to the Alford committee for reply. The resolution, acknowledging the existence of unemployment among engineers in the durable goods industries, maintained that "positive steps" be taken: ASME was to request the other engineering societies to join it in selecting and advancing projects beneficial to the nation and the community and capable of being accomplished only by engineers. It also requested the formation of a united bloc so that "a beneficial result may be obtained in Washington."

On September 19, 1934, the committee presented its report.[6] It was aware that estimates of unemployment ran as high

[5] "Capital Goods Industries: A Progress Report By a Special Committee of the ASME," *Mechanical Engineering, 56,* No. 2, 85-86, February (1934).

[6] "Durable Goods and Engineering Employment: A Report on the Present Situation by the ASME Committee on Capital Goods Industries," *Mechanical Engineering, 56,* No. 10, 579-582, October (1934).

as one out of every two engineers, but it felt that the future was still bright. It was mindful of and in agreement with certain findings of the Durable Goods Industries Committee [7] that had been elected, on March 8, by the Code Authorities: (1) these industries react more violently than do consumer industries to the business cycle; (2) the industries would not be able to take on more workers until sales increased; and (3) sales could not increase until public confidence was restored and private individuals began again to invest capital and extend credit for new undertakings.

The committee felt that while awaiting such recovery new construction and modernization ought to take place, a program that would be possible only through the co-operation of all levels of government, businesses, financial institutions, and civic organizations.

As to its definite recommendations concerning further alleviation of the unemployment problem among engineers, the committee asked for a thorough review of the manner by which employment opportunities were transmitted to ASME members by the Engineering Societies Employment Service, a more immediate means—perhaps the AEC—of informing engineers of Federal opportunities for engineering work and employment, and the stimulation of publicity on a local ASME section level for projects requiring engineers.

However, the committee was particularly emphatic that public confidence be restored. It is of interest to note how it suggested that this be accomplished:

1. Assuring private enterprise that the profit incentive will remain.

2. Recognizing that taxation is legitimately imposed only for revenue and not to redistribute wealth.

3. Removing the threat of inflation by advocating a permanent policy of a balanced budget.

4. Removing threats of arbitrary changes in our monetary policies.

[7] See "Report to the President of the United States on National Recovery and Employment by the Durable Goods Industries Committee," May 14, 1934, p. 11.

5. Clarifying the "Government's policies toward measures and trends which are inconsistent with our economic system."

6. Assuring companies at present under the temporary emergency NRA that they will not be subjected to unreasonable administrations.

The Alford influence here is unmistakable, for, as many of his associates still indicate, these views were not strange to him. In fact, the value of at least one of these reports by his Capital Goods Committee lies in its observations on the NRA Codes, a matter of great concern during the early days of the "New Deal."

In his private papers Alford indicated that he attached importance to the Progress Report of his committee, which was referred to above and which appeared in *Mechanical Engineering* in February, 1934, "not because of its permanent value, but to show the points of view toward the Codes of Fair Practice."

THE NRA CODES

In its progress report, one of the questions that Alford's Capital Goods Committee asked its correspondents was: "Has the NRA helped toward self-government in your industry?" Certainly this was a matter of more than pedagogic interest to management leaders, even though it was asked here essentially in an attempt to determine the factors that might affect the employment of engineers in the capital goods industries. Unfortunately, but probably not unexpectedly, the answers were not too definite, and an equal number of favorable and unfavorable replies were received. Between the extremes of "very decided advantage" and "no benefit" were the qualified answers that ranged from a feeling that the NRA control might be limited to the elimination of child labor and sweat shops to a fear that bureaucracy would be the direct result of any controls.

Consequently, it is hardly surprising to find that the Alford committee again brought up the subject in September, 1934, in its report. Here it took cognizance of a not too uncommon complaint concerning the restrictive nature of the Codes and suggested that some of them did have provisions that limited equipment size and productive output. The committee therefore suggested that a further study be made in regard to this matter.

According to Alford's private records,

When interest in the Codes of Fair Practice was at its height during 1934, I arranged, as Chairman of the Capital Goods Committee, to have two junior members of the American Society of Mechanical Engineers study the restrictions in the Codes. These two young engineers, W. E. Hopkins and J. F. Nelson, did good research work on this project. . . .

The resulting report,[8] presented to the ASME Council on December 3, 1934, was a comprehensive tabular presentation of "163 provisions limiting the extension and use of plant capacity and restricting industrial production."

In attempting to understand the "reasoning" of persons of import in both government and industry it is of interest to note that almost one third of these provisions were restrictions on capacity and equipment (from direct prohibition of extension of capacity in the iron and steel industry to restrictions on the offering of machinery as an inducement for sale by a seller of dry vegetable glue) and that the remainder involved restrictions on productivity and production (from allocation of production of crude oil to a restriction of a textile worker's production to that which existed on a previous date). However, it is pertinent to examine the brief statement prefacing this tabular disclosure, for here the Alford influence is unmistakable.

The restrictions are explained by the fact that businessmen and NRA officials shared the belief that the depression was the result of too many capital goods (manufacturing equipment) and too much production. Furthermore, there is a reference to Gantt's assertions that "overproduction has been the bugbear of American business," that workers "had to go bare-footed because they produced so many shoes," that "the way to get rich"

[8] "Code Restrictions on Machinery and Production," *Mechanical Engineering*, 57, No. 1, 9-14, January (1935).

is "to quit producing wealth," and that this country "never had real overproduction yet."

These points become meaningful and the Alford influence becomes more evident when considered with the statement of Gantt's biographer: [9] "During 1918 and 1919 Gantt began to fear the beginning of an 'economic catastrophe.' . . . He foresaw that when the impending business panic would come it would be attributed fallaciously to 'over-production,' and that lessening of output would seem to be the course taken by manufacturers and producers."

Despite this obvious inference, it is doubtful whether Alford considered everything about the Codes as unfortunate. A closer study of his more comprehensive view on this matter can be made in examining the papers delivered at the Sixth International Management Congress that was held in London, July 15 to 20, 1935, where Alford's paper discussed the "Management Aspects of the American Codes of Fair Practice." [10]

Alford's private files reveal how he was called on to write a paper for this Congress: "In February 1935 Harry Hopf met me in the Engineers' Club in New York City and told me of his great difficulty in getting satisfactory papers for the International Congress for Scientific Management to be held in London in the following summer. I offered to help . . ." Alford's choice of the subject of the paper was indicative of the importance he attached to it in general and to its management aspects in particular. The subject matter must have by now been well digested by him, for he, an unusually careful writer, asserted that he wrote the paper "in about a week's time." In characteristic and precise fashion, Alford added, in his private records, "I did not attend the Congress and do not know the fate of this contribution."

Perhaps Alford's is the only clear exposition of the Codes from the management viewpoint, for he considered them

---

[9] Alford, *Henry Laurence Gantt,* p. 278.

[10] In addition to the *Proceedings of Sixth International Congress for Scientific Management, London, 1935,* see also *Bulletin of the Taylor Society and Society of Industrial Engineers, 1,* No. 6, 19, October (1935).

worthy of attention as an experiment "in industrial self-government," and he was vitally interested in the fact that they included a planning process on the one hand and control rules on the other.

Because he felt that the planning aspects were improvisations (arising, for the most part, because these codes were necessarily hastily put together) and had not been subjected to the "deliberate consideration which must be a part of any planning, as that term is understood in industrial management," he felt that any appraisal, particularly for publication purposes, would have been misleading. Furthermore, his paper was for the meeting that took place in 1935, and he was genuinely suspicious that there might be some changes in the codes' structure in the offing. As for the "control" aspect, i.e., the related rules and regulations—and in a single year, 1934, the NRA issued 10,269 administrative orders—he analyzed, for his presentation to the International Management Congress, the first 500 of the 550 codes of Fair Practice that had been approved.

Alford took special pains to correct the popular belief (both in the United States and abroad) that the codes were a new management device; for scores of years before the 1930's, many procedures and acts had contributed to the idea. In fact, American business itself had for some time looked with favor on certain aspects of "business regulation, controlled production, and unfair trade practices, including uniform prices." Alford also showed—again an almost paradoxical concept—that up to 1930 it was the Federal Government itself which, except for the World War I period, had looked with disdain upon "such regulation."

After that war many businessmen seemed interested in continuing the "substantial savings" and the "effectiveness of operation" brought about by these means. Thus the Division of Simplified Practice was established in the Bureau of Standards of the Department of Commerce with the idea of "simplification of products." The number of business associations formed by business and industry increased and with them came intensified programs of studies in statistics, research, cost accounting, simplification, standardization, traffic, and other pertinent management matters.

With the debacle of 1929, however, each group sought a modification of the antitrust acts and looked to its own trade organization to force regimentation. More particularly, each trade association attempted to seek for its own members (1) benefits of technological and economic research, (2) restraint of production, and (3) checking of "unfair practices" (especially "price cutting"). As Alford correctly analyzed the situation, "without social supervision" the first aim would tend toward increasing technological unemployment, the second would increase obsolescence, and the third would increase profit at the expense of both the consumer and the wage earner.

That American industry was engaged in some concerted action before the 1930's is evident from the fact that a compilation and bibliographic listing in 1926 showed about one hundred "codes" covering aims, rules, and pledges. At about that time the Trade Relations Committee of the Chamber of Commerce of the United States was formed in order to encourage trade associations to adopt codes. The procedure then current was to submit such a code to the Federal Trade Commission and to the Justice Department before its adoption by the members. Although the fixing of prices and the restriction of production were illegal, about eighty codes were adopted. Hoover at this time stepped in and showed that these codes were frequently used as a "screen for illegal acts." Furthermore, his attorney general asserted that he felt that no government authority could police these codes.

By 1931, for example, the United States Chamber of Commerce suggested that action be taken to control production, so that it be better balanced with consumption: it consequently suggested that the antitrust laws be modified to allow business, under government supervision, to control production. As further measures, this body advocated old-age insurance and benefits, shorter working hours, and the formation of a National Economic Council. During the next year it even put itself on record for a "share-the-work" policy and industrial self-rule.

And, as an additional indication that related measures had actually reached up to the legislative state, records show that during the last Congress of the Hoover administration there was a bill (introduced by Black in the Senate and Connery in the House) advocating a 30-hour week for businesses engaged in interstate commerce.

These, then, were some of the details of the background events that finally terminated in the Industrial Recovery Act, approved by F. D. Roosevelt on June 16, 1933, with the underlying purpose "to put people back to work." The Blue Eagle drive resulted in the employment of about three and three-quarter million people and the addition of about three billion dollars to the national payroll.

It was Alford's contention that in the resulting codes business had hardly received as much as it had hoped for. And even though the businessmen themselves had a part in code preparation, their general reaction, as far as can be determined, was mixed. To their credit, many acknowledged the fact that labor ought to be protected from low wages and long hours. However, to their discredit some did plan to use the antitrust law exemptions as a ruse to raise prices.

Alford would have been expected to applaud the powers that set maximum working hours, fixed minimum wages, and prohibited child labor. But it is not easy to determine definitely Alford's reaction in 1935 to the very famous Section 7 (a) that gave "the right of collective bargaining to the workers." To put it bluntly he was plainly perturbed by the difficulty of interpreting and enforcing this feature which was causing many disputes and strikes at a time when more production rather than less production was of extreme importance.

However, there can be no such uncertainty as to his beliefs concerning the provisions based on the mistaken idea that we produced too many articles, too many goods, too many services and thus limited production. He took advantage of the opportunity afforded him by the International Management Congress to reiterate the findings that Hopkins and Nelson had made for his Capital Goods Committee.

Alford hesitated to draw for his international audience any general conclusions concerning the Codes, for he undoubtedly felt that these regulations were still in an immature stage. He had hoped that by the time of the next world management congress more definite points of view would have crystallized. However, before any such convention took place, the Codes together with the NRA had been removed from the American scene by the United States Supreme Court.

The Codes were not, as Alford had intimated, without their advantages: the general recognition of the planning aspects, the control phases and, above all, the great attention to costs and costing procedures.

SOME ASPECTS OF MANAGEMENT CONTROL

Among the most outstanding of the concepts of today's management is "Management Control." In its contemporary form its beginnings are credited to B. B. Somervell, who used it in connection with the Works Progress Administration in New York, took it with him in his post as head of the United States Army Service Forces, and finally put it to effective use at the Koppers Company. H. Nourse, J. Thurston, A. W. Rathe, to mention but a few contemporary advocates, are also connected with the use of this potent mechanism. Probably none of these leaders of "Management Control" would admit that as yet they have achieved the full measure of the latent worth of their creation. However, they have in reality effectively picked up and expanded a matter that J. P. Jordan stressed in connection with Alford's 1922 Report, namely, "cost control" is *the control.*" Among the basic concepts in today's management control is the effective use of "cost" figures in the determination of "facts."

As a further indication of the power of this *sine qua non* of management control, there is the fact that Alford himself realized the latent power of the evaluation of costs. This may not at first be apparent from the following notation in his private files:

In 1934 when I was an associate of Mr. G. Charter Harrison in a consulting practice, it seemed desirable to get on record the beginnings of the applications of standard cost procedures. I therefore wrote an article which gave the pertinent facts. It was published in *Mechanical Engineering* for August, 1934.[11]

However, a truer measure of his thoughts can be obtained from a closer examination of his theme.

In simplest terms, it was this: every major development in human history has left its distinctive mark in the form of some kind of change. As far as business and industry were concerned, these were no exceptions. The 1893 depression marked the end of the handicraft system and the beginning of the factory system in the United States. The unstable period before World War I brought about production planning. The 1921 recession gave rise to inventory control. The sad period brought on by the 1929 debacle, Alford expected, would also manifest itself in some revolutionary matter, namely, "to shift the essential managerial control from production to cost."

EARLY CONCEPTS OF COST CONTROL

Although *scientific* production control (beginning in the 1880's) may have predated the "not so well known" *scientific* cost control by about one third of a century, both had what Alford insisted was an "engineering origin." He seemed to have credited to Harrington Emerson the "earliest expression" in his insistence on a "two column" cost system—one for "actual" and the other for "standard" costs. Evidently Alford's assertion was based on the fact that this was a "revolutionary" concept that differed widely from the views most engineers had at that time. In fact, the then current "engineering" view maintained that all shop management experts could master the necessary accounting very easily and that the use of an expert accountant in the installation of a cost system in a plant was an "absurdity."

What Alford was trying to say was that "historical" costs—

11 Vol. 56, No. 8, pp. 466-467, "Cost Control: Its Importance Is Emphasized By the Trend of the Times."

although he incorrectly (according to modern terminology) used this term as identical with "job-order" costs—were the order of the day. He pointed to one of Taylor's reports to the Bethlehem Steel Company in which he not only considered such costs but looked upon them as necessary concomitants of his production control system. Even the far-sighted Gantt felt that the cost systems of his day were the invention of accountants doing the bidding of the financiers whose aim it was to place the responsibility for all the ills of business on the factory. Little wonder, then, that a well-known engineer of the time remarked: "The world has suffered from many devastating plagues, but none so destructive as that of the certified public accountant."

STANDARD COSTS

Alford quoted C. U. Carpenter to show that the cost systems developed at that time had one and only one function: to determine an article's cost. Thus, engineers generally "placed little value upon the costs compiled by the accountants," although a few envisioned systems embracing "the engineering quality of prediction or predetermination." According to Alford:

However, the honor of devising a system of predetermined costs belongs to an accountant, not to an engineer. G. Charter Harrison, who installed the first standard cost system in the United States, had the intensive thorough training in accounting, theory and practice of the British chartered accountant. This he supplemented by an extensive experience in the field of general and public accounting in the United States. Influenced largely by Emerson's views on cost, and by the possibility of determining the cost of an article before the cost was accumulated, Harrison installed his first "System of Standard Costs" in the plant of the Boss Manufacturing Company in 1911.

Harrison's early system was based on five fundamentals that have since been given wide acceptance:

1. Predetermination of Costs: In this connection it is of interest to note that W. B. Ferguson claimed that in determin-

ing a standard Emerson's "criterion of excellence" can be used for "determining what costs should be," while "past performance which represents the average cost of work under standard conditions" can be used for a standard of comparison.

2. Recognition of the Inevitability of Variations from Standard Costs: This, according to B. A. Franklin, was "the important point."

3. Analysis of Variance: This could be effected by pertinent questions and answers (e.g., Gantt's cost analysis of man and machine idleness) or by formulas (e.g., Harrison's on cost and production variation).

4. Application of the Law of Exceptions: This fundamental could now be applied to costing.

5. Application of the Law of Operating Rates: Since standards are set for labor, material, and overhead, these standards can be treated as "rates of input and are closely analogous to time rates," thereby making possible the control of their combined effect, the cost of the article.

There is no need to go into any details concerning the procedures for setting costs, but Alford's part in publicizing the use of standard costs is of importance here. Much of the basic literature, of course, stems from Harrison—particularly his two books, *Cost Accounting to Aid Production* and *Standard Costs.* However, C. F. Sanders, who was controller at one of the firms where Harrison made an installation, contributed a section (Section 26) on "Cost Accounting" to Alford's *Management's Handbook,* which also contained (Section 27) Harrison's own treatment of his "Cost and Profit Variation Formulas." Harrison and one of his former associates, H. J. Bock, were also contributors to Alford's *Cost and Production Handbook.*

Although standard cost systems are built on engineering fundamentals and require certain engineering prerequisites (e.g., "standard bills of material and standard times"), the installation, method of reporting, analyses, etc., are also in the domain of the accountant. In this connection, it is timely even now to point out one of the reasons that Alford gave for the occasional failure of some installations: "A lack of accounting knowledge

on the part of engineers; a lack of experience in the design of
methods and procedure on the part of industrial accountants;
and a lack of understanding of industrial operation on the part
of the public accountants." However, as to any rejection of the
standard cost method as being uneconomical, an accusation
then not uncommon, such a system if properly installed was
most economical because it was based on the Principle of Exceptions.

IMPORTANCE OF COSTS

Alford saw in costs the basis on which are built policy determination, budgeting procedures, sales program, profit program,
and the ". . . over-all control of business. That is, all of these
management procedures should properly not only be inter-
woven and interlocked, but be built up from the sure foundation of accurate costs." Certainly this is part of the gospel
of "Management Control."

Yet it was more than happy coincidence that took Alford
along this path. Many others besides Alford must have seen the
emphasis on costs as a natural concomitant of the troubled economic times. Few, however, had the foresight to understand its
significance. Others must surely have seen, with Alford, an
added impetus in the NRA Codes for the clarification of the
cost picture. Yet none saw, as did Alford, the gradual departure from what had up to this time been the key to industrial
control—quantity production.

For all this was just one link in Alford's chain. He saw the
control of costs as a dominant force also by virtue of the fact
that he recognized it as the natural result of his concept of
the control of the rates of input of the various cost factors.
Thus, his conclusion was unavoidable.

His unwavering faith in the progress of industrial management caused him to add the hope that once this more accurate knowledge of facts was obtained, it would be used as a
basis for a further improvement of industrial control.

WORK ASSIGNMENT

Alford's views on employer-employee relations, as already noted, were developed at a pace much slower than many would have expected from a person of such breadth of character and such depth of humanitarianism. However, once the influence of Gantt, Calder, and Colvin took root, these were matters of great concern to Alford.

It would have been disappointing if Alford had neglected to apply in this field his ever-present principle-formulating techniques. For this he chose a matter that had always been at the bottom of all employer-employee problems, work assignment,[12] and called the regulative principle he formulated the Principle of Work Assignment.

His work there is of special interest because it is an excellent instance of how the technical blends with the economic and the humanistic. The work is also interesting because of the occasion as well as the typical Alford method of attempting to solve some of the social problems by means of an engineering research.

During the close of the summer of 1934 there was, as Alford described it in his private papers, "a bitter, widespread strike in the textile industry." Although other matters at stake involved union recognition, collective bargaining, hours and wages, and some NRA labor provisions, one of the fundamental issues concerned the "stretch-out, specialization, work assignment, or the introduction of labor saving methods." As a result, the Textile Labor Relations Board appointed W. A. Mitchell as a common chairman for the three work assignment boards of the textile industries—cotton, silk, and wool. The Silk Textile Work Assignment Board was composed of an employee representative, E. L. Oliver, and an employer representative, J. W. Nickerson. It was the latter who, as Al-

[12] In his *Principles,* Alford defined this term as "fixing a fair day's work" (p. 453) and "the amount of work allotted to be performed in a specified period of time" (p. 455).

ford wrote in his private notes, "prevailed upon me to accept the appointment of chief engineer of this board." Alford's engineering research staff consisted of N. B. Cubberly, S. A. Hazen, C. C. Jessop, and J. A. Piacitelli.

Technically, the research staff was "to study work assignments," "to investigate" such matters as "stretch-out and excessive work assignments" complaints, employers' requests for "changes in work assignment," and to devise "a method for judging the reasonableness of the work effort," as well as to aid in the improvement of industrial relations.

Although thirty silk and rayon mills were observed, ranging in size from the industry's largest to the smallest, in Massachusetts, Rhode Island, Connecticut, New York, New Jersey, Pennsylvania, and Ohio, the study restricted itself to weaving operations. In contrast, as Alford expressed it, to the "usual industrial-engineering survey," no attempt was made to improve operations, shorten performance time, or lower costs, "the purpose was to secure creditable facts from which conclusions might be drawn."

For the record, its accomplishments were a theory and principle of work assignment and its reasonableness, and the determination of some times for certain weaving operations on particular types of silk and rayon fabrics. In addition, but outside the original scope, were a formula for determining loom assignments and some recommendations as to free-time allowances. Although it was suggested that a technique for establishing a work assignment could be formulated, it was also asserted that, because the industry was so large and its conditions so varied, limitations must be established to suit local particulars and peculiarities.

It is more than mere coincidence that at that time only three of all the mills under examination had established work assignments on the basis of time studies: one using "actual working time" of the weaver and two utilizing "estimated operating efficiency of the looms." For most of the plants, however, it was as if one of the most fundamental of all scientific management techniques never existed. The number of looms assigned to a weaver was usually decided on the basis of "judgment" and "guess," although many insisted that the matter was decided on the basis of "experience" and "market conditions." More often than not the decisions were made in an office many miles away from the plant. An on-the-scene investigation showed that some "stretch-out complaints" had their bases also in wage disputes, in a feeling of the lack of relationship between effort demanded and wage rates, and in the "lump of labor theory" in regard to the effect of increased loom assignments.

The general conclusions of the Alford study have found their way into his statement of his Principle of Work Assignment, given elsewhere in this study (Appendix, Part I). However, it is of importance to note how that principle came directly from the findings of the survey: [13]

A proper work assignment is the amount of work that can be done, performed with a reasonable expenditure of effort, in a period of time mutually satisfactory to worker and management, and the accompanying remuneration must be equitable and agreeable for the work performed and the effort expended. The three factors, (1) amount of work done, (2) the time during which it is to be performed, and (3) the wages paid therefor, are positively interrelated. No equitable and lasting decision can be made without giving due consideration to the other two.

In the study of the reasonableness of a work assignment, Alford's staff assumed the premise that the work must be "capable of being performed by a worker of average skill in the time specified with an amount of free time sufficient for personal needs and the relief of fatigue." The method of judging a work assignment was broken down into nine combinations of the amount of work to be done and the free time. These may be grouped as follows:

Group I: Work accomplishment equal to work assignment, and free time equal to, less than, or greater than the standard.

[13] See also: *Textile Manufacturing*, *61*, 491-492, December (1935). Alford, "Work Assignment in Silk and Rayon Manufacturing," in *Mechanical Engineering*, *57*, No. 11, 679-684, November (1935), presented by the Textile and Management Divisions, ASME Annual Meeting, New York, December 2-6, 1935.

Group II: Work accomplishment less than the work assignment, and free time equal to, less than, or greater than the standard.

Group III: Work accomplishment greater than the work assignment, and free time equal to, less than, or greater than the standard.

Two rules for procedure were then formulated:

Rule 1: If the work accomplished is the same as the work assigned (as in Group I), standard times are calculated for the number of occurrences observed. The work assignment is then judged excessive if the determined free time is less than the standard and is considered reasonable when the free time is the same or greater than the standard.

Rule 2: If the work accomplished is different from the work assigned (as in Groups II and III), "the number of occurrences that would have prevailed, if the actual work done had been equal to the work assignment, shall be computed." Then, if the free time determined is less than the standard, the work assignment is excessive. Again, if the determined free time is the same as or more than the standard, the work assignment is judged to be reasonable.

Since on almost every weaving job the work accomplished is different from that assigned, it was Rule 2 that was most frequently applied in the investigation. However, whichever rule was most frequently applied, it was necessary to establish standard times for even the most elementary operations. Because no acceptable classifications or suitable definitions were obtainable for the weaving operations, one of the first acts of the Alford staff was to formulate the required classification and definitions. Thus, under groupings of "work while loom is stopped," "work while loom is running," "patrolling, walking, and examining," and "free time," some twenty-five operations were defined.

For the actual determination of standard times, rayon fabrics were subdivided into five classes and silk into seven. The Alford associates then proceeded to obtain adequate time study information for "creditable" standards for at least three of these classes (plain gum silk, satin gum silk, and plain rayon acetate). Data came from time studies that the staff made in all of the mills. If the data were sufficient, the modes were used (otherwise arithmetic means), and all the resulting times were tabulated.

In the three instances where, because an operation was dependent on other factors, no values were given, a graph showing the relationship of the factors was shown. Thus, because a "walk to give attention" was "a function of work while stopped," a graphical interpretation of the relationship was given.

Alford's table failed to give values for two other items, "personal needs" and "inactive time," which "taken together make up the free time of the operator to be used for personal needs and for the relief from fatigue." Consequently, he suggested, as a "minimum standard for free time in silk and rayon weaving, 12.5 per cent of the total time." This would be equivalent to 60 minutes in a 480-minute shift: the median value for free times found by the time studies actually made was 59 minutes in a 480-minute shift.

Despite the fact that the staff did not offer any method for testing *in advance* the reasonableness of a work assignment, it did examine some formulas for this purpose. A brief analysis of some of these may be of value.

For such a purpose it must be understood that two determinations are necessary at the outset: (1) correct average amount of work (measured in "minutes") that a weaver must perform to produce "1,000 picks" of the fabric on which the work assignment is to be set and (2) standard allowance for free time. Thus,

$$\text{Work assignment per 1000 picks} = \frac{\left(\begin{array}{c}\text{Minutes per} \\ \text{work day}\end{array}\right)\left(1 - \begin{array}{c}\text{Per cent of free time} \\ \text{allowance}/100\end{array}\right)}{\text{Total minutes of work per 1000 picks}}$$

Even though the work assignment is fixed for the job, the number of looms assigned to a weaver or their speed ("picks thrown per minute") can be altered in order that the oper-

ator can produce the assigned work with satisfactory "loom efficiency" ("percentage of the full working day that the loom
actually runs"). It must be noted that an increased loom speed
is not always the answer, because warp and filling breakages
are more frequent at higher speeds. Usually time studies were
indicated whenever a loom speed change was made in order
to determine the effect.

The number of looms [14] that the weaver was to operate was
set by the formula

Number of looms

$$= \frac{\text{Work assignment in picks per work day}}{\left(\begin{matrix}\text{Minutes per}\\ \text{work day}\end{matrix}\right)\left(\begin{matrix}\text{Loom speed on}\\ \text{picks per minute}\end{matrix}\right)\left(\begin{matrix}\text{Loom effi-}\\ \text{ciency}/100\end{matrix}\right)}$$

But weaving requires that certain operations be performed
while the loom is stopped. Furthermore, if a weaver has more
than one loom assigned to him, an additional allowance must
be made for "interference time" (that is, the time during which
the stopped loom is waiting for attention from the weaver).
In any event, the total time would be the sum of the times
while running and those while stopped.

The time allowed for "interference" varies in some fashion
directly with the speed and skill of the weaver and inversely
with the number of looms he operates. The best determination would come from a time study and an analysis of many
cases. Not only was this done, but Alford presented a chart
for 2, 3, 4, 5, 6, 7, 8, and 9 loom strands, giving the relationship between "hand time" and "loom efficiency." On this basis,
since hand time was given by the formula,

$$\begin{matrix}\text{Hand}\\ \text{time } (\%)\end{matrix} = \frac{\left(\begin{matrix}\text{Time (in minutes per 1000 picks)}\\ \text{for work while loom is stopped}\end{matrix}\right)}{\left(\begin{matrix}\text{Total time (stopped plus running)}\\ \text{in minutes per 1000 picks}\end{matrix}\right)} \times 100$$

the loom efficiency could be obtained from the graph.

[14] Alford, "Looms per Weaver," Data from the Recent Silk and Rayon Work
Assignment Study, in *Textile World*, *61*, No. 1, 72-73, January (1936).

Hence, the work assignment and the loom efficiency could be stated, all on the basis of taking as the free time for personal needs and fatigue relief 12.5 per cent of total time.

It is doubtful how well these formulas worked, for Alford made no outright recommendations as to their adoption. With almost unbecoming facility he hurriedly passed over the manner in which the piece rate for the job is set in order to give earnings that would be "equitable and agreeable for the work performed." Surely here is a matter that cannot be determined as "readily" as he suggested.

Alford certainly expected that his recommendations when made and adopted would be tested in the field and then revised after further observance. Unfortunately this was not the case, for on June 16, 1935, the various textile work assignment boards disbanded with the ending of the National Industrial Recovery Act.

Many of his general findings were of benefit as indicators of the status of industrial engineering principles and techniques in general and their application to the textile field in particular. These were as meaningful as any of the observations that ever appeared in any of the ten-year histories for which he had become well known:

1. For the most part, industrial engineering principles and practice ("as understood by members of The American Society of Mechanical Engineers") were "unknown in the silk and rayon textile industry."

2. Work assignments based on time studies, with interrelated time production–wage analyses, were the exception rather than the rule in this industry.

Probably most perturbing of all his findings was his discovery that industrial engineers were being popularly condemned on the basis of the belief that their findings were being used to oppress workers. Although he cited the stretch-out as a manifestation of this situation, it must not be thought that he entirely discounted such contentions as mere gossip. Otherwise, would he have taken the time in his report at the ASME meeting to suggest that industrial engineers "re-examine their practices to make sure that they are discharging their full professional and societal obligations"?

That his moral beliefs were shaken is indicated by his having taken the occasion to warn the engineer not to "be party to fixing a work assignment" that demanded an "excessive effort" at an "inequitable" wage rate. Probably most indicative of his feelings on the matter was the fact that he told the meeting: "Let us not forget to honor the policy of that great leader whose memory we delight to honor, Gantt, who would not install his system of management unless he was convinced that his client would not use the new scientific methods to oppress labor." And that any person—much less an engineer—might practice something completely out of harmony with that which Gantt preached must have been unthinkable as far as Alford was concerned.

Although little was done by the industry concerning the technical recommendations, Alford's private files reveal that "the report of the Silk Board" was "based largely on the findings of the engineering report" of his staff. Thus the Board before its demise asserted:

The Board is clear in its conviction that a rigid restriction as to the number of machines to be run or the yards to be produced, even on the same fabric (and there are thousands of fabrics) would be unwise and unfair to workers and management alike. Work performed is not in proportion to machinery run, nor to pounds and yards produced; uniform piece rates per pound or yard, consequently, are unfair to workers as well as to management. . . .

Work assignments, to be consistent, and if they are to be adjusted in the interests of employers and employees, must be expressed and measured not in terms of units of machinery but in terms of actual work required.

Alford seemed pleased with the fact that Nickerson "complimented me" on reading the paper as reported in *Mechanical Engineering*. As his private files further reveal, Nickerson wrote in a letter dated November 18, 1935, "I think the article is excellent, both in contents and appearance in the place of honor." In fact, Nickerson publicly acknowledged the Alford contribution in his paper, "Work Assignment," [15] which he presented in March, 1936, to the American Academy of Political Science, where he referred his audience "for details concerning the engineering technique of textile work assignments," to the presentation of

. . . L. P. Alford, formerly Vice President of that Society (ASME), who supervised the engineering staff of the Silk Textile Work Assignment Board. Suffice it to record here that these engineers in their study of thirty typical silk and rayon mills in the United States, laid the foundation of a work which, if allowed to continue in conjunction to the arbitration methods recommended, by the Silk Board, would have done much to supplant conflicting arguments with demonstrable facts.

Additional testimony to the value of the Alford work here was given by a member of Alford's staff. The following passage is a quotation from a letter received by the author of this book from Joseph A. Piacitelli:

In this assignment, I had the privilege of working rather closely with him and under his general direction I was able to develop a time study procedure whereby one observer, during a single study period, was able to observe and record all elements of weaving operations. This procedure made it possible for the staff to make quick and effective analyses of the stretch-out problem. As a result the report prepared by him to the Board was an outstanding job.

[15] In the *Annals of the American Academy of Political and Social Science, 184* ("Problems of Organized Labor," edited by L. C. Marshall), 54-61, March (1936).

Chapter X

"SERVICE"

ALFORD—DURING THE EARLY 1930's

"The year 1937," Alford noted, "marked the close of one definite period in my professional work and the opening of another. The one that ended was nearly three and one-half years in government service; the one that commenced was in engineering education."

Although Alford still retained his connections with The Ronald Press Company after the sale of *Manufacturing Industries,* the depression found him pursuing additional interests elsewhere. As vice-president at Ronald between 1934 and 1937 he was "concerned with the procurement and publication of books, mainly business books and college texts." As for his outside endeavors, he once noted that since 1907 he had had "occasional consulting assignments." Consequently, there is nothing unusual in the fact that he continued along these lines.

For six months he was a partner, with Harrison, in G. Charter Harrison Associates, a consulting firm with a motto of "The Semaphore System of Executive Control" and with offices in the Chrysler Building in New York.

Alford's participation in the professional societies continued to be as vigorous as ever. As a matter of fact his influence was even greater than before. His enthusiasm was increased for he felt that the ills of the times required the services of the engineering profession. Also, his stature had been recognized by the profession, and his addresses and writings were assured of a receptive audience. And not content merely to talk about these matters, he served with a good deal of interest. Thus he was an administration member on two Codes of Fair Practice of the National Recovery Administration, and, between mid-January and mid-June, 1935, worked as chief engineer of the Silk Textile Work Assignment Board.

The year 1935 brought another great opportunity to Alford to work in the public interest. It was this year that he entered the Telephone Investigation.

THE TELEPHONE INVESTIGATION

It would hardly be necessary to pursue here in any great detail the investigation made of the American Telephone and Telegraph Company and its various subsidiaries. Much has already been written on this subject. And, perhaps more important, the investigation is significant here only insofar as it helps in rounding out Alford's accomplishments. Although the general facts surrounding this matter must be stated, they will be limited as much as possible and only those lesser known details which, up to now, have been confined to the relative security of the Alford private files will be added.

The study of monopolistic power was certainly not an innovation of Franklin Roosevelt's administration. The earlier Roosevelt earned a reputation and an appropriate appellation in this connection. Thus, although many Congressmen at various times had suggested an investigation of the telephone industry, it was only the creation of the Federal Communications Commission in 1934 that gave any concreteness and comprehensiveness to such an idea.

Sanctioned by Congress, the investigation was comprehensive, and the files, records, and correspondence of AT&T were thoroughly examined. The investigation is said to have cost the government about $2 million and the company $1.5 million. Seventy-seven staff reports were submitted. When all the information was in, both sides claimed a victory. The investigators asserted that it had found practices that required revision. The company, on the other hand, claimed that it had come through the examination with a clean bill of health.[1]

In any event, Commissioner Paul A. Walker, who was in charge of the investigation, submitted his "Proposed Report" to Congress for study, and it was also the basis on which the FCC issued on June 14, 1939, its final report. Despite the Brief submitted by the company, the FCC report succeeded in bringing into sharp focus the question of the place of monopolies in the economic system.

Among the Walker recommendations was his belief that the company, without impairing its admitted high caliber of service or disturbing its dividend payments, could reduce telephone rates by one fourth. Also, Walker criticized Bell's depreciation methods. He made other recommendations, but these are of greater interest to the study of Alford's contributions, for he played a larger part in their formulation.

Alford's part in the Telephone Investigation is readily available in five typewritten reports, neatly bound into six volumes, which he kept in his library in his Montclair home. Taken as *engineering economy* reports, they bear more than ample witness to Alford's abilities in this aspect of engineering problems. Interpreted, however, they divulge his philosophy of service and his earnest efforts for the public good.

Before even naming these staff reports on which he worked or even relating how he became involved in their preparation, it must be noted that the first thing that Alford did when he took on the task was to dispose of his shares of AT&T stock, an action typical of the openmindedness with which he approached a job. This action was not dictated by any law other than the one that he never violated, the moral law.

According to his own notes, Alford was solicited by H. W. Brooks, the engineer in charge of the Manufacturing Costs Unit of the Engineering Division of the Telephone Investigation of the Federal Communications Commission, to become associate engineer in charge of this unit. Alford accepted and assembled a staff to aid him. Two of his aids were C. L. Terrel

---

[1] Coon, *American Tel. & Tel.,* pp. 13 ff.

and J. A. Piacitelli. In this job, while he accomplished many things, none gave him as much pride as the part he himself played in connection with the hand telephone set. He prefaced his own copy of the "Hand Telephone Set" with the following observation: "An immediate result of the publication of this report was action by the Public Service Commissions of several states to relieve telephone subscribers of the surcharge on the hand telephone sets. At the beginning of 1938, the discontinuance and reduction of this charge were estimated to have brought savings up to $5,000,000 per year."

Although many telephone subscribers today still recall the extra charge, few persons know who, more than anyone else, was responsible for its removal. Sellman asserts that Alford informed him that when he first noted the method of manufacture of the hand set it occurred to him that its manufacture could not possibly entail extra costs. Of course, the detailed study that followed verified his early contention.

According to Lytle, Alford's pride in this accomplishment knew no bounds. Alford's other accomplishments could only be analyzed at various professional levels, but here was one multitudes of Americans could appreciate.

Even more remarkable, Alford noted in his copy that the cost of this report was small compared to the savings effected.

Of all the reports on which he worked, the longest pertains to "Permissible Costs." Over 800 typewritten pages, Alford bound them in two volumes. The contents may be determined from the subtitle: *Report on Western Electric Manufacturing Co., Inc., Manufacturing Cost of Telephone Apparatus and Equipment: Comparison of Western's Costs of Record with Maximum Permissible Costs and Justifiable Costs.* His own notes in this connection are indicative not only of how the report came to be written, but also Alford's difficulties with respect to it.

In April, 1936, Commissioner Walker called Alford and asked him what investigation, if conducted by the Manufacturing Costs Unit after July 1, 1936, would be most productive of significant results. Alford's reply was that "a study of the actual costs of manufacturing telephone equipment as produced by the Western Electric Company" would accomplish this. Walker then ordered Alford to present this proposal to C. G. Hill, and present a budget of time, personnel, and money. Brooks was temporarily absent at the time, but Alford relates what happened:

From the outset of these conferences, Mr. John Bickley, Chief Accountant of the Telephone Investigation, bitterly opposed my proposal. Previously he had preferred charges against me to Commissioner Walker, which had amounted to nothing except to injure himself.

After these conferences had continued for about three weeks without reaching a decision, Commissioner Walker asked me to make a special report to him on the relation of Mr. Bickley's program of work with the Western Electric Company, and the proposal of the Manufacturing Costs Unit. This I did, showing that Bickley had practically duplicated the work already under way by the Manufacturing Costs Unit, with the exception of the actual cost project, a matter with which he was obviously incapable of dealing.

The next step, probably taken at the suggestion of the White House, was to refer the issue to Justice Ferdinand Pecora of the Supreme Court of the State of New York. After listening for nearly a day to the presentations and arguments of Hill and Bickley, the Justice said: "If the engineers can do what they say they can do, then the study would be very much worthwhile."

Commissioner Walker then approved the proposal to investigate actual manufacturing costs of the Western Electric Company. However, he was somewhat skeptical of our ability to make the study, saying, "Western spends now eight million dollars per year on its accounting function. How can you get results with only a few thousand dollars I can allot for this work?"

My reply was "We will not make a study of everything, but only of a representative sample, and we are not operating an accounting system."

Alford found the study to be "the most complex and difficult problem I had ever attempted." It was, however, completed at an estimated cost of $125,000, and it was presented to Brooks, who in turn based on it his report to the FCC, on June 28, 1937.

When the work began, Alford "predicted that we would find Western's costs somewhat over 15 per cent high." Actually, "our finding is 21 per cent high."

Alford's group produced three other staff reports. One of these was "Cost Systems." Here was included: (1) a complete history of Western Electric, (2) an outline of Manfacturing Facilities, (3) analyses of the cost and accounting systems, and (4) a disclosure of Intra-Company Records, which showed Western's own unfavorable appraisal of its own cost methods.

The second of these remaining reports was the one on "Comparative Prices." Here the prices of telephone equipment and apparatus as manufactured by the Western Electric Company were compared to those manufactured by independent manufacturers. And, finally, there is the report on "Comparative Costs," which cost, according to Alford, about $50,000, and was presented to the FCC at the hearing on June 28, 1937.

In his library, too, one can find the culmination of his study. Not written by him but based on much of his work, this is the official *Report to Congress: Investigation of the Telephone Industry in the United States, Unanimously Adopted by the Commission, June 14, 1939* (76th Congress, House Document No. 340, U.S. Government Printing Office). It is of special interest because of his notation:

Early in my professional life I accepted and held to the doctrine that the manufacturing cost of any material or service purchased by a regulated public utility should be accurately accumulated and revealed on any occasion that might promote the public interest. An opportunity to act upon this belief came during my connection with the telephone investigation. I insisted that the manufacturers of telephone materials and equipment should be compelled to establish and maintain a cost system satisfactory to the Federal Communications Commission and be prepared to reveal the actual costs of whatever they produced to any person, or body, having the right to ask for them.

I was highly gratified to find this doctrine, or principle, of public utility regulation written into the first suggestion for new legislation in the following report of the Federal Communications to Congress.

It appears on page 611.

In his letter of July 26, 1937, Commissioner Walker went beyond simple appreciation and expressed his gratitude and praise, adding: "Your heart has been in the work, and you have served most faithfully. I feel confident that the report which has been produced, largely under your direction, will prove exceedingly valuable to regulating commissions and governmental bodies."

INDUSTRIAL ENGINEERING EDUCATION

Thorndike Saville, in his thought-provoking account of the "Achievements in Engineering Education," at the Centennial of Engineering, held in Chicago on September 4, 1952, claimed that engineering education in the United States had grown in accord with this country's geographic and industrial development. Furthermore, "a simple, single curriculum" has now begotten a score of "major curricula," and, in place of the six institutions of a century ago, there now are one hundred and forty-eight.

Industrial Engineering is one of these curricula, and reference has already been made to Lytle's famous study of *Collegiate Courses for Management* and his reference to the head of the first Industrial Engineering Department, Diemer. William S. Ayars who, prior to his retirement in 1939, was at Columbia University, and who had earlier in his career worked with Diemer at Pennsylvania State College, recounts some details of these early years.

Diemer had a "new idea," a matter that seldom meets with instantaneous and universal approval. Thus, during the first year, "there was by no means the most friendly of feelings toward him upon the part of his colleagues and assistants." However, Diemer's unpopularity was short-lived, for he more than "made good."

Because of his pioneering position, some of Diemer's ideas are of interest. He felt that shop experience was a prime prerequisite for all industrial engineering instructors. He also thought that he ought to meet his prospective students early in their careers. And, despite the fact that the freshman year was essentially made up of the same courses for all students, he managed to have a class with these beginners. To emphasize the breadth of the field, he used Gilbreth's *Primer of Scientific Management* as a text for them, and he required them to read Parkhurst's *Applied Methods of Scientific Management*, Diemer's own *Factory Organization and Administration*, and the discussions at Tuck School (Dartmouth) Conference. Other readings included Gantt's *Work, Wages, and Profits*, A. C. Humphrey's *Lecture Notes on Business Engineering*, and C. U. Carpenter's *Profit-making Management*.

Under Diemer's program, his students were subjected to as much mechanical engineering as the electrical engineering students, as much electrical engineering as the mechanical engineering students, and so on. Hence Diemer did not see much of his students after the first semester of the freshman year until the junior year. In the third year, the students' program included Machine Shop Time Study and Machine Shop Equipment, Methods, and Organization, for there was a course in Foundry and Pattern Shop Equipment, Methods, and Organization in the previous year: the lectures here were based on Taylor's *On the Art of Cutting Metals*, Becker's *High-speed Steels*, etc. Lectures in Time Study and courses in Principles of Economics, Money and Banking, Labor Problems, Transportation, and Logic (as a preliminary to a course in Psychology) were also in the junior year.

In the senior year, the student took, among others, courses in Factory Economics (Briscoe's *Economics of Efficiency*), Factory Accounts (probably akin to today's Production Control), Factory Planning (Day's *Industrial Plants* and Tyrell's *Planning of Industrial Buildings*), and Psychology.

Industrial Engineering was beginning to emerge as a separate curriculum just as the mechanical and electrical programs had done in the 1880's and 1890's. H. P. Hammond has shown how "the art preceded the science" in civil, mechanical, and mining engineering, while "the science preceded the art" in the electrical and chemical fields. The sequence in the case of industrial engineering is from the art. In the first place, this branch of engineering owes much to the mechanical engineers. Secondly, the reader need not be reminded of the art-versus-science controversy that raged in the early Taylor days. In any event, in accord with the Hammond thesis, the "corresponding curricula have been largely empirical or scientific in nature," and the industrial engineering curriculum certainly bears this out.

Today's consideration of the social-humanistic subjects in the engineering curriculum is well recognized. It would be difficult to say that the Diemer program was an early anticipation of the trend. Admittedly psychology, economics, logic, etc., are indicative of present-day concepts. However, their appearance was probably caused by Diemer's belief in their practical necessity rather than in any broad cultural pattern. Their presence, it seems, is merely a manifestation of the breadth of the management field. To be critical, the Diemer program may not have been broad enough: e.g., little if any attention was paid to the distribution phase.

However, this was per se the earliest industrial engineering department's program, even though it is not easy to determine exactly how much influence it exerted on curricula elsewhere.

ALFORD ON THE "OBJECTIVE OF INDUSTRIAL ENGINEERING COURSES"

Alford's attention was very early directed to an investigation of "the objective of industrial engineering courses." It took place at Schenectady, where, on June 17, 1925, at the request of his friend Roe, he spoke on the subject. Although Alford, in his 1922 Report for the ASME on the progress of management had noted the expansion of the collegiate program in industrial engineering, at Schenectady he was more concerned with a thorough analysis of the situation rather than a mere report of the generalities.

Because there had been on the one hand "the contributions of the engineers to the art of science and management," and on the other "the contributions of economists, businessmen, and bankers to the art and science of business," two types of curricula have developed. As the result of the former, there arose a modification of the older engineering curriculum, with basic engineering fundaments plus additional management subjects, while from the latter the regular commerce curriculum has added administration and perhaps some engineering courses.

The engineering type stressed the technical, production, or manufacturing methods, while the commerce type emphasized financial and commercial methods. Thus, the engineering schools' courses in the field have paid particular attention to product selection, design, development, and improvement; plant location, design, layout, and maintenance; and all the phases of production planning involving men, material, and machinery. Meanwhile, the commerce schools have emphasized economics, distribution, financing, governmental and social regulation, and industrial and business administration.

Yet it was Alford's feeling that all these courses had a common goal: an attempt to "fit students for positions of executing responsibility." Furthermore, when he later was actually intensively involved in engineering education, he was keenly aware that there were certain interrelationships among them. However, before engineering audiences he was in the early 1920's mainly concerned with the "engineering type," which he tentatively but not too happily—because curricula varied so widely—called "industrial engineering."

He found that these engineering courses were of three types:

a. Industrial engineering courses co-ordinated with the older engineering curricula.

b. Engineering curricula—e.g., mechanical, civil, electrical, or chemical with an option in industrial engineering.

c. Industrial engineering courses having mechanical, civil, electrical, and chemical engineering options.

Furthermore, in both course make-up and catalogue description they failed to display any "common defined objective and plan," they made no "balanced appeal to the student," and they lacked "reasonable uniformity of qualifications of the graduate." Admittedly, any course must be adapted to the institution, the funds and equipment it has, and the fields it serves. However, the existing divergence had exceeded even these limits.

It was Alford's belief that industrial leaders, whose counsel has frequently been sought, have added no little to the confusion. What is more, he felt "that advice from this source is of little value because of the specialized point of view which the average industrialist is compelled to take."

This divergence of plan and objective was even more serious in Alford's eyes because the field lacked any strong force of the type that Taylor exerted in the field of management. Naturally, Alford thought that the strong movement toward "the elimination of waste in industry" might supply the necessary unifying leadership.

Alford was firmly convinced that the term "industrial engineering" itself conveyed to the minds of prospective employers little information as to what the courses were or what the graduates could offer. On the other hand, the civil, mechanical, electrical, or chemical engineering concept conveyed a much more concrete picture. Finally, the students themselves had come to look at the courses as less "difficult" than the older engineering courses but more capable of affording to them immediately after graduation high-paying executive jobs.

The variety of names applied to the courses helped to confuse matters. On the basis of the three types of courses noted above, the number of names resulting from the possible combinations were many. Under the first category there were industrial engineering, engineering administration, administrative engineering, industrial administration, manufacturing engineering, management engineering, commercial engineering, and engineering management. Under the second category, each of the four older engineering curricula was coupled with each of the following: industrial engineering option, business option, and commercial option. Finally, for the third category the names listed above in the first category were coupled with each of the four older engineering courses as options. As weak as was the connotation of the title "industrial engineering" in his opinion, he felt that even it might have merit if the colleges adopted it or any other single name and adhered to it. The associated courses and degrees might then have had some amount of stability.

Incidentally, Alford had opened the pages of his magazines to this question even before his 1922 report. For instance, C. P. Bliss in the July, 1921, issue of *Management Engineering* had shown how, in the case of seven particular industrial engineering programs, certain individual subjects were treated. Thus students were exposed to mathematics courses 180 hours in one of these curricula and to 330 in another; yet the marketing courses were spread from a maximum of 210 hours in one of these to its complete absence in three programs. Again in the May, 1922, issue of *Management Engineering* Roe had shown the advantages of the co-operative plan, particularly as far as industrial engineering was concerned. Little wonder, then, that Lytle was called to NYU to foster such a program.

Alford, too, took cognizance of the wide range of teaching methods. In some cases, the engineering students were taught by members of the engineering faculty; in other cases, the business faculty came into the engineering school; in still others, the students were transferred to the business school; and outside lecturers were called in. The textbooks, if they did exist, were too descriptive and lacked concreteness; furthermore, they poorly classified and codified essentials. But Alford was hopeful for the so-called "experiential or case material," particularly because of the success of this method in the law and medical schools. In this connection it is possible that he was most impressed about the "co-operative feature" that allowed this type of material to be observed "at first hand and on the job."

Probably most critical of all aspects of industrial engineering courses, in Alford's mind, were their objectives. In most cases no statement of objectives ever appeared in print. In the few cases where the educators were bold enough to do so, their aims seemed to "indicate the purpose in one direction to train executives for industry and commerce, and in another to train specialists for the fields of manufacturing, selling, and administration."

Alford asserted that these views were essentially the same. He was particularly critical because none of these objectives aimed, as far as the student was concerned, at the development of his ability to think in terms of operating industrial affairs, the liberalization of his interests in the hope of increasing their usefulness, the emphasis upon human relations in industry, and the establishment of the correct personal attitude toward industry, the workers, and the public. He was particularly depressed, because the objectives of industrial engineering courses had not yet caught up with the prevalent concept of engineering expressed in the Preamble of the AEC Constitution as "the science of controlling the forces and utilizing the materials of nature for the benefit of man" and "the twentieth-century addition to the definition of 100 years ago in the words, 'and the art of organizing and directing human activities in connection therewith.' "

It was Alford's belief that what industry needed most were men who could deal "with operation in the broad." Hence he felt that the industrial engineering course must be the most severe and most rigorous of all the curricula in the engineering school. For, as he asserted, in closing his address in Schenectady: "To assume this quality of operation leaders must come forward having vision, technical knowledge, and administrative ability. Of these three qualifications no one can say which is most essential. I venture, therefore, to suggest 'Preparation for Industrial Leadership' as the outstanding objective of an industrial engineering course."

ALFORD AT NYU

Alford had the opportunity of carrying out this objective soon after 1937, for this year, he noted in his own private papers, "marked the close of one definite period in my professional work and the opening of another." He had been in government service for somewhat more than three years when he was called to New York University's College of Engineering at University Heights—the "capstone of my career."

The authoritative story of the development at New York University will eventually, it is hoped, be told by Dean William Remington Bryans. However, as far as the Industrial Engineering Department is concerned, he gives some interesting points. NYU had as early as 1914 courses in this field, even though the name given to them varied. Originally, the title carried a "Business and Engineering" connotation, although the next year it became "Industrial Engineering," and the following year, 1916, it returned to its original title. In 1919, Frank Newall came as the first Professor of Industrial Engineering, but it was Roe, having joined the faculty in 1921, who became the first head of the department.

Roe's appointment is still considered a most excellent one, for not only did he bring with him marked ability but also professional recognition. Newall, on the other hand, was handicapped, for he was neither an engineer nor an engineering graduate, even though he did have considerable shop experience: many still identify him with the efficiency men so prevalent at the time. The department was further enhanced in February, 1922, when Lytle, whose experience varied from an acquaintance with Gilbreth, Emerson, and Knoeppel to a career as an educator at Harvard, Georgia "Tech," and Cincinnati came and was given the administration of the co-operative program, as this aspect of training was then in the forefront. In 1923 NYU was most fortunate, for Porter, who in his work with Gantt had manifested the engineering abilities already recognized in other members of his family, filled the post left vacant by Newall's resignation.

The Department of Industrial Engineering continued to keep abreast of the times and strengthened its program from time to time. For example, in 1929 Roe had become alarmed by the fact that some students who were unable to keep up with the technical courses in other sections of the engineering college had drifted into this department—a situation against which, it will be remembered, Alford even before this time had warned. To cope with this emergency, it was suggested that more mechanical engineering subjects be included in the program and become an Industrial Engineering Option in Mechanical Engineering.

Typical of the progress and innovations in this department was Porter's course in Motion Study.[2] Established as early as 1928, it became the first ever to be given in an American college. Then too, Roe found the opportunity to develop those concepts in human relations, which he together with R. L. Sackett had advocated at SPEE, and which Clarence Davies found consistent with the precepts laid down by W. L. Abbott's Presidential Address before the ASME in 1926.[3]

Lytle[4] probably best expressed the ideas of the Industrial Engineering Department when he wrote: "In undergraduate work we cannot go far in giving students experience but we can train them to learn from experience. We cannot train much in leadership but we can train well for leadership. We cannot graduate managers but we can more definitely prepare minds for management."

It was then that, after deliberations and negotiations had stretched over five months, Alford was invited to join this department. The occasion was precipitated by the fact that Roe had reached retirement age. Saville, in writing to Rufus Smith, NYU Provost, early in the summer of 1937, not only declared

---

2 Saville, "Management and the Engineering College," in *Advanced Management, 16,* No. 5, 10-11, May (1951).

3 Eshbach, "Management of Men," *Proceedings of the 39th Annual Meeting,* SPEE, *39,* 637-654 (1932).

4 Lytle, "Collegiate Courses for Management: A Comparative Study of the Business and Engineering Colleges," 39th Meeting, SPEE, *39,* 806-839 (1932).

that Alford was being recommended jointly by both Roe and himself, but he reminded his correspondent that Kimball had considered him "perhaps the most outstanding man in the field."

By that time, Saville had already discussed with Alford the reorganization of the Industrial Engineering Department, for he was aware that here was a "great field" not only for public and industrial management, but especially valuable for its potential service for all departments of the College of Engineering. At the time, it was even thought that the department might take the lead in offering a degree of "Bachelor of Engineering" with no additional designation.

Certainly here were ideas consistent with Alford's thinking.

It was Roe himself who approached Alford in an attempt to persuade him to take up an educator's career. Although usually Alford could be counted on to react favorably whenever he was approached and convinced that he could through his efforts provide some important service to society, he was somewhat hesitant. He hardly pictured himself as an educator, and, in fact, some of his colleagues who had come with him through the agitated publishing offices appreciated his point of view.

Actually, he was no stranger to engineering education. Not only had he spoken on many occasions before collegiate circles —such as SPEE's Summer School in 1932—but he had even shared in an attempt at a more general educational endeavor. For example, four years before the 1933 World's Fair commemorating Chicago's centennial, the National Research Council had been requested "to prepare a scientific plan for the development of the exposition." The Council in turn passed the task on to the several scientific and engineering societies. W. L. Batt, the ASME representative, turned the matter over to a mechanical engineering committee. Alford was chairman of two of the fields allotted to ASME, management and materials handling.

In the management exhibit, Alford had the task of attempting to portray in "popular" fashion management, which in itself is seemingly "abstract in thought and intangible in application." He attempted to overcome this by portraying the working and home conditions (during four periods: 1833-1873-1913-1933) of a worker on a product well known to all, the shoe. (A product well known to Alford as well!) He suggested models and the treatment of interiors for the respective homes and shops. As to the ideas he presented for the materials handling exhibit, he stressed in the exhibits the ability of the equipment to handle greater loads, at greater speeds, with a "remarkable decrease in unit costs."

In view of such accomplishments, the Roe tactics in convincing Alford that he ought to succeed him at NYU were simple. He merely pointed out that Alford had really been teaching all his life. Alford accepted the challenge, but not before he had assured himself of help, if necessary.

Hagemann, who had been teaching, recalls that Alford had called him in, told him that he was considering accepting a teaching position somewhere in the area, and asked if he could, particularly because of his failing health, call on Hagemann for aid.

In this connection, the Alford appointment was all the more remarkable. In the first place, Alford was already sixty—just five years short of the retirement age. Secondly, Alford's coronary condition was not a favorable condition. As a matter of fact, it was just before his acceptance of the NYU offer that he had suffered a heart attack. Furthermore, he had not had a vacation in several years.

Nevertheless, he took on the NYU position with the vigor he alone could muster. He studied the present program in his typical analytical fashion. In order to determine overlapping of courses, he made a large chart on which the full contents of the courses were noted for easy comparison. He felt that the program should not be limited to the narrow confines of production. Study of job control, costs, statistics, and economics was fostered.

His first year at NYU he organized graduate courses in industrial engineering, for the College of Engineering had entered this field during the previous year. As he pointed out in an address at Purdue, in July, 1941, the young engineer after graduation often is given a position demanding some managerial and administrative responsibility and authority and, if he shows some ability here, his promotions follow along managerial rather than technological channels: hence the great need for graduate instruction in management. When he spoke at Purdue he could point to the fact that the registration in his department had increased from an enrollment of 2 in 1937-38 to 69, in 1940-41.

Two years after his arrival at NYU, he was prepared to take what he considered a decisive step. More fully convinced than ever that it was his department's duty to foster particularly the administrative aspects of the vision-technical knowledge-administrative ability triad, more determined than ever to divorce the program from even the slightest hint of dependence on the old efficiency [5] connotation that the "industrial engineering" title might suggest to some, and mindful of the trend toward a new name to describe the attempt to prepare students "for positions of leadership in administrative capacities," he petitioned the Faculty for permission to rename the department and its work.

The meeting was a stormy one, for many of his colleagues envisioned a return to the conditions prevailing before the Industrial Engineering Option of 1929. Alford's strength of personality, his vigorous arguments, his assertion that otherwise he must consider his work at NYU finished, and the conviction of many present at the conference that he alone could properly understand the potentialities of his suggestion, allowed establishment of the Administrative Engineering program under the "Department of Administrative Engineering."

In 1940-41 he tried to broaden the Administrative Engineering curriculum even further by including in it a Government

[5] Sellman relates that Alford felt so strongly about the connotation that the word "efficiency" evoked for many people that the two agreed among themselves not to use the word in their writings, if it could be avoided.

Option. Saville had in previous years attempted to bring some of these aspects to his civil engineering students in his Public Works course. Although that course was included in the broader program that Alford planned, the Government Option failed to attract many students, and it was abandoned.

Alford's activities at NYU were not confined to any classroom. He continued to maintain his professional associations. Still active at ASME, on its committees and in its functions, he found—or better, he made—time to testify before governmental bodies such as the Special Committee to Investigate Unemployment and Relief, chaired by James F. Byrnes, who was then (1938) Senator from South Carolina. Here Alford treated two aspects of the unemployment problem: (1) the relationship between wages and working hours and (2) the use of the "man-hour" to measure the fluctuation of industrial employment and unemployment.

He was active, too, with the Industrial Engineering Committee of SPEE. Here, for example,[6] he took the lead in attempting to secure some standardization of terms in management literature and management curricula. In one instance an author would use "administration" and "management" in accordance with his own desires and in the other a college would call its program by the name that would best describe the objectives it had set out for its graduating students. In the first case it must be admitted that Alford's own handbooks did much to set down certain standards of terminology. As for the curricula names, although the Alford aims still stand as vigorously as ever, the title he suggested is fast losing ground. But even Alford himself would not have regretted the renaming of his own department, about six years after his death, as the Department of Industrial and Management Engineering, if he were reasonably sure that it was a necessary step toward some standardized notation.

One more accomplishment of Alford's NYU days was the publication of his *Principles of Industrial Management* early

6 "Report of the Conferences: Industrial Engineering" (P. T. Norton, Jr.), in *The Journal of Engineering Education, 29,* No. 3, November (1938).

in 1940. Growing out of his lecture notes in his course in Industrial Management, he wrote the text in answer to several demands. The country had passed through a critical period, and the time was particularly ripe for a "restatement" of the fundamental management concepts of the leaders. Furthermore, there was a pertinent need for a presentation of management that would be effectively suited to the unstable conditions that, Alford felt, would be the general order of things for a long time. Also there was the need for a treatment that was *factual* and *quantitative* rather than *descriptive* and *qualitative*, along with the knowledge that the varying demands of the various management courses required a readily adaptable text.

The *Principles*—and it is to be noted that by now he felt that the term "law" was not entirely applicable—was the answer. Still stressing his fundamental concept of administration and management as "the art and science of getting work done," the book stresses throughout the concept of *control* in industry, built on a thorough and fundamental discussion of industrial history and philosophy. Because it actually bears his name as sole author on its title page, it may be looked upon as a manifestation of one of his most renowned capabilities. Erik Oberg of *Machinery* magazine expressed it in a letter to Roe on April 17, 1942, as his "rare ability of drawing upon the experience and knowledge of other people in the many fields in which he could not possibly be an authority himself." "He was able," Oberg added, "to co-ordinate the work of others with his own, welding all the different contributions to a work into a complete whole, so edited that it might have been the work of one man." And, although Oberg was probably referring to the handbooks, this ability is particularly evident in the *Prinicples* text.

The rigorous schedule that Alford established for himself made more and more demands on his ailing health. He walked more slowly. He appreciated more his New York apartment, which saved him from the arduous trips to Montclair.

Miss Albert, the Department's secretary, fondly recalls his systematic nature—his orderly desk and his custom of giving his daily dictation early in the morning so that she could plan her work accordingly. Fearful that he might be subject to a heart attack while at his desk, he told her that, in such an event, a remedial pill might be found in the upper pocket of his vest.

Ever punctual, no one, no student, no matter how humble, ever found him to be late for an appointment. Often this was indeed an accomplishment, particularly when he spent an uncomfortable night owing to his health. A favorite of the students, they affectionately called him "The King."

The 1941 Christmas Recess was as filled with activity for him as any other period of time during his lifetime. Except for the Christmas party at which his students paid their respects to him, the close of the year was, for him, merely a time during which he could do more work. In his busy schedule he found time to act as host to members of the Academy of Management, which met at University Heights. He continued his work despite the fact that, according to Sellman, he had been warned by a heart specialist that a recent cardiogram indicated that he ought to rest much more. Actually he worked up until December 30, when he was taken to the Flower and Fifth Avenue Hospital. On January 2, one day before his sixty-fifth birthday, he was dead.

His orderliness, however, took hold. His lectures had been prepared and were in order, even though he was no longer present. He must have given thought to the fact that the time would come when a successor would have to be named for him. It is said that he seemed to have looked favorably upon J. M. Juran, who was beginning to be known in the management field.

Juran claims that he never met Alford at the telephone company, when they were on "opposite sides," but that their first actual contact was at a SPEE meeting held at NYU. Mindful of the papers at the Seventh International Management Congress, Alford requested one paper on quality control, and Levinger suggested Juran, who was under him at Western Electric. Alford must have been impressed, for, in his *Principles,* he quotes from what was then an unpublished manuscript of

Juran. Juran relates that he went to the Alford home in Mont-clair on more than one occasion. However, the war changed any immediate plans, for Juran took on a position with the Lend-Lease Administration. Eventually Juran was in Alford's post at NYU.

Although much of the credit for the orderliness and con-tinuity in the Administrative Engineering Department must go to Porter, who took on the chairmanship, Alford left behind a systematic plan.

Probably most representative of the attitude taken on Al-ford's death was the spontaneous action on the part of some of his students, who wrote a letter to the *NYU Heights Daily News,* the campus newspaper, extolling the man who had clearly demonstrated that "the goal of his life was service to humanity." Certainly Alford would have been proud of this letter, for he would undoubtedly have been aware that his students were applying to him that very virtue that he had applied to Gantt.

There may have been other matters that he considered un-finished at the time of his death. But it is doubtful if anyone sensed the urgency he felt was connected with the lack of re-search in the management field. In establishing the work of his department in the graduate field he was indeed disturbed by the fact that the March, 1941, issue of *The Journal of Engineering Education* had published the findings of the Committee on En-gineering Research, 1939-40, which indicated that, of 1,141 theses in 73 colleges and universities, only 19 of the titles in-dicated any concern with any phase of the management field. Alarmed that these represented only 1.7 per cent, he felt it was a challenge to engineering educators and their agencies!

This was no new discovery, for he had been concerned with this disturbing fact some time before. It is particularly appro-priate, since it concerns the future and hope of management, that some attention be paid, now that most of Alford's work has been considered, to this important aspect of management's progress.

As far as Alford was concerned, his interest in this problem began long before he entered the engineering teaching profession. It was ever-present, particularly in his work with professional societies.

RESEARCH—THE FUTURE OF ENGINEERING, MANAGEMENT, INDUSTRY, AND SOCIETY

During his lifetime, Alford's interest in professional development was extended over so many societies—ASME, AEC, Institute of Management, NACA, SPEE, SIE, Sigma Xi, Academy of Management, Instytut Nankowej Organizacji—that it would not have been humanly possible for one man to work intensively in all of them. However, he concentrated his efforts on at least three—ASME, AEC, and the Institute—and made more than average contributions to others. The posts he held in many of these societies and the written and oral discussions that he contributed further indicate the extent of his participation.

His connection with the Institute of Management should be examined more closely for it was in the early formative meetings of this "society" that he expressed publicly what he had often intimated privately—the aims and purposes of a *management research organization*. His private files reveal: "I was active from the first in planning for and organizing the Institute of Management. As a member of the organizing committee I helped to draw up the charter and the by-laws and became one of its first vice-presidents."

As a Fellow of the Institute, he found in the first technical session,[7] which was held in Chicago, on October 31, 1927, an opportunity to air his views publicly. The Institute was by virtue of its charter the Research Group of the American Management Association. (It has since been absorbed by that latter organization.)

As a further manifestation of his foresight, Alford was con-

[7] Alford, "Function of the Institute of Management," *Proceedings of the Institute of Management*, No. 2. American Management Association, 20 Vesey Street, New York, 1928.

cerned here with a matter which even today has hardly been touched, much less achieved, to any degree, namely, Management Research.

Even though he knew and was highly appreciative of the fact that American industry was becoming so aware of the need for research that it was beginning to make large contributions to educational and other institutions for this purpose, he was highly critical of the fact that so little of these funds were used for research in the management field itself. Alford was aware of the relative "newness" of the discoveries concerning the fundamentals of management as compared with researches in the "older" *sciences*. To demonstrate this fact, he was fond of using an analogy once suggested by H. J. Thorkelson: if each year should be represented by one second, then the records of the earliest prehistoric man were written about five days ago, Cro-Magnon man was still with us until yesterday afternoon, and the Chinese had just begun their study of astronomy about an hour and a quarter ago. Of course, since Taylor was with us just a few seconds ago, it would hardly be expected that management research would be in full swing at this moment.

Alford felt that a management organization in general and a management research organization in particular had great opportunities. It could promote scientific methods of research in management problems, determine formula and standardization procedures, encourage, "through professional recognition," those who were furthering management, and finally provide a forum for the interchange of management information.

Alford was a little disturbed by the relatively small amount of theoretical work that was done in the management field, a matter certainly not nearly so neglected in other *sciences*. He was, therefore, hopeful that a management research organization might serve as a forum where management theories and hypotheses (e.g., Taylor's idea that "High Wages and Low Labor Cost go together," [8] Alford's own thesis that "Management Fundamentals Have Had an Evolutionary Origin," etc.) could be presented and examined, where management research meth-

[8] Alford himself later applied his kmh method to this very notion.

ods (e.g., Methods of Time Study, Motion Study, Cost Finding, Determining of Purchasing Power of Counties, Measuring Office Output, Determining Cost Obligations of Industrial Pension Plans, Forecasting Sales Demand, Forecasting Cash Requirements, etc.) could be exhibited and discussed, and finally where management laws, principles, analytical formulas, and experimental and experiential factors (e.g., Smith's Law of Division of Labor, Babbage's Law of Transfer of Skill, Taylor's Formulas for Cutting Metals, Kimball's Formula for Minimum Production Cost, the American Engineering Standards Committee's Preferred Numbers Series, Barber's Valve and Fittings Index, Davis' Formula for Most Economical Lot Size, the American Table of Mortality, etc.) could be displayed and disseminated.

Then, too, as a "clearing house," a management research organization would be in a position to record projects so that others need not duplicate these efforts but rather build on and take counsel from them. And lastly, this type of organization might take positive action as a source of recognition, honor, encouragement, and assistance.

He felt "it was a striking commentary on American thoughtlessness and underevaluation that very few professional honors have been awarded here for management achievement," while American management proponents received honors from foreign countries. And, as an instance of an exception, he pointed to F. A. Halsey, who had received the ASME Medal for his wage plans, as one who "stands almost alone in this regard." The importance Alford attached to this matter is well indicated by the pride he took in connection with the awards he himself received and by the eagerness with which he served on the ASME's Committee on Honors and Awards.

While at NYU he found an excellent opportunity to foster an interest in research even though it was not limited to management research. Acting with Maurice Holland, a friend of the University, there was established in the Department of Administrative Engineering the first graduate course in the Management of Research and Development. Originally conducted by means of a series of lectures by well-known research directors, this important and popular course eventually came under the guidance of Masson.

In general, though, Alford's belief as to what a management research organization needs most is clearly expressed in the heading that he and the other organizers of the Institute had inscribed on all membership certificates: "The Institute of Management is dedicated to research." As far as *management* is concerned, he was a strong devotee of its being "the art and science of organizing, preparing, and directing human efforts which control the forces and utilize the materials of nature for the benefit of mankind." As for *research,* he divided it into two categories: *pure* ("investigation, experiment, or study intended to discover some new fundamental law, force, or element") and *applied* ("investigation, experiment, or study intended to disclose some new application of scientific law, natural force, or useful material"). But probably most important and most meaningful of all three terms was the verb: ". . . dedicated—implies devotion to some worthy end with solemnity of motive and earnestness of purpose." And it is obvious that he believed that "In a professional organization that end can be none other than the public welfare."

A further manifestation of Alford's high hopes in research is a letter that he wrote during the last months of his life. He wrote this in answer to one he had received. Although he was generally prompt, the unusual speed with which he replied is clearly indicative of the fact that it pertained to matters to which he had already devoted considerable thought.

The first letter was written on October 3, 1941, by B. H. White, vice president of the Liberty Bank of Buffalo. On behalf of the Research Advisory Service, an organization sponsored by a group of progressive commercial banks, White asked Alford for his opinion on a very pertinent subject: What should be done now to prepare to meet the economic and business adjustments that were sure to come with the war's end?

Alford's two-page reply was in the mails by October 6. Essentially, he emphasized and underlined the statement that "manufacturers should now strengthen and expand their re-search facilities." He believed that laboratory facilities should be expanded if they exist, and be established if they do not exist; that more attention must be paid to both immediate and long-range planning; that existing products must be further improved and new adaptations must be studied; that new prod-ucts must be developed, and above all that the costs of all products must be lowered.

Clearly here is a dictum that even today is still applicable and that, in the long run, can but lead to a further improve-ment of the public welfare. Here again is the Service Motive, the *sine qua non* of engineering to which he devoted his life.

APPENDIX

APPENDIX

PART I

ALFORD'S LAWS AND PRINCIPLES

NOTE: This appendix not only gives the statements of Alford's Laws and Principles, but attempts in tabular fashion to indicate their logical and chronological development from his first statement of them in his ASME paper (1926), through his later restatements in his *Laws of Management* book (1928), his *Cost and Production Handbook* (written in 1933), and his textbook, *Principles of Industrial Management* (written in 1939), to the posthumous statement that appeared in the *Production Handbook* (1944), so much of whose work he had performed before his death in 1942. (These four books are publications of The Ronald Press Company.) Furthermore, the groupings given here may serve as a guide for the fundaments discussed in the body of the text, where the same headings and classifications may be found.

1926 LAWS	1928 LAWS	1933 LAWS	1939 PRINCIPLES	AFTER 1941 PRINCIPLES
DIVISION OF WORK (SPECIALIZATION OF THE JOB): Subdividing work so that one or a few manual or mental operations can be assigned to a worker improves the quality and increases the quantity of output.	Same.	Same.	Same.	Same.
DIVISION OF EFFORT (SPECIALIZATION OF THE INDIVIDUAL): Assigning to each worker one or a very few manual or mental operations that he is particularly adapted to perform improves the quality and increases the quantity of output.	Same.	Same.	Same.	Same.
Corollary: FUNCTIONAL MANAGEMENT (FUNCTIONAL FOREMANSHIP OR SPECIALIZATION OF THE MANAGEMENT): The highest managerial efficiency is obtained by functionalizing the duties of the executive.	As the scope of an executive's responsibility is narrowed his efficiency increases.	Same.	Same.	Same.
TRANSFER OF SKILL (SPECIALIZATION OF TOOLS AND MACHINES): The attention and skill required to use a tool or operate a machine is inversely as the skill transferred to its mechanism.	Same.	Same.	Same.	Same.
SIMPLIFICATION (SPECIALIZATION OF PRODUCT): Concentrating upon the manufacture of a single or a few types and sizes of product tends to improve the quality and lower the production cost.	Same.	Same.	Same.	Same.
STANDARDIZATION: Fixing the types, sizes, and characteristics of a product reduces its cost of manufacture.	Predetermined results, established procedures, and fixed types, sizes, and characteristics of product improve operations and reduce the cost of manufacture.	Same as 1928.	Same.	Same.
Corollary 1: Interchangeable manufacture reduces the [manufacturing] cost and, all other characteristics being equal, produces a product of maximum serviceability.	Same.	Same.	Same.	Same.

1926 LAWS	1928 LAWS	1933 LAWS	1939 PRINCIPLES	AFTER 1941 PRINCIPLES
STANDARDI-ZATION (CONT'D)	Corollary 2: A standard, in order that it shall raise rather than lower the standard of products, should deal with those elements or principles which are sufficiently understood and recognized to be stable. It should be concurred in by the most competent experts, so that their consensus as crystallized in the standard can be expected to control production for a reasonable period. However, a standard should deviate to the least possible extent from economical current practice, and where practices vary over a large range, effort should be made to follow the main path of common practice, if thereby economy and utility do not have to be sacrificed.	1928's Corollary 2 omitted.	Corollary 2: An engineering standard is always progressive, never ultimate.	Omitted.
			Corollary 3: 1928's Corollary 2.	Omitted.
	Corollary 3: The value of a standard increases rapidly with the extent to which its provisions are based upon, and are therefore verifiable by measurement. Therefore, those elements of a standard which depend upon, or are decided by, personal judgment unaided by instrumental measurement should be reduced to a minimum.	1928's Corollary 3 omitted.	Corollary 4: 1928's Corollary 3.	Omitted.
	Corollary 4: Difficulty of arriving at a standard is increased by the number of departments of an industry or conditions of application which it must serve and satisfy.	1928's Corollary 4 omitted.	Corollary 5: 1928's Corollary 4.	Omitted.
	Corollary 5: Every standard should be subject to revision from time to time in order that it should continue to reflect the available and applicable knowledge of the art.	1928's Corollary 5 omitted.	Corollary 6: 1928's Corollary 5.	Omitted.
	Corollary 6: Standardization focuses attention upon the essential elements of the object under consideration and thereby transfers competition to a field where it has positive social value.	1928's Corollary 6 omitted.	Corollary 7: 1928's Corollary 6.	Omitted.

1926 LAWS	1928 LAWS	1933 LAWS	1939 PRINCIPLES	AFTER 1941 PRIN- CIPLES
LEADERSHIP: Wise leadership is more essential to successful operation than extensive organization or perfect equipment.	Same.	Same.	Same.	Same.
			OBJECTIVE: In order that all secondary considerations may be subordinated, the essential preliminary to a contemplated action is a clear, complete statement of the objective or purpose of the action, prepared in the form of an established policy or set of instructions. (Urwick)	Omitted.
			OBJECTIVE: Each part and subdivision of the organization should be the expression of a definite purpose in harmony with the objective of the undertaking.	Same.
			UNDERTAKING: The necessary preliminary to all corporate activity is a clear complete statement of the objective of an activity, formulated as a policy or a set of instructions; the resulting action must subordinate all secondary considerations to that of the stated object.	Same.
AUTHORITY AND RESPONSI- BILITY: Responsibility for the execution of work must be accompanied by the authority to control and direct the means of doing work.	Same.	Same.	Same.	Same.
			ULTIMATE AUTHORITY: The responsibility of a higher authority for the acts of its subordinates is absolute.	Same.
			FORMAL AUTHORITY: A clear line of formal authority must run from the top to the bottom of an organization for control.	Same.
			SPAN OF CONTROL: The number of supervisory subordinates reporting to a superior should preferably be limited to no more than five or six. [The number of workers reporting to a group leader or foreman should be no more than ten or twelve.] (Graicunas)	Same.

312

1926 LAWS	1928 LAWS	1933 LAWS	1939 PRINCIPLES	AFTER 1941 PRIN- CIPLES
EXCEPTIONS: Managerial efficiency is greatly enhanced by concentrating attention solely upon those executive matters which are questions of policy, or are variations from routine, plan, or standard.	Same.	Same.	Same.	Same.
			ASSIGNMENT OF DUTIES: The duties of every person in an organization should be confined as far as possible to a single leading function. (Taylor)	Same.
			WRITTEN DEFINITION: The duties, authority, responsibility, and relations of everyone in the organization structure should be clearly and completely prescribed in writing.	Same.
			CO-ORDINATION: The smooth, frictionless, effective attainment of the objective of an organization is secured through the co-ordination of all activities performed. (Urwick)	Same.
			FACT CONTROL: Any fact gains its real significance through its relation to all other facts pertaining to the situation.	Same.
			HOMOGENEITY: An organization to be effective and to operate without friction should bring together only duties and activities that are similar or directly related.	Same.
			ORGANIZATION EFFECTIVENESS: The final test of an organization is smooth and frictionless operation.	Same.

1926 LAWS	1928 LAWS	1933 LAWS	1939 PRIN-CIPLES	AFTER 1941 PRIN-CIPLES
ECONOMIC PRODUCTION: PRODUCTION WHEN RELATIVE RATE IS	Same.	Same.	Same.	Same.

1. INCREASING: The unit cost of production decreases when the rate of increase in output increases faster than the rate of input or use of the production factors.

2. DECREASING: The unit cost of production increases when the rate of increase in output increases at a lower rate than the rate of input or use of the production factors and the unit cost of production increases when the rate of output decreases and the rate of input or use of the production factors increases.

	Corollary: For the same percentage change, the production factor labor alone has three times the effect on production of the production factor fixed capital alone.	Corollary: Same as 1928.	Same.	Same.

MASS PRODUCTION:
1. Large-scale production tends to increase operating efficiency and competitive power.

2. In large-scale production the unit time of production tends to approach the actual operating time as a limit.

	Same. Also known as Interchangeable Manufacture.	Same.	Same.	Same.

	SIMULTATION OR CO-ORDINATION:	Same.	Same.	Same.

1. The minimum over-all production time for [a group of] operations on an item of product is obtained by the maximum overlapping, or simultaneous performance, of the several work units. (Blanchard)

2. The minimum over-all production time for a group of simultaneous operations tends to approach the time of the longest work unit as its limit.

1926 LAWS	1928 LAWS	1933 LAWS	1939 PRIN-CIPLES	AFTER 1941 PRIN-CIPLES
PLANNING OR MENTAL LABOR: The mental labor of production is reduced to a minimum by planning, before work is started, what work shall be done, where the work will be done, and when the work shall be done.	Same.	Same.	Same.	Same.
PRODUCTION CONTROL: The highest efficiency in production is obtained by producing the required quantity of product, of the required quality, at the required time, by the best and cheapest method.	Same.	Same.	Same.	Same.
		OPERATING PERFORMANCE: Operating performance is controlled most directly through control of the rates of expenditures of labor, materials, and expense. (Alford & Hannum)	Same.	Same.
MANUFACTURING COST: Only those expenditures and charges which have made an essential contribution to the production of a manufactured item shall be allocated to the cost of that item.	Same.	Same.	Same.	Same.
Corollary (INDIRECT EXPENSE): The indirect expense chargeable to the output of a factory shall bear the same ratio to the indirect expense necessary to run the factory at normal capacity as the output in question bears to the normal output of the factory.	Same.	Same.	Same.	Same.

MATERIALS CONTROL AND HANDLING

1926 LAWS	1928 LAWS	1933 LAWS	1939 PRINCIPLES	AFTER 1941 PRINCIPLES
MATERIALS CONTROL:				
1. The highest efficiency in the utilization of materials is obtained by providing the required quantity, of the required quality and condition, at the required time and place.	Same.	Same.	Same.	Same.
2. The highest efficiency in the storage of materials, tools, and supplies is obtained by providing a definite place to store every item, keeping every item in its assigned place, and keeping an adequate record thereof.	Same.	Same.	Same.	Same.
	3. Quickening material turnover reduces the expense of material control.	Same.	Same.	Same.
FLOW OF WORK: The greatest economy in progressing materials through a manufacturing plant is secured when the materials move a minimum distance when passing from operation to operation.	Same.	Same. Also governing law for Mat'ls Handling Principles: Wherever possible (a) reduce handling; (b) shorten up handling and transportation.	Omitted.	Same as 1926, 1928.

AFTER 1941 PRINCIPLES

The following principles on HANDLING MATERIALS, which appear in the *Production Handbook,* do not appear in any of Alford's previous works:

1. Economy in the control of work in process (materials in process) is increased by reducing to a minimum the time for banking and handling materials.

2. Economy in handling materials is increased by moving them in a straight line.

3. All other factors being constant, handling materials by gravity is more economical than handling by power.

MATERIALS CONTROL AND HANDLING: AFTER 1941 PRINCIPLES (Cont'd)

4. Economy in handling materials is improved by increasing the proportion of use time to idle time of the transporting unit.

5. Economy of handling materials is increased by increasing the speed of the transporting unit to the point of where the cost of securing the increased speed is equal to the resulting savings in handling costs.

6. The productivity of mobile materials handling equipment units is increased by providing smooth floors, wide aisles, easy turns, and ample approaches to doorways and elevators.

7. Economy in handling materials is increased by replacing equipment and methods with more efficient equipment and methods when the cost of replacement is less than the resulting savings accumulated over a reasonable period of time.

8. The unit cost of handling materials decreases as the quantity handled increases up to the capacity of the transporting unit.

QUALITY CONTROL AND INSPECTION

1926 LAWS	1928 LAWS	1933 LAWS	1939 PRINCIPLES	AFTER 1941 PRINCIPLES
1. The quality of manufactured goods is a variable with an upward trend under conditions of competitive manufacture.	Same.	Same.	Same.	Same.
2. Control of quality increases output of salable goods, decreases cost of production and distribution, and makes economic mass production possible.	Same.	Same.	Same.	Same.
3. The inspection function in manufacturing (measuring and judging production) for highest efficiency must be independent of, but co-ordinate with, the functions of engineering, production, and sales.	Same.	Same.	Same.	Same.
				4. The conformance of finished product to its design specifications and standards should be accomplished by avoiding the making of nonconforming material rather than by sorting the good from the bad after manufacture is completed.

1926 LAWS	1928 LAWS	1933 LAWS	1939 PRIN-CIPLES	AFTER 1941 PRIN-CIPLES
PRODUCTIVITY OF THE INDIVIDUAL WORKER: The highest individual productivity is possible only when the worker is given the highest class of work for which his natural abilities fit him.	Same.	Same.	Same.	Same.
DEVELOPMENT OF SKILL: 1. SPEED (FACILITATION): As the newly acquired nerve path is strengthened, the new response tends to proceed more rapidly.	Same.	Same.	Same.	Same.
2. ACCURACY (ELIMINATION): As the new connections between impressions and memories improve, there are fewer useless and erroneous movements, the responses become more precise and likewise more accurate.				
3. LEARNING: Under usual conditions an average worker acquires skill rapidly during the first half of the training period, then more slowly for a time, if at all, and finally at a rapid rate until average proficiency is attained.	Same.			
HAND MOTIONS (Gilbreths'): 1. Both hands should work and rest at the same time. 2. Both hands should begin and complete their "therbligs" at the same instant. 3. The arms should move in symmetrical directions whether the same or opposite. 4. The paths of fast motions should be taught and learned. 5. The sequence of the fewest "therbligs" is usually the best way of doing work.	Same.	HAND MOTIONS: Same as 1926, 1928.	HUMAN MOTIONS: (Twenty Rules)	HAND MOTIONS: Same as 1926, 1928, 1933.
MOTION TIME (Segur): Within practical limits the times required by all expert workers to perform true fundamental motions are constant.	Same.	Same.	Omitted.	Same as 1926.
BARTH'S LAW OF DELAY ALLOWANCE.	Omitted.	Omitted.	Omitted.	Omitted.

WAGE PAYMENT

1926 LAWS	1928 LAWS	1933 LAWS	1939 PRINCIPLES	AFTER 1941 PRINCIPLES
WAGES:				
1. RELATIVE WAGES: Wages tend to lower when the supply of labor exceeds the demand; wages tend to rise when the supply of labor is insufficient to satisfy the demand.		Same.	Same.	Same.
2. WAGE LEVEL: The normal wage level of each country depends upon and corresponds to that country's general average productivity of labor.	Corollary: High wages accompany high production.	3. Cor'y: High wages accompany high operating performance.	Same.	Same.
		Same.	Same.	Same.
TASK AND WAGE INCENTIVE: 1. The average worker accomplishes the most when assigned a definite amount of work to be done in a given time. (Taylor)	**Same.**	Same.	Same.	Same.
2. An adequate wage incentive for the accomplishment of a definite task influences a workman to maintain his maximum output.	2. A wage incentive for the accomplishment, etc. 3. Incentive wage rates must be based on such simple mathematical rules that the worker will have no difficulty in determining unaided the amount of money he earns in doing a job. (Barth)			
WAGE RATE: Wage rates on standardized jobs should never be changed except a material change has previously been made in conditions, methods, or equipment.	BASE TIME OR RATE CHANGE: Base time on standardized jobs should never be changed except in those cases where a substantial change has previously been made in conditions, methods, or equipment.	BASE TIME, etc.: Same as 1928.	Same.	Same. PAYMENT FOR RESULTS: The amount of wages or salary paid to a worker should have a direct, logical relation to the quality of work done by the worker.

WAGE PAYMENT (Cont'd)

1926 LAWS	1928 LAWS	1933 LAWS	1939 PRINCIPLES	AFTER 1941 PRINCIPLES
HOURS OF WORK: All other factors influencing production being constant, a decrease in the hours of work increases the hours of leisure of the workers, an increase in the hours of work increases the comfort [as the result of greater earnings] of the workers. (Cox)	Same.	Same.	Instead of Cox's HOURS OF WORK, Alford illustrated how principles, discerned from trends, may be formulated. Thus: Hours of work in industry tend constantly to shorten. Money wages in industry tend constantly to increase.	Cox's HOURS OF WORK, as in 1926, 1928.
			WORK ASSIGNMENT: A reasonable work assignment is the amount of work to be done in a given time, for a wage mutually satisfactory to worker and management, and capable of being performed by a worker of average skill in the time specified with an amount of free time sufficient for personal needs and for the relief from fatigue.	Same.

OTHER FUNDAMENTS

1926 LAWS	1928 LAWS	1933 LAWS	1939 PRINCIPLES	AFTER 1941 PRINCIPLES
MAINTENANCE: Anticipating repairs and replacements prevents interruption due to bad order or brokendown equipment.		Same.	Same.	Same.
	SAFETY: Maximum productivity is dependent upon the reduction of accidents to an irreducible minimum. (Am. Eng'g Coun.)	Same.	Same.	Same.
LABOR SAVING EQUIPMENT (ASME: Hagemann & Shepard).	Same.	Omitted.	Omitted.	Omitted.
ECONOMIC LOT SIZE (Davis).	ECONOMIC MANUFACTURING LOT SIZES (ASME: Raymond): Economic Lot Formula (Raymond); Approximation (Lehoczky); Economic Purchase Quantities (Davis).	ECONOMIC MANUFACTURING LOT SIZES: Omitted.	Omitted.	Omitted.
LAW OF PROFIT: A steady and reasonable profit can only come as the reward for rendering essential service.		Omitted.	Omitted.	Omitted.

OTHER FUNDAMENTS (Cont'd)

1926 LAWS	1928 LAWS	1933 LAWS	1939 PRINCIPLES	AFTER 1941 PRINCIPLES
LAW OF DISCRIMINATION: Sensations increase in arithmetical progression as the stimuli increase in geometrical progression. (Weber)	SERIES: In manufacturing the series of greatest economy is the one that will satisfy the conditions with the fewest terms. (Geometric Series, Preferred Numbers, etc.)	SERIES: Omitted.	Omitted.	Omitted.
			INDUSTRIAL PLANT LOCATION: The most advantageous location for an industrial plant is one where the sum of the manufacturing and distributing costs are at a minimum.	Omitted.

1939 PRINCIPLES

The following principles, like the PRINCIPLE OF INDUSTRIAL PLANT LOCATION, appear only in Alford's *Principles of Industrial Management*.

ADMINISTRATION AND MANAGEMENT RESEARCH:

ATTITUDE OF MIND: Every research problem should be approached without passion, prejudice, or self-interest, realizing that every effect in administration and management has a cause.

DEFINITION OF THE PROBLEM: The problem involved in every research project should be stated in simple terms, and divided into its constituent parts to facilitate attack and avoid waste of time, effort, and money on obvious features, or on those already solved.

OBJECTIVE: The objective of every research project should be clearly and definitely stated to aid in reducing the cost of the investigation to a minimum.

LIMITATION ON PROCEDURE: As a first step in initiating a research project, determine the limitations of the procedure to be followed.

OTHER FUNDAMENTS: 1939 PRINCIPLES (Cont'd)

LOGICAL PROCEDURE: Exclude from the procedure any investigation or study that does not contribute directly to the objective.

QUALIFICATIONS OF THE RESEARCH DIRECTOR: The person selected to act as a director of a research project should have a sufficient knowledge of the subject being studied to avoid fallacies and malobservations.

ANALYSIS: Every research problem should be analyzed initially to its elements to make sure that all needful information will be gathered, and all pertinent observations made; analysis by judgment should be supported by specimen instrumental observation wherever possible.

TESTIMONY: Documentary evidence should be weighed against the experience and integrity of the author; personal testimony should be put in writing and evaluated against the credibility of the one who has testified; all testimony should be interpreted in its relation to other information.

IDENTIFICATION AND CLASSIFICATION: Every fact and item of information should be clearly identified, and related facts should be grouped into logical divisions or classes.

HUMAN PURPOSE: Wherever the objective of the administration or management research is to reach a decision on human conduct, the purely logical judgment of the facts disclosed should be modified by the quality of the purpose which motivated the conduct.

EXPERIMENTAL TEST: Whenever practicable, the thesis or hypothesis upon which the objective of the research is based should be submitted to experimental test, by setting up the governing conditions, and discovering whether the results therefrom are as indicated by the findings of the theoretical study.

PART II

ALFORD CHRONOLOGY

1877 Born January 3 at Simsbury, Connecticut.

1884-1890 Attended local grammar school.

1890-1893 Attended Plainville, Connecticut, High School.

1893-1896 Attended Worcester Polytechnic Institute.

1896 Received B.S. in E.E., June, from WPI.
Shop Foreman at McKay Metallic Fastening Association, 1896-1897, at Winchester, Massachusetts.

1897-1899 Shop Foreman at McKay-Bigelow Heeling Association.

1899 Production Superintendent at McKay Shoe Machinery Company, 1899-1902.

1900 Married Grace Agnes Hutchins, January 1, at Winchester.
Junior Member ASME.

1902 Mechanical Engineer, United Shoe Machinery Company, Boston plant.
Lived at West Somerville, Massachusetts.

1903 Transferred to Beverly plant of the United Shoe Machinery Company.

1904 L. P. Alford's son, Ralph I., born August 3.

1905 Received Professional M.E. Degree from WPI.

1906 Head, Mechanical Engineering Department, United Shoe Machinery Company.

1907 Associate Editor, *American Machinist.*
Moved to New York, New York, first to West 110th Street and then to West 106th Street.

1908 Engineering Editor, *American Machinist,* 1908-1911.
Sent to Newfoundland to observe A. G. Bell's experiments with cellular wings and airfoils.
Member ASME.

1910 Sent to Birmingham, England, to deliver paper on the "Development of High-speed Drilling Machines," before a combined meeting of IME and ASME, July 27.
Toured England, Belgium, France, Germany, and Switzerland.
Moved to Irving Street, Montclair, New Jersey.

1911 Editor in Chief, *American Machinist,* 1911-1917.

1912 Administration, Sub-Committee of the Meetings Committee, ASME, 1912-1917; Secretary, 1912-1916; Chairman, 1917.

1913 Meetings Committee, ASME, 1913-1919; Chairman, 1914-1918.

Invited to attend the Joint Meeting of ASME and the Verein Deutscher Ingenieure.

Toured Germany, Switzerland, Denmark, Sweden, France, Belgium, England, and Scotland.

1916   Chairman, Machine Tools, Sub-Committee of the Research Committee, ASME, 1916-1917.

1917   Chairman of two Special Committees: Machine Tool Standardization, 1917-1919, and Cutting Action of Machine Tools, 1917-1918, of the Research Committee, ASME.

Chairman, ASME Junior Prizes Committee.

Chairman, War Labor Board, 11th District, State of New Jersey.

Editor in Chief, *Industrial Management,* 1917-1920.

Moved to 9 North Mountain Avenue, Montclair, New Jersey.

1919   Special Committee on Aims and Organization, ASME.

1920   Vice-President, ASME, 1920-1922.

Vice-Chairman, Constitution and Bylaws, ASME.

Vice-Chairman, ASME Special Committee on Industrial Engineering.

Member of Joint Engineering Conference Committee.

Chairman of the ASME Delegation at the Engineering Organizing Convention, Washington.

Secretary, American Engineering Council, 1920-1921.

Member of ASME Delegation to AEC for all but two years of the Council's life, 1920-1940; also served as Chairman of the Delegation and Vice-President of the Council.

1921   Editor, *Management Engineering,* 1921-1923.

Chairman, Special Committee on Organization of Society Activities, ASME.

Member of the Waste in Industry Committee, AEC.

1922   Vice-President, The Ronald Press Company, 1922-1934.

Member of the Twelve Hour Shift in Industry Committee, AEC.

1923   Editor, *Manufacturing Industries,* 1923-1928.

Full Membership, Sigma Xi, WPI.

1924   Executive Committee, Management Division, ASME.

1925   Elected to the Board of Trustees of the National Museum of Engineering and Industry as ASME Representative.

Member of the General Committee on Preferred Numbers of the American Engineering Standards Committee and Chairman of its Working Committee.

1926   Standing Committee on Professional Divisions, ASME, 1926-1927.

1927 Awarded the Melville Gold Medal, ASME.

Organizing Committee of the Institute of Management, where he also served as President and Fellow.

1928 Chairman, Survey Committee, Management Division, ASME, 1928-1929.

Special Research Committee on Lubrication, ASME, 1928-1934.

Executive Chairman, Committee on Safety and Production, AEC.

Consultant for *Manufacturing Industries,* 1928-1930, after the periodical's sale in 1928.

1929 Committee on Recent Economic Changes, National Board of Economic Research.

Chairman of the Materials Handling and Management Committees for ASME for the Exhibition at the Chicago Century of Progress Exposition.

Accepted invitation for presentation of a paper, "Scientific Industrial Management," at the World Engineering Congress, Tokyo, October 30. (Alford's paper was read by Roe.)

1930 Chairman, Working Committee on Preferred Numbers, American Engineering Standards Committee.

ASME representative, Alfred Noble Prize.

1931 ASME Representative, International Management Congress Committee of the U.S.A.

Committee on Balancing Production, Distribution, and Consumption, AEC, 1931-1936.

Awarded Henry Laurence Gantt Gold Medal, ASME and the Institute of Management.

1932 Awarded Doctor of Engineering Degree (*honoris causa*) by WPI.

Sub-Committee on Metal Cutting Data (of the Special Research Committee on Cutting of Metals), ASME, 1932-1942; Chairman, 1935-1942.

1933 Biography Committee, Special Committee of Publications Committee, ASME, 1932-1942.

Awarded Certificate of Appreciation from the Officials of A Century of Progress Exposition.

1934 Chairman, Special Committee of Council on Capital Goods Industries, ASME, 1934-1935.

Special Committee of Council on Policies and Budget, ASME, 1934-1936.

ASME Representative at National Management Council.

Reduced active role at The Ronald Press Company, but officially retained his Editorship and Vice-Presidency until
1937 and his Directorship until his death (1942).

Continuing his management consulting practice, he was a
partner with G. Charter Harrison for a short time.

Administration Member on two Codes of Fair Practice, NRA.

1935   Special Committee of Council on Public Affairs, ASME,
1935-1936.

Standing Committee on Awards, ASME.

Chief Engineer, Silk Textile Assignment Board, January-
August.

Associated Engineer in Charge of Manufacturing Costs Unit
of the Federal Communications Commission, 1935-1937.

Invited to present paper on "Management Aspects of the
American Codes of Fair Practice" for the International
Congress for Scientific Management, London, Summer,
1935.

1936   Chairman, Standing Committee on Awards, ASME, 1936-
1942.

Fellow, ASME.

1937   Special Committee of Council on Procedure for Selection of
Honorary Members and John Fritz Medalist, ASME, 1937-
1938.

ASME Representative at the National Management Council, 1937-1942.

Medals Committee, Special Committee of the Honors and
Awards Committee, ASME, 1937-1938.

Professor of Administrative Engineering and Chairman of
the Department of Industrial Engineering, College of Engineering, New York University, 1937-1942.

Industrial Engineering Committee, SPEE, 1937-1942.

1938   Delegate to the International Management Congress, Washington.

Special Committee on Certificate and Pin for Fellow Grade,
ASME, 1938-1939.

1939   Special Committee of the Council for Frederick W. Taylor
Memorial, ASME, 1939-1942.

General Committee, Management Division, ASME, 1939-
1942.

1941   ASME Representative on Gantt Medal Award Board, 1941-
1942.

Honorary Member, ASME.

1942   Died, January 2, at Flower Hospital, New York, New York.

PART III

BIBLIOGRAPHY OF L. P. ALFORD'S WORKS

Books, Articles, Papers, and Other Writings (Published and Unpublished) Credited to Alford's Sole Authorship

"Power Problems in Connection With the Development of Plans for a Manufacturing Plant," Thesis for the Mechanical Engineer Degree. Worcester Polytechnic Institute, 1905.

"Development of High-speed Drilling Machines," Excerpt Minutes of *Proceedings* of the Joint Meeting of the Institution of Mechanical Engineers and the American Society of Mechanical Engineers, Birmingham, England, 981-985, July 27, 1910.

"Development of High-speed Drilling Machines," Abstract, *Transactions, ASME, 32,* 766-710, 1910.

Bearings and Their Lubrication, New York, McGraw-Hill Book Company, 1911.

"Scientific Management in Use," *American Machinist, 36,* No. 14, 548-550, April 4, 1912.

"Respeeding of Lathes," *American Machinist, 41,* No. 23, 973-977, December 3, 1914.

"Respeeding of Machine Tools," *American Machinist, 41,* No. 24, 1017-1024, December 10, 1914.

"Standardizing Lathe Tool Posts," *American Machinist, 41,* No. 25, 1062, December 17, 1914.

"Standard Taper Sockets and Shanks," *American Machinist, 41,* No. 26, 1112-1115, December 24, 1914.

"Standard Boring-bar Cutters, Gibs and Keys," *American Machinist, 41,* No. 27, 1148, December 31, 1914.

"Industrial Motor Applications: Machine Tools," pp. 1181-1201, *Standard Handbook for Electrical Engineers,* Frank F. Fowle, Editor in Chief, 4th ed., New York, McGraw-Hill Book Company, 1915.

"Machine Tools and Machine Shop Practice," pp. 1396-1466, *Mechanical Engineers' Handbook,* Lionel S. Marks, Editor in Chief, New York, McGraw-Hill Book Company, 1916.

"The Status of Industrial Relations," *Transactions, ASME, 41,* 163-186, 1919.

"The Value of Team Work Among Engineers," in *The Practical Applications of Industrial Engineering, Proceedings* of the Society of Industrial Engineers, Philadelphia Spring Conference, 269-272, March 24-26, 1920.

"Ten Years' Progress in Management," *Transactions, ASME, 44,* 1243-1276, 1922.

"Ten Years' Progress in Management," *Mechanical Engineering, 44,* No. 11, 699-703, November, 1922.

"Industrial Motor Applications: Machine Tools," pp. 1220-1237, *Standard Handbook for Electrical Engineers,* Frank F. Fowle, Editor in Chief, 5th ed., New York, McGraw-Hill Book Company, 1922.

"Management," pp. 1276-1321, *Accountants' Handbook,* Earl A. Saliers, Editor, New York, The Ronald Press Company, 1923.

"Motion Time Analysis: A New Step in Operation Study and Rate Study," *Manufacturing Industries, 12,* No. 5, 341-345, November, 1926.

"Laws of Manufacturing Management," *Transactions, ASME, 48,* 393-418, 1926.

"Laws of Manufacturing Management," *Mechanical Engineering, 49,* No. 4, 301-305, April, 1927.

"Way to Reduce the Cost of Accident," *Manufacturing Industries, 14,* No. 2, 121-124, August, 1927.

"Function of the Institute of Management," *Institute of Management Studies,* No. 2, New York, American Management Association, 1927.

"Representative Policies and Methods for Purchasing New Equipment," *Manufacturing Industries, 14,* No. 4, 277 ff., October, 1927.

"Can We Afford New Equipment?" *Manufacturing Industries, 15,* No. 1, 27-30, January, 1928.

"America's Most Spectacular Manufacturing Achievement," *Manufacturing Industries, 15,* No. 1, 11, January, 1928.

"How Is the Cost of New Manufacturing Equipment Charged to Product?" *Manufacturing Industries, 15,* No. 2, 107 ff., February, 1928.

"When Is Equipment Scrapped and How Is Its Value Charged Off?" *Manufacturing Industries, 15,* No. 3, 199-202, March, 1928.

"Who Does the Buying of Equipment in Manufacturing Plants?" *Manufacturing Industries, 15,* No. 4, 279-282, April, 1928.

Laws of Management Applied to Manufacturing, New York, The Ronald Press Company, 1928.

"Functions of the Institute of Management," *Proceedings* of the Institute of Management, October 1, 1927, New York, American Management Association, 1928.

"Preferred Numbers as a Tool of Management Research," *Institute of Management Series,* No. 14, New York, American Management Association, 1929.

"Industry: Technical Changes in Manufacturing Industries," pp. 96-166, in *Recent Economic Changes in the United States,* vol. 1, New York, McGraw-Hill Book Company, 1929.

"Planning for the Century of Progress, Chicago, Illinois, 1933-1934," Unpublished, 1929.

"An Opportunity in Management," *Enterpriser,* University of Illinois, 1929.

"Scientific Industrial Management," Paper Number 341, World Engineering Congress, Tokyo, Management Session, October 30, 1929.

"Organization for Production Control," Selected Papers of the Summer School for Engineering Teachers, Papers of the Production Division of the 1929 Session: Mechanical Engineering, Society for the Promotion of Engineering Education, No. 12, February, 1930.

"Fundamentals of Management Applied to Industrial Enterprises," *Mechanical Engineering, 51,* No. 10, 744-746, October, 1929.

"Progress in Manufacturing, 50th Anniversary, ASME," *Mechanical Engineering, 52,* No. 4, 401-403, April, 1930.

"Management's Responsibility for Industrial Accidents," *Mechanical Engineering, 52,* No. 12, 1048-1050, December, 1930.

"After the Depression—What?" *Factory and Industrial Management, 81,* No. 4, 604-606, April, 1931.

"Some Economic Factors in an Industrial Program," *Annual Industrial Conference,* Pennsylvania State College, June, 1932.

"Appraisal of Economic Forces," *Mechanical Engineering, 55,* No. 6, 345-346, June, 1933.

"A Declaration of Abundance," Paper for the American Engineering Council, Unpublished, October 13, 1933.

"Management Aspects of American Codes of Fair Practice," London, International Congress for Scientific Management, 1935.

"Ten Years' Progress in Management (1923-1932)," *Transactions, ASME, 55,* MAN-55-2, 1-16, 1933.

"Cost Control," *Mechanical Engineering, 56,* No. 8, 466-467, August, 1934.

Henry Laurence Gantt: Leader in Industry, New York, ASME; also Harper & Brothers, 1934.

"Work Assignment in Silk and Rayon Manufacturing," *Mechanical Engineering, 57,* No. 11, 679-684, November, 1935.

"Work Assignment in Silk and Rayon Manufacturing," *Textile Manufacturer, 61,* 491-492, December, 1935.

"Looms per Weaver: Data From Recent Silk and Rayon Work Assignment Study," *Textile World, 86,* No. 1, 72-73, January, 1936.

Principles of Industrial Management, New York, The Ronald Press Company, 1940.

WORKS EDITED BY ALFORD, ALSO CONTAINING HIS OWN INDIVIDUAL CONTRIBUTIONS

"Manufacture of Artillery Ammunition" by Members of the Editorial Staff of the *American Machinist,* L. P. Alford, Editor in Chief, New York, McGraw-Hill Book Company, 1917.

Foremanship, Books I, II, III, and IV, L. P. Alford, Directing Editor, New York, Association Press (YMCA), 1921.

Management's Handbook by a Staff of Specialists, L. P. Alford, Editor in Chief, New York, The Ronald Press Company, 1924.

Cost and Production Handbook, L. P. Alford, Editor, New York, The Ronald Press Company, 1934.

WORKS BY ALFORD AS CO-AUTHOR

"Factory Construction and Assignment," with H. C. Ferrell, *ASME Journal,* 1139-1166, June, 1911.

"The Principles of Management," with A. H. Church, *American Machinist, 36,* 857-862, May 30, 1912.

"Leadership in Industry: A Suggestion Proposed for the Manufacturers' Committee of the Sesqui-centennial," with Lee Galloway and Theodore Skinner, September, 1923 or 1925.

"A Basis for Evaluating Manufacturing Operation," with J. E. Hannum, *Transactions, ASME, 51,* MAN-51-2, 9-15, 1929.

"A Basis for Evaluating Manufacturing Operation," Abstract, with J. E. Hannum, *Mechanical Engineering, 51,* No. 3, 181-185, March, 1929.

"Measuring Operating Performance by Kilo Man-Hour," with J. E. Hannum, *Mechanical Engineering, 54,* No. 12, 821-824, December, 1932.

"Applications of the KMH Method of Analyzing Manufacturing Operations," *Transactions, ASME, 55,* MAN-55-7, 59-66, 1933.

"Man-Hour Planning," with J. E. Hannum, Unpublished, 1934.

"DISCUSSIONS" BY ALFORD AT ASME

"Industrial Service Work in Engineering Schools," *Transactions, ASME, 36,* 180 and 184, 1914.

"Standard Cross Sections and Symbols," with L. Ormay, *Transactions, ASME, 36,* 969-974, 1914.

"Industrial Preparedness," *Transactions, ASME, 38,* 62, 1916.

"Cutting Tool Research," *Transactions, ASME, 39,* 206-207, 1917.

"Code of Ethics," *Transactions, ASME, 40,* 98-99, 1918.

REPORTS OF COMMITTEES ON WHICH ALFORD SERVED, WHERE AL-
FORD'S WORK RANGED FROM ACTIVE PARTICIPATION TO COMPLETE
PREPARATION OF THE REPORT

"The Present State of the Art of Industrial Management," Sub-
committee on Administration of ASME, *Transactions, 34,* Majority Report, 1131-1150; Minority Report by M. H. Vaughan,
1151-1152, 1912.

Waste in Industry, Committee on Elimination of Waste in Industry of the Federated American Engineering Societies. Published
by the Federated American Engineering Societies, Washington;
Distributed by McGraw-Hill Book Company, New York, 1921.

The Twelve Hour Shift in Industry, Committee on Work Periods
in Continuous Industry of the Federated American Engineering
Societies, New York, E. P. Dutton & Company, 1922.

*Safety and Production: an Engineering and Statistical Study of
the Relationship Between Industrial Safety and Production,* Committee on Safety and Production of the American Engineering
Council, New York, Harper & Brothers, 1928.

*Table of Preferred Numbers, American Engineering Standards
Committee, AESC* Z 17-1927, New York, American Engineering
Standards Committee, 1927.

"The Balancing of Economic Forces: Suggested Lines of Attack on
the Interrelated Problems of Consumption, Production, and Distribution," Committee on the Balancing of Economic Forces,
First Progress Report to the American Engineering Council, *Mechanical Engineering, 54,* No. 6, 415-423, June, 1932.

"The Balancing of Economic Forces," Committee on the Balancing
of Economic Forces, American Engineering Council, "Part I: An
Analysis of Forty Causes of Business Instability," *Mechanical Engineering, 55,* No. 4, 211-224, April, 1933; and "Part II: An
Analysis of Twenty-three Plans for Business Stabilization," *Mechanical Engineering, 55,* No. 5, 295-304, May, 1933.

"Capital Goods Industries: A Progress Report," ASME Capital
Goods Committee, *Mechanical Engineering, 56,* No. 2, 85-86,
February, 1934.

"Durable Goods and Engineering Employment," ASME Capital
Goods Committee, *Mechanical Engineering, 56,* No. 10, 580-582,
October, 1934.

"Code Restrictions on Machinery and Production," ASME Capital
Goods Committee; Report written by W. E. Hopkins and J. F.
Nelson. *Mechanical Engineering, 57,* No. 1, 9-14, January, 1935.

"The Balancing of Economic Forces, Part III: A Catechism of
Fundamental Factors," Committee on the Balancing of Economic

Forces, American Engineering Council, Unpublished, Written
January 10, 1936, Revised April 18, 1936.

"American Standard Preferred Numbers," Sectional Committee of
the American Standards Association, American Engineering and
International Standard, ASA Z 17.1-1936, New York, American
Standards Association, April 14, 1936.

"Report on Work Assignment in Silk and Rayon Manufacturing,"
L. P. Alford, Chief Engineer of the Silk Textile Work Assignment Board, Unpublished, 1935.

Staff Reports of the Manufacturing Costs Unit of the Engineering Division of the Telephone Investigation of the Federal Communications Commission, L. P. Alford, Associate Engineer in
Charge of Unit

"Comparative Costs," Unpublished, 1935-1937.

"Comparative Prices," Unpublished, 1935-1937.

"Hand Telephone Set," Unpublished, 1935-1937.

"Permissible Costs," Two Volumes, 1935-1937, Unpublished.

ADDRESSES BY ALFORD

"The Engineer's Place in Reconstruction," Society of Industrial
Engineers, New York, 1919.

"The Golden Rule in Industry," Industrial Conference, Blue Ridge,
North Carolina, July 2, 1920.

"Cost Accounting and Industrial Waste," Convention of the Re-
fractories Accountants Institute, New York, October 24, 1921.

"The Purpose of Industry," Joint Meeting for Foremen and Executives, New Haven, January 18, 1921.

"The Foreman and His Job," YMCA, Cambridge, January 20, 1921.

"The Foreman's Relation to Production," Long Island Industrial
YMCA, February 23, 1921.

"Trend of American Industry," Supervisors' Club, April 13, 1921.

"Multiplying Expense," Worcester, December 15, 1921.

"The Federated American Engineering Societies," St. Louis, June
2, 1923 (?).

"Economic Trend of Industry," Reading, April, 1922.

"Factory Management," York, Pennsylvania, February, 1923.

"Story of Industry," Scranton, April 21, 1924 (?).

"What Management Has Accomplished," Newport News, Virginia,
April 10, 1925.

"The Objective of Industrial Engineering Courses," Schenectady,
July 17, 1925.

"Research in Management," Chicago, January 21, 1927.

"Management's Part in Maintaining Prosperity," Columbus, Ohio,
October 24, 1927.

"Place of Cost Accounting in Management," Dayton, Ohio, January 22, 1929.

"Accounting Aid to Industrial Management," Indianapolis, February 20, 1929.

"Future of Management," Brooklyn Polytechnic Institute, March 7, 1929.

"Safety and Production," Franklin Institute, March 10, 1929.

"The Foreman's Side of Profits," Utica, March 18, 1929.

"The Contributions of Industry to the Modern State," New York, April 3, 1929.

"Development of a Cost Reduction Program in Manufacturing Industry," National Association of Cost Accountants, Springfield, Massachusetts, April 17, 1929.

"The New Economics: Establishing Standard Rate Levels Based on Production Value," Blue Ridge, North Carolina, August 3, 1929.

"Trends in Industrial and Production Management," Society of Industrial Engineers, October 23, 1929.

"The Contributions of Henry Laurence Gantt to Modern Industry," 1932 Summer School for Professors of Engineering, Stevens Institute of Technology, Society for the Promotion of Engineering Education, July, 1932.

"Budgetary Control," National Association of Cost Accountants, Binghamton, May, 1934 (?).

"An Analysis of the Basis of Morale in Industry," Society for the Advancement of Management, Washington, May 22, 1941.

"Graduate Instruction in Management," Purdue University, July 1, 1941.

OTHER ADDRESSES

"Responsibility of Management," Buffalo.

"Purpose of Industry," Cambridge.

"Engineer in Industrial Leadership," Chicago.

"Co-operation of United States Industry," Detroit.

"Engineering Leadership in Industry," Detroit.

"Parallels Between Labor Saving Machinery and Labor Saving Management," Elizabeth, New Jersey.

"Trained Intelligence in Every Day Work," University of Illinois.

"Does Employment Management Pay?" Greensboro, North Carolina.

"Basis of American Prosperity," Hoboken.

"Management and Administration," New Jersey Executive Club, Jersey City.

"The Federated American Engineering Societies and the Elimination of Waste in Industry," Minneapolis.

"Materials," New Bedford, Massachusetts.

"The Professional Engineer," Cooper Union, New York.

"Industry: Past and Present," Scranton.

"History of Management," Somerset County (New Jersey) Foremen's Club.

"Leadership in Industry," Toledo.

"Work in Industry," Toledo.

"Accident Prevention," Delaware Safety Council Institute, Wilmington.

"Current Organization Problems," July 16, 1942.

"Elimination of Waste."

"Engineer in Industrial Readjustment."

"Industrial Strides."

"Maintaining Quality in Industry," July 16, 1941.

"Materials and Their Control."

Alford noted that, between 1910 and 1938, he had delivered lectures at the following institutions:

Alabama Technical Institute
Brooklyn Polytechnic Institute
Columbia University
Cornell University
Drake University
Harvard University (Graduate School of Business Administration)
University of Illinois
New York University
Pennsylvania State College
University of Pittsburgh
Pratt Institute
Purdue University
Worcester Polytechnic Institute
Yale University (Sheffield Scientific School)

TRANSLATIONS OF ALFORD'S WORKS

"Lois, principes et règles," Translation of Alford's "Laws of Manufacturing Management" by CH.-B. Thumen, in *Mon Bureau*, 295-298, July, 1928 and 345-348, August, 1928.

"Les lois de l'organisation industrielle," Translation of Alford's *Laws of Management* by M. P. Hervé, Geneva, International Management Institute, 1930.

"Die Gesetze der industriellen Betriebsführung," Authorized Translation of Alford's "Laws of Manufacturing Management" by

Walter Niedlich, Geneva, International Management Institute, 1930.

Handbuch für industrielle Werkleitung, Translation of Alford's *Management's Handbook,* Fritz Fröhlich, Berlin, Vereines deutscher Ingenieure (VDI-Verlag), 1930.

Posthumous Works

Production Handbook, L. P. Alford and John R. Bangs, Editors, and George E. Hagemann, Staff Editor, New York, The Ronald Press Company, 1944.

Principles of Industrial Management, L. P. Alford and Henry R. Beatty, rev. ed., New York, The Ronald Press Company, 1950.

Interviews With L. P. Alford

"The Importance of the Modern Engineer in the Scientific Administration of Economic Activities," by Louis Levine, New York, *The World,* Sunday, September 26, 1920.

"The American Engineer Council's Check-up of the Elements Responsible for the Appalling Nationwide Industrial Waste," by Charles W. Wood, New York, *The World,* Sunday, November 12, 1921.

Books Acknowledging Debt to L. P. Alford

Budgeting by Prior Sinclair (The Ronald Press Company).

Control of Quality by G. S. Radford (The Ronald Press Company).

Cost Accountants' Handbook, Theodore Lang, Editor (The Ronald Press Company).

Gantt Chart by Wallace Clark (The Ronald Press Company and Pitman Publishing Corporation).

Graphic Production Control by C. E. Knoeppel (Engineering Magazine Company).

Principles of Industrial Organization by Dexter S. Kimball (McGraw-Hill Book Company).

PART IV

ADDITIONAL BIBLIOGRAPHY

American Machinist
Editorials
What the American Machinist Stands For, *33*, No. 2, 85, July 14, 1910.
Increasing Rates and Reducing Costs, *33*, No. 24, 1127, December 15, 1910.
F. W. Taylor and the Steel Mills, *34*, No. 9, 463, March 9, 1911.
Are Twelve Hours a Day Too Much? *36*, No. 24, 967, June 13, 1912.
The Geometric Progression for Feeds and Speeds, *41*, No. 23, 1003-1004, December 3, 1914.
Special Correspondence
Shop Efficiency and Railroad Rates, *33*, No. 24, 1097-1098, December 15, 1910.
American Society of Mechanical Engineers
"The ASME Today," *Mechanical Engineering, 61*, No. 10, 745-747, October, 1939; *61*, No. 11, 825-828, November, 1939; *62*, No. 2, 138-142, February, 1940.
Discussions of Alford Papers
"The Present State of the Art of Management," *Transactions, 34*, 1153-1229, 1912.
"Status of Industrial Relations," *Transactions, 41*, 186-208, 1919; *Mechanical Engineering, 41*, No. 6, 513-516, 566, June, 1919; *41*, No. 7, 572-580, July, 1919.
"Ten Years of Progress in Management," *Transactions, 44*, 1274-1296, 1922.
"Laws of Manufacturing Management," *Transactions, 48*, 418-438, 1926; *Mechanical Engineering, 49*, No. 4, 305-308, April, 1927.
"A Basis for Evaluation of Manufacturing Operation, *Transactions, 51*, 16-24, 1929.
"Fundamentals of Management as Applied to Industrial Enterprises," *Mechanical Engineering, 51*, No. 10, 964, October, 1929; *52*, No. 3, 239, March, 1930.
"Ten Years' Progress in Management, 1923-1932," *Transactions, 55*, MAN-55-2, 16-21, 1933; *Mechanical Engineering, 55*, No. 4, 264, April, 1933.

"Balancing of Economic Forces," *Mechanical Engineering, 54,* No. 7, 519, July, 1932; *54,* No. 8, 588, August, 1932; *54,* No. 10, 734, October, 1932; *54,* No. 12, 879, December, 1932; *55,* No. 7, 454-457, July, 1933.

"Appraisal of Economic Forces," *Mechanical Engineering, 55,* No. 6, 345-346, June, 1933.

"Application of KMH Method of Analyzing Manufacturing Operations," *Transactions, 55,* 66-72, 1933.

"Hours and Awards," *Mechanical Engineering, 61,* No. 4, 302-304, April, 1939.

"Progress in Industrial Management," *Transactions, 51,* MAN-51, 1-6, 1929; *52,* MAN-52-1-4, 1930.

"Ten Years' Progress in Management," *Transactions, 65,* 213-260, 1943.

ANDERSON, E. H., and SCHWENNING, G. T. *The Science of Production Organization,* New York, John Wiley & Sons, 1938.

BABBAGE, CHARLES. *On the Economy of Machinery and Manufacture,* London, Charles Knight, 1832.

BARTH, CARL. "The Barth Standard Wage Scale," *Manufacturing Industries, 10,* No. 6, 357, December, 1925.

BOHENIK, A. F. "The American Engineering Council," Unpublished.

BORAH, W. E. *Report from Committee on Education and Labor, Amending S. 6172 to Regulate Method of Directing Work of Government Employees,* Srp. 931, 62nd Cong., 2nd Sess., In V.3:6122, July, 1922.

BRANDEIS, L. D. *Scientific Management and Railroads, Being Part of the Brief Submitted to the ICC,* New York, Engineering Magazine Company, 1912. For Full Brief, see *Interstate Commerce Commission Reports,* vol. 20. Also *Evidence Taken in the Matter of Proposed Advances in Freight Rates by Carriers,* 61st Cong., 3rd Sess., Senate Document No. 725, November 21, 1910.

BURNHAM, JAMES. *The Managerial Revolution,* New York, John Day Company, 1941.

CALDER, JOHN. "Overvaluation of Management Science," *Iron Age, 91,* 605-606, March 6, 1913.

———. "Review of Principles of Management," *American Machinist, 35,* 965-966, July 20, 1911.

CAMERON, W. H. "The Attitude of the Employer Towards Accident Prevention and Workmen's Compensation," *Transactions, ASME, 37,* 899-907, 1915.

CHURCH, A. H. "Has Scientific Management Science?" *American Machinist, 35,* No. 3, 108-112, July 20, 1911.

CHURCH, A. H. "The Meaning of Scientific Management," *Engineering Magazine, 41*, No. 1, 47-101, April, 1911.

——. *Production Factors in Cost Accounting and Works Management*, New York, Engineering Magazine Co., 1916.

——. *The Science and Practice of Management*, New York, Engineering Magazine Co., 1914.

CIVILIAN EXPERT BOARD. *Report on Industrial Management of U.S. Navy Yards*, Prepared by Direction of Hon. George Von L. Meyer, Secretary of the Navy, Washington, U.S. Government Printing Office, 1912.

COBB, T. W., and DOUGLAS, P. H. "A Theory of Production," *American Economic Review, 18*, No. 1, *Supplement,* March, 1928.

COLVIN, F. H. "Management at Watertown Arsenal," *American Machinist, 37*, No. 11, 424-427, September 12, 1912.

——. *Sixty Years with Men and Machines*, New York, Whittlesey House, McGraw-Hill Book Company, 1947.

COOKE, M. L. *How About It?*, Philadelphia, M. L. Cooke, 1917.

——. "Unemployment Scores," *Bulletin, Taylor Society, 6*, No. 4, 163-170, August, 1921.

COON, HORACE. *American Tel & Tel*, New York, Longmans, Green & Co., 1939.

COPLEY, F. B. *Frederick W. Taylor: Father of Scientific Management*, 2 vols., New York, Harper & Brothers, 1923.

CRISSEY, F. E. "The Taylor System Again," *American Machinist, 34*, 1182, June 22, 1911.

CROZIER, WILLIAM. "Scientific Management," *Bulletin, Taylor Society, 6*, No. 5, 213-216, October, 1921.

——. "Scientific Management in Government Establishments," *Bulletin, Taylor Society, 1*, No. 5, 1-8, October, 1915.

DE LEEUW, A. L. "The Final Measure of Industrial Efficiency," *Management Engineering, 1*, No. 3, 141-146, September, 1921.

DEMOND, C. D. "The Barth Standard Wage Scale: Discussion and Reply," *Manufacturing Industries, 11*, No. 3, 373, March, 1926.

DEPARTMENT OF LABOR. "Report on the Measurement of Technological Unemployment, Submitted by the Secretary of Labor," November 14, 1931, Later Incorporated in Report 964 of the U.S. Senate, Under Senate Resolution 483 of the 71st Congress, June 30, 1932.

DODGE, J. M. "A History of the Introduction of a System of Shop Management," *Transactions, ASME, 27*, 720-729, 1906.

DOUGLAS, P. H. *The Theory of Wages*, New York, The Macmillan Co., 1934.

DRURY, H. B. *Scientific Management: A History and Criticism*, New York, Columbia University Press, 1915.

DRURY, H. B. "Scientific Management and Progress," *Bulletin, Taylor Society,* 2, No. 4, 1-10, November, 1916; 3, No. 1, 7-22, February, 1917.

EMERSON ENGINEERS. *Harrington Emerson (1835-1931).* Privately Prepared, 1951.

ENGINEERING MAGAZINE EDITORIAL. "Science Versus Systems," 40, No. 6, 952, March, 1911.

ESHBACH, O. W. "Management of Men," *Proceedings,* 39th Annual Meeting, Society for Promotion of Engineering Education, 39, 637-653, 1931.

EVANS, H. A. "Detailed Instruction for Machine Shop Methods," *American Machinist, 31,* 645-649, April 23, 1908.

———. "Do Taylor's Methods Increase Production?" *American Machinist, 34,* 1133-1134, June 15, 1911.

———. "Effect of the Taylor System: What Is to Become of the Mechanic?" *American Machinist, 33,* 1085, December 15, 1910.

———. "Output Under Scientific Management," *American Machinist, 34,* 1202-1203, June 29, 1911.

———. "General Instruction for Machine Shop Methods," *American Machinist, 31,* 610-614, April 16, 1908.

———. "Reduction in Cost of Navy Yard Work," *American Machinist, 33,* 1200-1202, June 30, 1910.

———. "Scientific Factory Management," *American Machinist, 33,* 1108, June 16, 1910.

FEDERAL COMMUNICATIONS COMMISSION. *Investigation of the Telephone Industry in the U.S., A Report of the FCC to Congress,* 76th Cong., House Document No. 340, Washington, U.S. Government Printing Office, 1938.

FILIPETTI, GEORGE. *Industrial Management in Transition,* Chicago, Richard D. Irwin, 1946.

FINLEY, D. E. *Report From the Committee on Printing, Favoring H.C.R. 45, To Print Hearings on Taylor and Other Systems of Shop Management, Held Under Special Committee Appointed Under HR 90,* August 12, 1912, Hrp. 1173, 62nd Cong., 2nd Sess., VE:6138, Washington, U.S. Government Printing Office, 1912.

FRANKLIN, B. A. *Open Shop Review,* 185, May, 1926.

GANTT, H. L. *Industrial Leadership,* New Haven, Yale University Press, 1916.

———. *Organizing for Work,* New York, Harcourt, Brace and Howe, 1919.

———. *Work, Wages, and Profits,* New York, Engineering Magazine Company, 1916.

GILBRETH, F. B. *Primer of Scientific Management,* 2d ed., New York, D. Van Nostrand Company, 1914.

GILBRETH, F. B., and ASSOCIATES. "Lecture Notes on Scientific Management," Written Up and Compiled by W. S. Ayars, a Member of the First Summer School of Scientific Management, F. B. Gilbreth and Associates, Providence, R.I., August 4-September 1, 1913, Unpublished.

GOING, C. B. *Principles of Industrial Engineering,* New York, McGraw-Hill Book Company, 1911.

HAGGARD, H. W. "Physiology for the Engineer," *Mechanical Engineering, 61,* No. 1, 8-12, January, 1929.

HALL, E. D. "Quality Control," *Manufacturing Industries, 16,* No. 1, 17-19, July, 1928.

HATHAWAY, H. K. (editor and compiler). "Tributes to Taylor," *Transactions, ASME, 37,* 1459-1496, 1915.

HINE, C. D. L. *Modern Organization,* New York, Engineering Magazine Co., 1912.

HOUSE OF REPRESENTATIVES SPECIAL COMMITTEE to Investigate the Taylor and Other Systems of Shop Management, *Hearings.* Under Authority of HR 90, 62nd Cong., 2nd Sess., 3 Volumes, Washington, U.S. Government Printing Office, 1912.

HOXIE, R. F. *Scientific Management and Labor,* New York, D. Appleton & Company, 1915.

HUDSON, F. C. "The Machinist's Side of Taylor," *American Machinist, 34,* 773, April 27, 1911.

HUNT, E. E. *Scientific Management Since Taylor,* New York, McGraw-Hill Book Company, 1924.

HUTTON, F. R. "The Mechanical Engineer and the Function of the Engineering Society," *Proceedings, ASME, 29,* 595-632, 1907.

INSTITUTION OF MECHANICAL ENGINEERS. Excerpts of the *Proceedings* of the Joint Meeting with ASME, July 27, 1910, pp. 981-1009, Westminster, S.W., 1910.

JOHNSON, J. R. "A Manager's View of the Taylor System," *American Machinist, 34,* 885-886, May 11, 1911.

JURAN, J. M. (editor). *Quality Control Handbook,* New York, McGraw-Hill Book Company, 1951.

———. "Transition in Corporation Controls," *Advanced Management, 13,* No. 3, 126-130, September, 1948.

KIMBALL, D. S. "Another Side of Efficiency," *American Machinist, 35,* 263-265, August 10, 1911.

———. *I Remember: Autobiography,* New York, McGraw-Hill Book Company, 1953.

———. *Principles of Industrial Organization,* New York, McGraw-Hill Book Company, 1913.

KIMBALL, D. S. "Review of Principles of Management," *American Machinist, 35,* 965, July 20, 1911.

KNOEPPEL, C. E. "Installing Efficiency Methods," New York, Engineering Magazine Company, 1915.

LEPAWSKY, ALBERT. *Administration: The Art and Science of Organization and Management,* New York, Alfred A. Knopf, 1949.

LEWIS, WILFRED. "An Object Lesson in Efficiency," in Thompson, *Scientific Management,* pp. 232-241.

———. "Fifty Years of Scientific Management," *Manufacturing Industries, 15,* No. 4, 249-252, April, 1925.

LYTLE, C. W. "Collegiate Courses in Management," *Proceedings,* 39th Annual Meeting, Society for the Promotion of Engineering Education, *39,* 806-839, 1931.

———. *Job Evaluation Methods,* New York, The Ronald Press Company, 1946.

———. *Wage Incentive Methods,* rev. ed., New York, The Ronald Press Company, 1942.

MARSHALL, L. C. *Business Administration,* Chicago, University of Chicago Press, 1921.

McKNIGHT, C. H. "Reducing Material Waste," *Mechanical Engineering, 54,* No. 2, 109-112, February, 1933.

MEYERS, G. J. "The Science of Management," in Thompson, *Scientific Management,* pp. 132-152.

MORRISON, C. J. "Confusing Use of the Term Scientific Management," *American Machinist, 34,* 1181, June 22, 1911.

NICKERSON, J. W. "Work Assignment," *Annals,* American Academy of Political and Social Science, *184,* 54-61, 1936.

NORTON, P. T., JR. "Report of the Conferences: Industrial Engineering," *Journal of Engineering Education, 29,* No. 3, 197-198, November, 1938.

OSBORNE, W. "Echoes of the Oil Country," *American Machinist, 34,* 1036-1037, June 1, 1911.

PAGE, A. W. *The Bell Telephone System,* New York, Harper & Brothers, 1941.

PERSON, H. S. "Progress in Scientific Management," *Mechanical Engineering, 69,* No. 11, 893-897, November, 1947.

———. "The Genius of Frederick W. Taylor," *Advanced Management, 10,* No. 1, 2-11, January-March, 1945.

POLAKOV, WALTER. "The Measurement of Human Work," *Management Engineering, 2,* No. 2, 911-913, February, 1922.

PORTER, H. F. J. "The Higher Law in the Industrial World," *Engineering Magazine, 29,* 641-645, August, 1905.

———. "The Realization of Ideals in Industrial Engineering," *Transactions, ASME, 27,* 343-347, 1906.

RATHE, A. W. "Management Control," *Advanced Management, 15*, No. 3, 8-11, March, 1950.

RAUTENSTRAUCH, WALTER. *The Economics of Business Enterprise*, New York, John Wiley & Sons, 1939.

REUTER, F. J. "The Break Even Chart," *Manufacturing Industries, 11*, No. 4, 290, April, 1926.

RECENT ECONOMIC CHANGES COMMITTEE, *Recent Economic Changes in the U.S.*, Report by a Committee of the President's Conference on Unemployment, 2 vols., New York, McGraw-Hill Book Company, 1929.

REDFIELD, W. C. *The New Industrial Day*, New York, Century Co., 1912.

———. "Scientific Spirit in Management," *American Machinist, 36*, No. 16, 612-615, April 18, 1912.

RICE, J. M. *Scientific Management in Education*, New York, Hinds, Noble & Eldridge, 1913.

ROE, J. W. "Measurement of Management," *Transactions, ASME, 45*, 825-840, 1923.

SAVILLE, THORNDIKE. "Achievement in Engineering Education," *Journal of Engineering Education, 43*, No. 4, 222-235, December, 1952.

———. "Achievement in Engineering Education," *Advanced Management, 16*, No. 5, 10-11, May, 1951.

SHEWHART, WALTER. "Finding Causes of Quality Variances," *Manufacturing Industries, 11*, No. 2, 125-128, February, 1926.

SMITH, ADAM. *An Inquiry Into the Nature and Causes of the Wealth of Nations*, 2 vols., Everyman's Library, New York, E. P. Dutton & Company, 1910.

STILSON, C. H. "Letter on Scientific Management," *American Machinist, 35*, 175-176, July 27, 1911.

SWEET, J. E. "Dedication of Memorial Tablet to Robert Henry Thurston," *Transactions, ASME, 32*, 52-54, 1910.

TARDY, W. B. "A Plea for a Standard Organization," etc., *Journal, American Society of Naval Engineers, 23*, 681 ff.

———. "Scientific Management and Efficiency in the U.S. Navy," *Engineering Magazine, 41*, No. 4, 545-568, July, 1911.

TAYLOR, F. W. "On the Art of Cutting Metals," *Transactions, ASME, 28*, 30-279, 1907.

———. "A Piece Rate System, Being a Step Toward Partial Solution of the Labor Problem," *Transactions, ASME, 16*, 856-903, 1895.

———. "The Principles of Scientific Management," Special Ed., Confidential Circulation, New York, Harper & Brothers, 1911.

———. *Scientific Management* (Collection of Two Papers and Testimony of Taylor, with Foreword by H. S. Person), New York, Harper & Brothers, 1947.

TAYLOR, F. W. "Shop Management," *Transactions, ASME, 24,* 1337-1456, 1903.

TAYLOR SOCIETY (H. S. Person, editor). *Scientific Management in American Industry,* New York, Harper & Brothers, 1929.

————. *Frederick Winslow Taylor: A Memorial Volume,* New York, 1929.

————. "Fiftieth Anniversary of ASME," *Bulletin, Taylor Society, 15,* 62, April, 1930.

THOMPSON, C. B. *Scientific Management: A Collection of the More Significant Articles Describing the Taylor System,* Cambridge, Harvard University Press, 1914.

————. *The Theory and Practice of Scientific Management,* Boston, Houghton Mifflin Co., 1917.

THOMPSON, S. E. "History of Scientific Management in America," *Mechanical Engineering, 61,* No. 9, 671-675, September, 1939.

THURSTON, R. H. "President's Inaugural Address," *Transactions, ASME, 1,* 14-29, 1880.

TOWNE, H. R. "Axioms Concerning Manufacturing Cost," *Transactions, ASME, 34,* 1111-1123, 1912.

————. "The Engineer as Economist," *Transactions, ASME, 7,* 428-432, 1886.

————. "Foreword" to *Taylor's Shop Management,* Person's Collection, pp. 5-11.

————, SMITH, O., CALDER, J., HIGGINS, A., and FALKENAU, A. "The Human Element in Scientific Management," *Iron Age, 89,* 912 ff., April 11, 1912.

TUCK SCHOOL OF ADMINISTRATION AND FINANCE. "Scientific Management: Report of the First Conference," Hanover, N.H., Dartmouth College, 1912.

TUGWELL, R. G. *Industry's Coming of Age,* New York, Harcourt, Brace & Co., 1927.

URWICK, L. *The Elements of Administration,* New York, Harper & Brothers, 1944.

————. "Management's Debt to Engineers," *Advanced Management, 17,* No. 12, 5-12, December, 1952.

————. *Management of Tomorrow,* London, Nisbet & Co., 1933.

————. "The Principle of Direction and Control," in *Dictionary of Industrial Administration,* London, Pitman & Sons.

————. *The Meaning of Rationalisation,* London, Nisbet & Co., 1929.

————, and BRECH, E. F. *The Making of Scientific Management,* vol. I: *Thirteen Pioneers,* Reprint, London, Pitman & Sons, 1951.

WILSON, W. B. "Report for Committee on Labor, Amending HR

90, Authorizing Committee to Investigate Taylor and Other Systems," etc., June 24, 1911; Hrp. 52, 62nd Cong., 1st Sess., in VA:6134.

Wilson, W. B. "Report for Committee on Labor, Favoring HR 2305 to Regulate Method of Directing Work of Government Employees (so as to Prohibit Use of Stop-Watch, etc.)," July 5, 1912; Hrp. 1001, 62nd Cong., 2nd Sess., in VJ:6133.

———. "Report from Special Committee to Investigate Taylor and Other Systems," etc., March 9, 1912; Hrp. 403, 62nd Cong., 2nd Sess., in VB:6135.

Wish, Harvey. *Society and Thought in Early America*, New York, Longmans, Green & Company, 1950.

PART V

ABBREVIATIONS USED

AEC   American Engineering Council
AESC   American Engineering Standards Committee
AIChE   American Institute of Chemical Engineers
AIEE   American Institute of Electrical Engineers
AIMME   American Institute of Mining and Metallurgical Engineers
AMA   American Management Association
ASA   American Standards Association
ASCE   American Society of Civil Engineers
ASEE   American Society for Engineering Education (formerly SPEE)
ASME   American Society of Mechanical Engineers
ASRE   American Society of Refrigerating Engineers
IES   Illuminating Engineering Society
IME   Institution of Mechanical Engineers
IRAA   Industrial Relations Association of America
IRE   Institute of Radio Engineers
MIT   Massachusetts Institute of Technology
NACA   National Association of Cost Accountants
NACT   National Association of Corporation Training
NEMA   National Electrical Manufacturers Association
NICB   National Industrial Conference Board
NPA   National Personnel Association
NYU   New York University
SAE   Society of Automotive Engineers
SAM   Society for (the) Advancement of Management
SIE   Society of Industrial Engineers
SPEE   Society for the Promotion of Engineering Education (now ASEE)
WPI   Worcester Polytechnic Institute

INDEX

INDEX

349